CRITICAL PERSPECTIVES ON WORK AND EMPLOYMENT

Series editors
Irena Grugulis, Leeds University Business School, UK
Fredrik Movitz, Stockholm University, Sweden
Chris Smith, Royal Holloway University of London School of Management, UK
Chris Warhurst, University of Warwick Business School, UK

Critical Perspectives on Work and Employment combines the best empirical research with leading edge, critical debate on key issues and developments in the field of work and employment. Extremely well regarded and popular, the series has links to the highly successful International Labour Process Conference.

Formerly edited by David Knights, Hugh Willmott, Chris Smith and Paul Thompson, each volume in the series includes contributions from a range of disciplines, including the sociology of work and employment, business and management studies, human resources management, industrial relations, and organizational analysis.

Further details of the International Labour Process Conference can be found at www. ilpc.org.uk

Published:

Mingwei Liu and Chris Smith
CHINA AT WORK

Kirsty Newsome, Philip Taylor, Jennifer Bair, Al Rainnie
PUTTING LABOUR IN ITS PLACE

Marco Hauptmeier and Matt Vidal
COMPARATIVE POLITICAL ECONOMY OF WORK AND EMPLOYMENT RELATIONS

Carol Wolkowitz, Rachel Lara Cohen, Teela Sanders and Kate Hardy
BODY/SEX/WORK

Chris Warhurst, Françoise Carré, Patricia Findlay and Chris Tilly
ARE BAD JOBS INEVITABLE?

Irena Grugulis and Ödül Bozkurt
RETAIL WORK

Paul Thompson and Chris Smith
WORKING LIFE

Alan McKinlay and Chris Smith
CREATIVE LABOUR

Maeve Houlihan and Sharon Bolton
WORK MATTERS

Chris Warhurst, Doris Ruth Eikhof, and Axel Hunschild
WORK LESS, LIVE MORE?

Bill Harley, Jeff Hyman and Paul Thompson
PARTICIPATION AND DEMOCRACY AT WORK

Chris Warhurst, Irena Grugulis, and Ewart Keep
THE SKILLS THAT MATTER

Andrew Sturdy, Irena Grugulis, and Hugh Willmott
CUSTOMER SERVICE

Craig Prichard, Richard Hull, Mike Chumer, and Hugh Willmott
MANAGING KNOWLEDGE

Alan Felstead and Nick Jewson
GLOBAL TRENDS IN FLEXIBLE LABOUR

Paul Thompson and Chris Warhurst
WORKPLACES OF THE FUTURE

More details of the publications in this series can be found at https://he.palgrave.com/series/critical-perspectives-on-work-and-employment/14937

Critical Perspectives on Work and Employment Series
Series Standing Order ISBN 978–0–230–23017–0

You can receive future titles in this series as they are published by placing a standing order. Please contact your bookseller or, in the case of difficulty, write to us at the address below with your name and address, the title of the series and the ISBN quoted above.

Customer Services Department, Macmillan Distribution Ltd, Houndmills, Basingstoke, Hampshire, RG21 6XS, UK

The New Digital Workplace

How New Technologies Revolutionise Work

Edited by
Kendra Briken,
Shiona Chillas,
Martin Krzywdzinski
Abigail Marks

First published 2017 by
PALGRAVE

Palgrave in the UK is an imprint of Macmillan Publishers Limited,
registered in England, company number 785998, of 4 Crinan Street,
London, N1 9XW.

Palgrave® and Macmillan® are registered trademarks in the United States,
the United Kingdom, Europe and other countries.

ISBN 978–1–137–61013–3 paperback

This book is printed on paper suitable for recycling and made from fully
managed and sustained forest sources. Logging, pulping and manufacturing
processes are expected to conform to the environmental regulations of the
country of origin.

A catalogue record for this book is available from the British Library.

A catalog record for this book is available from the Library of Congress.

Contents

Part II Clouds, Crowds, and Big Data – Changing Regimes of Control, Changing Forms of Resistance and Misbehaviour

Part III The Digital Workplace (Worker) – Gendered, Self-Exploitative and Vulnerable?

Part IV Epilogue

List of Illustrations

Tables

Figures

Acknowledgements

The editors would like to thank all the contributors for producing their chapters under severe time restrictions and for their understanding replies to increasingly frantic emails that needed to be answered promptly. Our thanks also go to Palgrave, who accommodated the timeline with consummate professionalism. The book chapters were selected from papers presented at the International Labour Process Conferences over the past two years, in Athens and particularly Berlin, where the conference theme 'Working Revolutions: Revolutionising Work' provided the impetus for many of the chapter contributions. We would also like to acknowledge the encouragement and support of the series editors: Irena Grugulis, Chris Smith, Fredrik Movitz and Chris Warhurst.

Notes on Contributors

Michael Allvin is an associate professor at the Department of Sociology, Uppsala University. His research focuses on work, organisations and governance. He has previously written books and articles on the individualisation of work and on the new boundaryless work.

Andreas Boes (PD, Dr) is an expert on the informatisation of society and the future of work. Since 2007, he has established a research team on this topic at the Institute for Social Science Research in Munich (ISF München), where he is also a member of the board of directors. He is a member of the directorate of the Munich Center for Internet Research (MCIR) and is a lecturer at the Technical University of Darmstadt. After having studied sociology, political science, economics and education at Philipps-University Marburg, Boes worked as a researcher at ISF Marburg as well as the Technical University of Darmstadt, where he finalized his habilitation on informatisation and societal change.

Kendra Briken is a chancellor's fellow at the Department of Human Resource Management at the University of Strathclyde. Her main research interests include the broad area of changes in and at work. Over the last years, she investigated in commercial security and police forces, focusing on the labour process and transnational security value chains. Her most recent projects focus on the integration of new technologies in community pharmacies, and in fulfilment centres.

Florian Butollo is an assistant professor at the Department of Labour, Industrial and Economic Sociology at the University of Jena, Germany. He is author of *The end of cheap labour? Industrial transformation and 'social upgrading' in China* (Campus, 2014).

Shiona Chillas is a lecturer in management, based in the Institute for Capitalising on Creativity in the School of Management, University of St Andrews where she has worked since gaining her PhD in the Department of HRM, University of Strathclyde. Her research interests include graduate labour markets, new technology at work, and creative labour and she is currently working on the role of design in fledgling business start-ups. She is published in *Organization, Social Science and Medicine* and *New Technology, Work and Employment.*

Premilla D'Cruz holds a PhD from the Tata Institute of Social Sciences, Mumbai, India, and is a professor of organisational behaviour at the Indian Institute of Management Ahmedabad, India where she teaches micro organisational behaviour and workplace creativity. Premilla's research interests include workplace bullying, emotions at work, self and identity, organisational control, and ICTs and organisations. Premilla is currently studying workplace cyberbullying and experiences of crowdsourced work in India and is also part of a 15-country study of cross-cultural underpinnings of workplace bullying. Premilla has been a visiting scholar at several European and Australian universities and has received (along with Ernesto Noronha) numerous multi-lateral and bi-lateral research grants. She is currently the president of the International Association on Workplace Bullying and Harassment (IAWBH).

Jörg Flecker is a professor of sociology and the head of the Sociology Department at the University of Vienna, Austria. Previously, he was the scientific director of the working life research institute (FORBA) in Vienna. His main research interests include changes in work, new technologies, the labour market, transnationalisation, employment relations, and the political extreme right. For more than 15 years he has worked on delocalisation of ICT-enabled work and restructuring of service value chains and in 2016 he published the edited volume *Space, Place and Global Digital Work* with Palgrave Macmillan.

Tobias Kämpf (Dr) is a senior researcher at the Institute for Social Science Research in Munich (ISF München), where he is co-responsible for the research projects 'Wing' and 'Digit-D'. His area of expertise encompasses the consequences of globalization and digitisation on modern labour societies with a special focus on highly qualified knowledge-work. Kämpf studied sociology at Ludwig-Maximilians-University Munich and holds a PhD from the Technical University of Munich. He has been lecturing at the Technical University of Darmstadt as well as the Friedrich-Alexander-University Erlangen-Nuremberg.

Martin Krzywdzinski heads the research group Globalization, Work and Production at the Berlin Social Science Center (WZB) and is steering committee member of the international automobile research network GERPISA. He completed his PhD in political science at the Free University Berlin and has conducted numerous international research projects dealing with production systems, work organisation and employment relations. His research interests include globalisation processes, global value chains and multinational companies as well as technological change and innovation. He has published in *Work, Employment & Society, International Journal of Human Resource Management, European Journal of Industrial Relations, European Urban and Regional Studies, Industrial Relations Journal* and others. Together with Ulrich Jürgens he authored *New Worlds of Work. Varieties of Work in Car Factories in the BRIC Countries* (Oxford University Press, 2016).

Barbara Langes is a researcher at the Institute for Social Science Research in Munich (ISF München), where she is currently writing her PhD thesis. Her research focus lies on new organisational concepts for highly qualified knowledge-work within a new phase of informatisation. She has studied philosophy, logic and philosophy of science as well as sociology at Ludwig-Maximilians University of Munich, the University of Tasmania in Australia as well as the University of St Andrews in Scotland. She is a lecturer at the Technical University of Darmstadt.

Thomas Lühr is a researcher at the Institute for Social Science Research in Munich (ISF München), where he is currently writing his PhD thesis. He is especially interested in the long-term consequences of the industrialization of knowledge-work. His focus is on the change of the status of highly qualified employees within businesses and its implications for the development of the middle class. Lühr studied political science, sociology as well as peace and conflict studies at Philipps-University Marburg. He is a lecturer at the Technical University of Darmstadt.

Boy Lüthje holds the Volkswagen Endowed Chair for Industrial Relations and Social Development at the School of Government of Sun Yat-Sen University, Guangzhou, China. His recent publications include *From Silicon Valley to Shenzhen: Global production and work in the IT industry* (Rowman & Littlefield 2013, with Stephanie Hürtgen, Peter Pawlicki and Martina Sproll) and *Beyond the iron rice bowl. Regimes of production and industrial relations in China* (Campus 2013, with Siqi Luo and Zhang Hao).

Gavin Maclean is a research assistant at the Employment Research Institute, Edinburgh Napier University. His research interests include examining forms of cultural and social production, particularly work in the cultural industries and open source software communities. His has worked on several research projects that have examined inequality in work, employment and unemployment. He holds a PhD from Heriot-Watt University which looked at the art-commerce conflict in the recorded music industry.

Abigail Marks is a professor of work and employment studies at Heriot-Watt University, Edinburgh. Her research is focused on the ICT sector, social stratification and work, identity and the experience of work and unemployment for people with diagnosed mental health conditions. Abigail is currently the director of the Centre for Research on Work and Wellbeing. She has published in journals such *as Work, Employment and Society, Sociology, Human Relations* and the *British Journal of Industrial Relations*. Abigail is currently on the editorial board of the *Journal of Management Studies* and *New Technology, Work and Employment*.

Fredrik Movitz is an assistant professor in sociology and researcher at the Department of Sociology, Stockholm University, where he also lectures in organisation theory and management. His research has largely centred on work and organisation in technical sectors, industrial dynamics, unregulated working conditions and industrial relations. Currently, he is focusing on changes in work and organisation within the Swedish financial sector and broader processes of financialisation.

Ernesto Noronha holds a PhD from the Tata Institute of Social Sciences, Mumbai, India, and is a professor of organisational behaviour at the Indian Institute of Management Ahmedabad, India. Ernesto currently teaches research methodology, sociology of work and employment, and organisational dynamics to postgraduate and doctoral students. Ernesto's academic interests lie in workplace ethnicity, technology and work, labour and globalization, and qualitative research methods and he is involved in research projects on knowledge process offshoring, telework, Indian IT expatriates in the Netherlands, non-standard work, and collectivization in India's IT and ITES-BPO sector. Ernesto has received multi-lateral and bi-lateral grants including from the ILO, the DFG and the NWO and has been a visiting faculty and scholar at various universities in Europe, the US and Australia.

Sabine Pfeiffer is a sociologist of work and a professor of sociology at the University of Hohenheim in Stuttgart, Germany. Her main fields of research are in work studies, innovation studies, and food studies with special focus on virtual work. Sabine Pfeiffer is also a senior research fellow with the Institute for Social Science Research in Munich. Her recent publications have addressed unemployment, nutritional poverty, organisational standards in production and innovation work, living labouring capacity and the Industrial Internet.

Annika Schönauer is senior researcher and member of the management board of the working life research institute (FORBA). Her main research interests include changes in service work, transnationalisation, delocalisation of ICT-enabled work, restructuring of service value chains and working time. Annika Schönauer studied Sociology and Ethnology at Vienna University, completed a postgraduate training programme for further professional qualification in the social sciences (SOQUA) and finished her PhD thesis on restructuring and quality of work in the call centre sector in 2012. After collaborating in a number of research projects on tourism, migration, the labour market and the liberalisation of the service sector, she joined the working life research institute (FORBA) in Vienna in 2005. In 2015 she was a university assistant at the Sociology Department at the University of Vienna, Austria.

Philip Schörpf is a junior researcher at the Working Life Research Institute (FORBA) and at the Centre for Social Innovation (ZSI) in Vienna. He was a social worker between 2010 and 2014 and worked at the Department for Sociology at the University of Vienna from 2014 to 2016. His research interests include crowdwork and virtual work, outsourcing and offshoring of work, creative labour and social innovation. Philip Schörpf studied socioeconomics at the Vienna University of Economics and Business and currently works on his PhD in Sociology.

Christina Teipen is a professor of social sciences with a focus on economic sociology at the Berlin School of Economics and Law. Her research fields are the sociology of work and industrial relations with an emphasis on global value chains and the video games industry. Previously, she has held research positions at several universities, most recently at the Berlin Social Science Center (WZB). She has published in journals including *Economic and Industrial Democracy* as well as *British Journal of Industrial Relations*.

Paul Thompson is a professor of employment studies at the University of Stirling and an adjunct professor, School of Management, Queensland University of Technology. Informed by labour process theory, his research interests focus on social media and employment relations; control, resistance and organisational misbehaviour; financialisation, value chains and the changing political economy of capitalism. He has published eleven books and over 60 refereed journal articles, and his work has been translated into Japanese, French, Italian, Spanish, German, Hungarian and Swedish. He is currently the convenor of the International Labour Process Conference and co-editor of the Palgrave Series titled Management, Work and Organization.

Mascha Will-Zocholl is a lecturer of social sciences at the Hessian University of Police and Administration, University of Applied Sciences, Wiesbaden. Her main fields of research are the sociology of work, especially implications of new technologies on work and organisation, emerging topologies of work, trust in cooperation. Recently, she analysed societal perceptions of meaningful work. She has conducted studies in automotive engineering, among physicians and in social work during her research positions at Goethe-University Frankfurt and Technische Universität Darmstadt.

Adrian Wright is a senior lecturer at the University of Central Lancashire where he is also a member of the Institute for Research into Organisations, Work and Employment (iROWE). Adrian completed his doctoral research in 2016 where he investigated enterprise and entrepreneurialism in the digital games sector. Broadly, his research interests include changing forms of work and employment in the technology sector and work arrangements in the new economy.

Labour Process Theory and the New Digital Workplace

Kendra Briken, Shiona Chillas, Martin Krzywdzinski and Abigail Marks

The digitalisation of work has become a key topic in public and academic debate over the past few years. The leading prophets have promised nothing less than a 'digital revolution' that radically changes labour markets (Brynjolfsson and McAfee, 2012). 'This time, it's different', promise others (Ford, 2015). The difficulty – but also the fascination – with this ongoing discussion on digitalisation is that it brings together very different technological and social developments. While the public debate focuses on a rather black-and-white picture, the academic debate provides a more nuanced insight into the changing world of work.

On one hand, we can observe a new phase of technological change in traditional manufacturing industries, which is linked to the development of the Internet of Things, new robotic approaches, wearable computing and other technologies (such as 3D printers) and is described using terms such as 'advanced manufacturing techniques', 'digital manufacturing techniques', 'the smart factory' or '*Industrie 4.0*' (Lucke et al., 2008; IDA, 2012; Forschungsunion and Acatech, 2013). On the other hand, there are (relatively) new Internet-based business models and companies in which data generation and management play a central role extended in scale and scope. Though business models and companies are diverse and range from huge transnationals like Google, Facebook, Amazon and Uber to smaller, more niche-related businesses, an important feature is that they all distinguish themselves from 'traditional' companies (Lazonick, 2009). As we can see, it is precisely the employment relationship that is challenged, as well as existing forms of control and resistance.

1

Even though we know that some of the concepts are either at the test stage, niche developments or just clever marketing strategies, this does nothing to alter the fact that both Braverman's (1974) thesis of a degradation of work as well as the old 'engineering utopias' of an automated factory run by a few knowledge workers are back on the public agenda and open for debate (see Ford, 2015). From a labour process perspective, the current debates reflect a long-standing tradition. Since capitalist production obeys the 'imperative to constantly renew production' (Hall, 2010), technology-driven changes in the workplace have been key to labour process analysis. In this regard, the following macro-level questions are at stake: How are employment structures and industries changing? What jobs are under pressure to rationalise? Where are new forms of work and employment emerging? Moreover, there are more subtle issues and questions that require exploration.

- How are the skills and competency requirements, and thus also the basis for power relations in companies, changing? Where are competencies being devalued, and where are new, critical skills originating?
- How are control regimes and approaches to performance regulation changing within companies? Is there an increase in surveillance and a subordination of labour to self-regulating technical systems? Or, are new opportunities for worker self-organisation evolving?
- What room for autonomy and worker discretion do new technologies allow for? Can we observe new forms of resistance?

The key aim of this collection is to address some of these issues by inviting writers from around the world to discuss the impact of changes regarding jobs and labour in the digital economy. These contributions were selected from papers presented at the 2015 (Athens) and 2016 (Berlin) International Labour Process Conferences. Themes familiar to labour process researchers emerge in the chapters. Chief among these are issues such as how technology facilitates job loss via substitution and the potential of technology to deskill existing workers. An overarching theme is cost-cutting strategies as the driver for new technologies at work.

Part 1: Robots and Virtualities – The Changing Face of Manufacturing Work

Terms like 'digital manufacturing techniques', 'advanced manufacturing techniques', 'cyber-physical systems', 'smart factory' or – particularly in Germany – *Industrie 4.0* frame public debate on the transformation of manufacturing work through new automation concepts. The core elements of these concepts include the spread of the Internet of Things in factories, which is discussed under the heading 'cyber-physical systems'. German labour-studies scholar Dieter Spath understands this term as referring to 'objects [machines and components] equipped with their own decentralised steering mechanisms, which are interconnected via an internet of data and services and are independently self-steering' (Spath and Ganschar, 2013, p. 23). Another key feature is the spread of flexible robots, who, in line with the slogan that 'the robots are leaving their cages', can now directly interact with people. Finally, the use of assistance systems in manufacturing work is considered crucial for the new era: for example, smart eyeglasses or watches.

With regard to the social consequences of this development, there are diametrically oppositional scenarios. On the one hand, there are the providers of the new technological solutions – as well as trade associations and governments – who see the new technologies as a driver of growth and a potential engine for the creation of new, highly skilled jobs (MIT Technology Review, 2016; Forschungsunion and Acatech, 2013; President's Council of Advisors on Science and Technology, 2011). On the other hand, there are authors who emphasise the potential for major social upheaval. What these latter, pessimistic scenarios have in common is that they link new technologies to a substantial leap in the objectification of human (production) knowledge; this devalues human labour and increases the complexity of the systems, which also makes management by experts increasingly less controllable.

In this vein, Frey and Osbourne (2013) claim that in the medium term, 70–90 per cent of manufacturing jobs may be rendered unnecessary by new advanced manufacturing technologies. Brynjolffson and McAfee (2014) present a similar argument: they see the risk of rapidly rising social inequality linked to this development. It is suggested that ordinary workers will increasingly have to compete with 'smart' automation concepts; their wages will stagnate or fall in the medium term; and meanwhile the incomes of the highly skilled workers who can control the new technologies will rise rapidly.

As Howcroft and Taylor (2014) note, many of the bright promises made by the supporters of the new manufacturing technologies and many of the dark scenarios painted by their opponents are far from novel. The relationship between technology, skills, work organisation and control is a central theme of labour process theory (LPT). At the same time, the current discussion is suffering due to a dearth of empirical data suitable for assessing the varied interpretations and predictions. Almost all existing studies base their arguments on estimates (or in some cases, on speculation) about what is technologically and technically feasible. Against this backdrop, it is worth looking at earlier discussions on technology and work in the context of LPT.

A linchpin of the debate was Braverman's *Labor and Monopoly Capital* (1974) revisiting Marx's theory. According to Braverman, technology is deployed by management to improve control over the work process and the workers: Braverman argued that companies use (and will further use) automation to replace or simplify skilled jobs to such an extent that they can be performed by unskilled workers. This strengthens the position of the company in the labour market and reduces the power of the workers.

Braverman's universalist thesis of deskilling was contested within labour process research (cf. Wood, 1982; for a critique, see also Attewell, 1987). Thompson and Harley (2007, p. 149) stress that 'the notion of the workplace as a contested terrain is a central motif of LPT'. This means that the acceptance of new technologies is a site of potential conflict. Workers' responses to technology and their capacity to limit management prerogative must also be accounted for (Hall, 2010). It should not be assumed that workers' knowledge and experience can be completely replaced by automation – they remain an important resource for management, in turn forcing management to ensure consent is maintained when introducing new technologies. Hence, LPT does not argue that deskilling is an inevitable long-term trend in capitalist societies; it instead emphasises that the interest of management in controlling the work process represents a major constraint on upskilling (Thompson and Harley, 2007, p. 157), because highly skilled workers have reservoirs of knowledge not controlled by management.

Much of the empirical research on the use of automation has focused on the automotive industry, which has been at the forefront of the use of industrial robots since the 1970s and in the use of computer-integrated manufacturing (CIM) since the 1980s. Closely paralleling today's debates, some authors in the 1980s anticipated a trend towards upskilling in response to technological change (Adler, 1988; Katz and Sabel, 1985), while others perceived a move to deskilling (Shaiken, 1985; Shaiken et al., 1984). Over time, a more nuanced assessment of the change process emerged from empirical analyses. These studies identified a polarisation of skill requirements: while deskilling trends prevailed in direct production, workers in maintenance areas noticed an upskilling of their work (Jürgens et al., 1993; Milkman and Pullman, 1991; Gallie 1991); ambitious attempts to integrate production and maintenance tasks were not entirely successful (Jürgens et al., 1993, p. 214).

Some 20 years after the debate on CIM and the use of robots, the topic of automation is returning to the forefront of discussion with renewed intensity. In this context, LPT lends itself as a research approach for a number of reasons: the first reason for this is that it favours in-depth case studies, which are necessary for understanding the changes that are underway. The second advantage of the LPT approach is its understanding of the 'workplace as a contested terrain', which prevents it from advancing deterministic theses. Hence, LPT counsels scepticism towards both optimistic and pessimistic, apocalyptic scenarios of all-encompassing technological monitoring (Warhurst and Thompson, 1998). LPT emphasises the importance of the subjective knowledge and experience that companies still depend on in the work process; it emphasises the capacity of the workers (and their representatives) to resist, and it underscores the fact that workplaces are also social constructs, which cannot be organised according to technical concerns only. The contributions in this section of the book focus on such debates, updating and introducing new theoretical frameworks and offering contemporary evidence for their claims.

Pfeiffer's research departs from core labour process theory and takes Burawoy as her main influence. One of Burawoy's most important points of departure from Braverman is that rather than being 'coerced' by the capitalist system, workers participate in the system and consent in various ways to the very system which constrains them. Following in Burawoy's footsteps, Pfeiffer looks at the origins and the development of the current discussion on advanced manufacturing systems and in particular the German debate on *Industrie 4.0*. She demonstrates that these concepts are very strongly encouraged by political and economic elites in Europe and North America to protect the lead the Global North has in the competition with emerging economies. While public presentations of these concepts emphasise opportunities – such as the opportunities to improve job quality, create healthy and creative jobs and increase prosperity – the actual manufacturing concepts emphasise the objectives of rationalisation and standardisation. The technical possibilities of new manufacturing technologies risk promoting deskilling and a 'digital despotism' in the workplace.

Butollo and Lüthje analyse China's manufacturing sector in the light of policymakers' drive to make China more competitive in the global marketplace. The 'Made in China 2025' initiative that references the German *Industrie 4.0* scenario and proposes large-scale robotisation of manufacturing in China prioritises economic growth above social and/ or environmental considerations. Although China has assumed a leading position in transforming the infrastructures of electronic commerce (network capitalism), the authors see little new (or promising) for workers in Chinese manufacturing and suggest that widespread reform in the basic institutions of socioeconomic regulation is a far more pressing problem than a programme of substituting workers with robots, which in any event is an example of neo-Taylorist rationalisation strategies. The long-term effects on the labour market, and specifically on migrant workers in China, have been overlooked in the strategy.

Will-Zocholl critically assesses the promised benefits of digitisation by examining how digitisation and virtualisation practices occur in another familiar territory for labour process researchers, automotive engineering. She notes conceptual differences in informatisation, digitisation and virtualisation, which are progressively more particular in scope and worthy of differentiation in research accounts. The findings, focusing on the tacit knowledge of engineers, lead her to argue that attempts to standardise the profession have not been successful. She argues that digitisation is not a straightforward transfer from the physical to the digital world: in this context localised knowledge and practices prevail, and fragile professional cooperation is explained by differences in the training of engineers, localised software packages and an inability to transfer virtual prototypes back to the physical world.

Part 2: Clouds, Crowds, and Big Data – Changing Regimes of Control, Changing Forms of Resistance and Misbehaviour

In the second part of this book, we focus on the digital workplace and how the integration of new technologies changes the employment relationship. On one hand, Ford (2015) and Carr (2014) describe scenarios in which workers will become mere servants of ever 'smarter' computers and robots, whose complexity will increasingly defy workers' capacity for understanding. Moore and Piwek (2015) emphasise the opportunities for control and monitoring that are opened up by the new wearable technologies (on the role of social media as an instrument of control, see McDonald et al. (2016)). Reports on the use of wearables at Tesco and Amazon show that this technology can be used to analyse employees' productivity data, movements and interactions. The case of a Tesco distribution centre in Ireland has become notorious as an exemplar of the 'dark side' of technology (Wilson, 2013; Rawlinson, 2013; Moore and Robinson, 2015). In this case, warehouse workers wear 'smart' bracelets that assign their tasks and measure their movements, and their pay is directly linked to their measured work performance. The emergence of performance management systems controlled by technology is critically assessed (Taylor, 2013), and some empirical evidence shows how much the monitoring system still depends on direct control regimes (Briken et al., 2016). In this book we will focus on new(er) forms of contracts influencing employment relations.

For some decades now, researchers have emphasised the 'culture of labor market flexibility' in the information and communications technology (ICT) sector (Carnoy et al., 1997, p. 47; Benner, 2002), which is based on the use of temporary contracts and outsourcing/offshoring and on a very high mobility of high-skill workers among firms. The use of cloud technologies allows for large-scale storage in virtual spaces (in very material locations) and for cloud computing. The parallel use of hardware infrastructures offers new options for employers in terms of time and spatial relations. Tasks can be redefined and outsourced directly but also by using technology-mediated channels. Labelled as online outsourcing by the World Bank (Kuek et al., 2015), this technique allows employers as clients to outsource wage labour to a 'large distributed, global labour pool of remote workers, to enable performance, coordination, quality control, delivery, and payment of such services online' (Kuek et al., 2015, p. 1). Tasks can be outsourced to the crowd as micro-tasks – that is, as small jobs without special skills requirements – or as macro tasks – that is larger assignments, sometimes with high skills requirements. Typical micro-tasks include writing short texts such as product descriptions, conducting web searches or categorising images and videos. These individual tasks come with pay that may range from a few cents to a few euros. By contrast, macro tasks, which are typically outsourced in the field of software programming or design, can take little time or up to several weeks. Although some authors see crowdwork as a key element of the 'Global Digital Economy' (Huws, 2014, 2015), which is leading to the development of a global 'cybertariat', there are few empirical studies on this form of work organisation. In the field of micro-tasks, the available studies highlight the competition between crowdworkers as a central element of the control regime. But the limited information that is currently available on this subject refers only to individual platforms, especially to Amazon Mechanical Turk (Silberman et al., 2010; Irani and Silberman, 2013). Here, the excessively low wages established through the market mechanism seem to be accompanied by the greater dependence of crowdworkers on clients' evaluations of their work. Clients have the power to block crowdworkers from tasks arbitrarily and without explanation and may reject finished tasks without payment. Initial efforts by unions have been made to help organise crowdworkers (for an overview of Europe, see Valenduc and Vendramin, 2016, p. 41f; for the US, see Irani, 2015), and early studies have interrogated the new work identities that are emerging (Lehdonvirta and

Mezier, 2013); however, there are few empirical studies that discuss the changing employment relationship.

This is where *Schörpf, Flecker and Schönauer* make an important empirical contribution to the debate in analysing how the now triangular employment relation between crowdworkers, employers/clients and platform operators creates new forms of control and/or allows for dissent. The authors describe the strategies and structures of crowdsourcing platforms for creative work and the temporal aspects of creative crowdworking. The design of the online platforms provides a framework within which clients offer tasks and workers present themselves and perform work. The platforms' terms and conditions give a general framework defining its intermediary function. Some aspects like the blurred boundaries of work are common in the self-employed world of work. However, the authors show how standardised measures around reputation differ from the reputation in direct social settings because it is, as the authors point out, 'standardised and one-dimensional'.

D'Cruz and Noronha draw on empirical evidence from ICT workers in India to understand the scope and character of workplace bullying in the (new) digital workplace. Far from removing such behaviour, the authors find that different and more pervasive forms of bullying occur in the digital workplace, noting that online abuse is transmitted more broadly, that bullying tactics are more difficult to resolve and that they in fact become more pervasive. The ICT sector might be at the forefront of digital labour, but existing (and in this case negative) forms of workplace behaviours are reproduced in a more sophisticated form, often with the tacit acceptance of managers.

Movitz and Allvin present longitudinal data on the role of technologically related change in digitised workplaces, specifically in a Swedish bank. They chart the stimulus for, and progress of, various change programmes through the lens of intergroup conflicts around the ownership of IT systems. The authors acknowledge that their claim that change programmes are politically infused is not new, representing classic capital and labour power conflicts over jobs and resources. However, they argue that individualised employment relationships produce intergroup conflicts; groups of workers, who make temporary alliances that cross professional and departmental structures, struggle against each other, with limited evidence of collectivisation against the will of senior management. The authors see cutting costs as a major organisational driver for technological change, resulting in job losses, a reconfiguration of power structures and failed and failing change programmes. Irrespective of the promise of efficiency and effectiveness driving the rationalisation of IT systems, technology is side-lined in the change process, and the threat of job loss, relocation and loss of influence are key sites of inter-group and intragroup conflict.

Last but not least, *Boes Kampf, Langes and Luhr* discuss the scope and momentum of digital transformation, again making use of the informatisation approach that incorporates social processes in digitisation. Their evidence is based on a study of knowledge workers (broadly defined), and they locate their research in the 'historical development of work and organization', suggesting that the contemporary digital workplace is at the forefront of a 'paradigm shift' in the nature of work. Industrialisation underpinned by complementary mental labour is no longer sustainable, they argue; instead, information is now the dominant mode of production. This new world of work offers possibilities of empowerment and increases in mental productive forces, yet the evidence presented seems to lean more towards a reduction in autonomy and increased control over workers across the occupational hierarchy. Boes et al. surface a key theme around the pace of technological change, a point that is mentioned only in passing in other chapters in the book. At the same time, they suggest that from the 1990s onwards, digitalisation has also encompassed the creation of a new sphere of social action. It is precisely here where they suggest that the world of work is at a crossroads. Either the digital sphere of social action could lead to the use of opportunities to support the empowerment of employees, interlinking knowledge resources and increases in mental productive forces, or new production models will create a 'control panopticon of data and a new extent of exchangeability' at all skill levels.

Part 3: The Digital Workplace (Worker) – Gendered, Self-Exploitative, and Vulnerable?

In the third part of the book, we take a closer look at the ways in which the digital workplace reproduces and reinforces existing inequalities. Broadly speaking, from the literature we know that motivation to engage in creative work is influenced by the idea of working in a very specific sector where entrepreneurial ideas and innovative spirit are valued (Marks and Huzzard, 2010). For complex, highly skilled tasks such as the design, programming and testing of software applications, intrinsic motives such as recognition, fun and challenge are emphasised. Companies in the ICT sector cultivate the image of being a 'creative employer'; they seek to maintain flat hierarchies and promote a corporate culture that heavily emphasises direct, informal relations (Barrett, 2004; Baldry et al., 2007; Hodgson and Briand, 2013). Performance is managed via reputation systems and competitions. We also find elements of 'gamification' here, which stimulate emotional needs like the pursuit of success (Blohm and Leimeister, 2013, p. 275). As *Maclean, Marks and Chillas* show in their contribution to this volume, the acceptance of these forms of employment relations builds on the recruitment of a particular type of employee and becomes crucial for an often neglected aspect in LPT approaches, namely the underlying reproduction of gender relations. Their chapter focuses on the theme of reproduction and transformation that is a guiding question for researchers of technological developments. The authors take the under-representation of women in ICT work as a focus, arguing that technology in a broad sense reinforces structural inequalities. Their chapter introduces two theoretical resources, the work of Pierre Bourdieu and recent work on affordances as lenses through which to view reproductive tendencies, both of which might usefully provide explanatory frameworks to complement labour process analyses, particularly in the social realm. The authors argue that early socialisation is key to understanding under-representation, in a social world that is structured by androcentric principles. At the same time, the suggested theoretical framework goes beyond gender analysis and may also be applied to other structural inequalities.

The aforementioned lack of formal rules and guarantees at the organisational level exploits a high degree of self-control and self-rationalisation that seems to be ingrained in the knowledge worker in many parts of the ICT sector (Howcroft and Bergvall-Kareborn, 2013; Mayer-Ahuja and Wolf, 2009). The informality of workplace cultures frequently prompts the expectation that workers can be contacted by peers or supervisors by email at any time (Mazmanian et al., 2006); however, the resulting breach in the work-life boundary leads to dissatisfaction among software workers (Scholarios and Marks, 2004). Moreover, organisations rarely live up to the 'creative dream' and frequently return to bureaucratic structures (Baldry et al., 2007).

Wright's chapter shows some of the ways in which this paradoxical situation is perceived by the employees in examining the digital games sector as a sub-set of creative labour (Smith and McKinlay, 2009). He notes the lure and fascination attached to careers in the creative sector. Creative careers are seen as requiring workers to make sacrifices in work-life balance and requiring them to adopt an enterprising mentality. The analysis shows that passion, commitment to work, an entrepreneurial attitude and the need for attachment are the ways in which these workers rationalise exploitative working practices such as unpaid work and long hours. Digital workplaces are far from the brave new world of work, and individualised working practices fully normalise self-exploitation in the sector. The resultant work intensification and working for low pay are seen as acceptable trade-offs that are needed to make connections in the industry and also to feel part of an occupational community. Working *with* technology is shown to act in a way that distances workers from each other, something that must actively be worked *at* to gain and maintain social relationships.

Paradoxically, the perception of software programming as creative work coexists with a growing standardisation of work in software companies. As Beirne et al. (1998) show, there have been attempts to standardise and industrialise software development work from as early as in the 1960s, and most commonly, programmers have defended their need for autonomy. In the last decade, we have witnessed a new wave of flexible methods allowing for standardisation at a new qualitative level. What are called the 'agile' approaches rely on iterative and incremental processes including failure feedback loops and different time loops which become more and more standard for process organisation in software development and other digital workplaces (Popendieck and Popendieck, 2003). Like lean production, what is called the 'scrum' process emphasises empowered teams, standardised and collective forms of knowledge and the continuous improvement of processes. These approaches co-opt the team spirit and seem to enforce collaborative or co-productive working relationships since they claim to reduce bureaucratic controls. At the same time, the transparency of each and every task increases under such regimes and, with it, the measurability of this work and the pressure on employees to perform. While some research has been done on the question of how the processes of the formalisation and standardisation of work in the Internet-based industries influence skill requirements and employees' skill profiles, as well as control and discretion, not many studies investigate this question in different national settings.

Teipen's chapter examines working conditions in the video-game industry, integrating the varieties of capitalism and global value chain approaches with labour process analysis in an attempt to cover macro- and micro-level dimensions of work and employment. To illustrate the proposition, she provides empirical cross-national evidence of video-game developers in Germany, Sweden and Poland, an ambitious yet fruitful project. She finds that despite significant variation in institutional arrangements in these countries, the labour process of game developers is remarkably similar, attributed to the vulnerable position of game development studios in the sectoral value chain. Even in high-skilled work such as this, numerical flexibility and insecurity dominate. Echoing Wright, she notes that self-exploitative practices are endemic.

Conclusion

How revolutionary is the technological transformation in the 'new digital workplace' and how revolutionary will its impact on work be? Without wishing to deny the importance of the ongoing changes, we must nevertheless stress that transformation is an open and contested process. The questions of which scenarios will prevail at the end and whether we are dealing with gradual or disruptive changes are open to debate. Predictions on the effects of digital technologies – whether they take the form of optimistic upskilling promises or of pessimistic deskilling and surveillance scenarios – are currently rather speculative in character. In this regard, *Briken and Thompson* critically assess some of the big-picture narratives. Their argument is that contemporary social theory and the ongoing debate on 'postcapitalism' (see Mason, 2015; Srnicek and Williams, 2015) has generally put forward rather flawed conceptions of the pathways between (1) developments in capitalist political economy and (2) digitalised work and employment relations. The chapter begins with a brief commentary on some of the general characteristics of social theory concerning the workings of capitalism before its more detailed exposition and critique of increasingly influential variants – cognitive and postcapitalism or digital capitalism. Drawing on other labour process research, within that critique, the authors' observations point towards a more realistic picture of digital capitalism at work, including the importance of the financialisation of the economy. Briken and Thompson's argument invites readers to reflect on the plea made nearly 30 years ago in the introduction to an edited collection drawing on the 3rd and 4th International Labour Process Conferences, entitled *New Technology and the Labour Process* (Knights and Willmott, 1988):

> [it is] only through historical comparisons that a fuller understanding of the significance of contemporary developments in new technology may be gained. (Burnes et al., 1988, p. 3)

Although it is now almost three decades later and the pace of technological change has speeded up significantly, there are remarkable similarities in the concerns present in both that volume and this book. Both note that research is located in the aftermath of crises (in 1988 of energy, inflation and fiscal, which have perhaps been updated to environmental, financial and regulatory in this book), and the themes of substitution as well as the inevitability of technological development loom large in contributed chapters. As in our book, engineers in the 1988 book are a key focus of the empirical evidence, and the introduction celebrates the exchange of ideas between German (in those days, West German) industrial sociologists and Anglo-American labour process theorists. Unsurprisingly, control regimes, skill trajectories, power relations, work intensification, substitution, the role of technology in the labour process and cost-cutting strategies are discussed and critiqued, around the twin themes of continuity and change. Animating questions such as 'how new is new?' are explored much in the same way as authors in this volume address in their own analyses, albeit contextualised within contemporary workplaces. The missing element in our book is, however, clear evidence of collectivisation and resistance: it appears that individual-isation of employee relations, an emerging threat in 1988, has strengthened to become a dominant feature in the digital workplace. Where collectivi-sation appears in the current volume, it is almost an oddity, or mentioned in passing, rather than the norm, which is portrayed in the 1988 book. We can only speculate as to the place of technology in strengthening individu-alised employment relations which is evident in the digital workplace and in contemporary researchers' concerns. However, we contend that the lack of attention to collectivisation represents a 'line in the sand' and is a provoca-tion for future research in technological workplace developments.

We can then say that in some respects the digital workplace offers the promise of radical change, but in many cases, it seems that 'business as usual' prevails. There is no clear and final response to the questions about changing employment structures, the skills, control regimes and the spaces for autonomy that we raised at the beginning of this introduc-tion. However, the contributions reinforce how necessary it is to analyse experiences with new technologies in practice, to identify the spectrum of different approaches that can be used, as well as their conditions and consequences. What is certain is that this research requires perseverance, and obviously, even industrial revolutions do not take place overnight.

REFERENCES

Adler, P. S. (1988) 'Automation Skill and the Future of Capitalism', *Berkeley Journal of Sociology*, 33, 1–36.

Attewell, P. (1987) 'The Deskilling Controversy', *Work and Occupations: An International Sociological Journal*, 14, 3, 323–46.

Baldry, C., P. Bain, P. Taylor, J. Hyman, D. Scholarios, A. Marks, A. Watson, K. Gilbert, G. Gall and D. Bunzel (2007) *The Meaning of Work in the New Economy* (Basingstoke and New York: Palgrave Macmillan).

Barrett, R. (2004) 'Working at Webboyz: An Analysis of Control Over the Software Development Labour Process', *Sociology*, 38, 4, 777–94.

Beirne, M., H. Ramsay and A. Panteli (1998) 'Developments in Computing Work: Control and Contradiction in the Software Labour Process', in P. Thompson

▶

and C. Warhurst (eds), *Workplaces of the Future* (London: Macmillan Education UK), pp. 142–62.

Benner, C. (2002) *Work in the New Economy: Flexible Labor Markets in Silicon Valley* (Oxford: Blackwell Publishers).

Bergvall-Kareborn, B. and D. Howcroft (2013) 'The Future's Bright, the Future's Mobile': A Study of Apple and Google Mobile Application Developers', *Work, Employment & Society*, 27(6): 964–81.

Blohm, I. and J. M. Leimeister (2013) 'Gamification', *Business and Information Systems Engineering*, 5(4): 275–8.

Braverman, H. (1974) *Labor and Monopoly Capital. The Degradation of Work in the Twentieth Century* (New York: Monthly Review Press).

Briken, K., P. Taylor and K. Newsome (2016) 'Work Organisation, Management Control and Working Time in Retail Centre', paper presented at the 34th ILPC, 4–6th April, Berlin.

Brynjolfsson, E. and A. McAfee (2012) *Race Against the Machine: How the Digital Revolution is Accelerating Innovation, Driving Productivity, and Irreversibly Transforming Employment and the Economy* (Lexington: Digital Frontier Press).

Brynjolfsson, E. and A. McAfee (2014) *The Second Machine Age. Work, Progress, and Prosperity in a Time of Brilliant Technologies* (London and New York: W. W. Norton & Company).

Burnes, B., D. Knights and H. Willmott (1988) 'Introduction', in D. Knights and H. Willmott (eds), *New Technology and the Labour Process* (Basingstoke and London: Macmillan), pp. 1–19.

Carnoy, M., M. Castells, C. Benner and International Labour Organization (1997) 'Labour Markets and Employment Practices in the Age of Flexibility: A Case Study of Silicon Valley', *International Labour Review*, 136, 1, 27–48.

Carr, N. G. (2014) *The Glass Cage: Automation and Us* (New York: W.W. Norton & Company).

Ford, M. (2015) *The Rise of the Robots: Technology and the Threat of Mass Unemployment* (London: Oneworld).

Forschungsunion and Acatech (2013) *Umsetzungsempfehlungen für das Zukunftsprojekt Industrie 4.0: Deutschlands Zukunft als Produktionsstandort sichern; Abschlussbericht des Arbeitskreises Industrie 4.0* (Berlin and Frankfurt, Main: Forschungsunion Wirtschaft – Wissenschaft/Deutsche Akademie der Technikwissenschaften).

Frey C. B. and M. A. Osborne (2013) 'The Future of Employment: How Susceptible are Jobs to Computerisation?' Oxford Martin School working paper (Oxford: Oxford University).

Gallie, D. (1991) 'Patterns of Skill Change: Upskilling, Deskilling or the Polarization of Skills?', *Work, Employment & Society*, 5, 3, 319–51.

Hall, R. (2010) 'Renewing and Revising the Engagement between Labour Process Theory and Technology', in P. Thompson and C. Smith (eds), *Working Life: Renewing Labour Process Analysis* (London: Palgrave Macmillan), pp. 159–81.

Hodgson, D. and L. Briand (2013) 'Controlling the Uncontrollable: "Agile" Teams and Illusions of Autonomy in Creative Work', *Work, Employment and Society*, 27, 2, 308–25.

Howcroft, D. and P. Taylor (2014) '"Plus ca change, plus la meme chose?"—Researching and Theorising the "New" New Technologies', *New Technology, Work and Employment*, 29, 1, 1–8.

Huws, U. (2014) *Labor in the Global Digital Economy: The Cybertariat Comes of Age* (New York: NYU Press, Monthly Review Press).

Huws, U. (2015) 'iCapitalism and the Cybertariat: Contradictions of the Digital Economy', *Monthly Review*, 66, 8, 41–57.

IDA (2012) *Emerging Global Trends in Advanced Manufacturing* (Alexandria, VA: IDA).

Irani L. (2015) Justice for 'Data Janitors' (Public Books). http://www.publicbooks.org/nonfiction/justice-for-data-janitors.

Irani, L. C. and M. S. Silberman (2013) Turkopticon: Interrupting Worker Invisibility in Amazon Mechanical Turk, *Proceedings of the SIGCHI Conference on Human Factors in Computing Systems*: ACM, 2013. 1, 611–20.

Jürgens, U., T. Malsch and K. Dohse (1993) *Breaking from Taylorism: Changing forms of work in the automobile industry* (Cambridge: Cambridge University Press).

Katz, H. C. and C. F. Sabel (1985) 'Industrial Relations & Industrial Adjustment in the Car Industry', *Industrial Relations*, 24, 3, 295–315.

Knights, D. and H. Willmott (eds) (1998) *New Technology and the Labour Process* (Basingstoke and London: Macmillan).

Kuek, S. C., C. Paradi-Guilford, T. Fayomi, S. Imaizumi, P. Ipeirotis, P. Pina and M. Singh (2015) *The Global Opportunity in Online Outsourcing* (Washington, DC: World Bank).

Lazonick, W. (2009) *Sustainable Prosperity in the New Economy? Business Organization and High-Tech Employment in the United States* (Kalamazoo, MI: W.E. Upjohn Institute).

Lehdonvirta V. and P. Mezier (2013) Identity and Self-Organization in Unstructured Work, working paper, series 1, COST action IS 1202 (Hertfordshire: University of Hertfordshire).

Lucke, D., C. Constantinescu and E. Westkämper (2008) 'Smart Factory – A Step towards the Next Generation of Manufacturing', in M. Mitsuishi, K. Ueda and F. Kimura (eds), *Manufacturing Systems and Technologies for the New Frontier: The 41st CIRP Conference on Manufacturing Systems May 26–28, 2008, Tokyo, Japan* (London: Springer, 115–18).

Marks, A. and T. Huzzard (2010) 'Employability and the ICT Sector: A Study of Employees in Scottish Small Businesses', *New Technology Work and Employment*, 25, 2, 167–81.

Mason, P. (2015) *PostCapitalism: A Guide to our Future* (London: Allen Lane).

Mayer-Ahuja, N. and H. Wolf (2009) 'Beyond the Hype: Working in the German Internet Industry', in A. McKinlay and C. Smith (eds), *Creative Labour. Working in the Creative Industries* (London: Palgrave Macmillan), pp. 210–33.

Mazmanian, M., J. Yates and W. Orlikowski (2006) 'Ubiquitous Email: Individual Experiences and Organizational Consequences of Blackberry Use', *Academy of Management Annual Meeting Proceedings* (Atlanta: August 8, D1–D6).

McDonald, P., P. Thompson and P. O'Connor (2016) 'Profiling employees online: shifting public–private boundaries in organisational life', *Human Resource Management Journal*. doi:10.1111/1748-8583.12121

Milkman, R. and C. Pullman (1991) 'Technological Change in an Auto Assembly Plant: The Impact on Workers' Tasks and Skills', *Work and Occupations*, 18, 2, 123–47.

MIT Technology Review (2016) *Industrial Internet of Things: Here Today, Here to Stay* (Cambridge, MA: MIT Technology Review).

Moore, P. and L. Piwek (2015) 'Unintended Consequences: The Dark Side of the Quantified Self', paper commissioned by the Sustainable Societies Network.

Moore, P. and A. Robinson (2015) 'The Quantified Self: What Counts in the Neoliberal Workplace', *New Media & Society*, 18, 2774–92.

Popendieck, M. and T. Popendieck (2003) *Lean Software Development: An Agile Toolkit* (Salt Lake City: Addison Wesley).

President's Council of Advisors on Sciences and Technology (2011) 'Report to the President on Ensuring American Leadership in Advanced Manufacturing' (Washington, DC: White House).

Rawlinson, K. (2013) 'TESCO Accused of Using Electronic Armbands to Monitor Its Staff', *Independent*, 13 February 2003.

Scholarios, D. and A. Marks (2004) 'Work-Life Balance and the Software Worker', *Human Resource Management Journal*, 14, 2, 54–74.

Shaiken, H. (1985) *Work transformed: Automation and labor in the computer age* (New York: Holt, Rinehart, and Winston).

Shaiken, H., S. Kuhn and S. Herzenberg (1984) 'The Effects of Programmable Automation on the Work Environment: A Case Study of an Auto Assembly Plant', in U.S. Congressional Office of Technology Assessment (ed.), *Computerized Manufacturing Automation: Employment, Education and the Workplace (Vol. 2)* (Washington, DC: Office of Technology Assessment), pp. 293–357.

Silberman, M. S., L. Irani and J. Ross (2010) 'Ethics and tactics of professional crowdwork', *XRDS*, 17, 2, 39–43.

Smith, C. and A. McKinlay (2009) 'Creative Labour: Content, Contract and Control', in A. McKinlay and C. Smith (eds), *Creative Labour. Working in the Creative Industries* (London: Palgrave Macmillan), pp. 29–50.

Spath, D. and O. Ganschar (2013) *Produktionsarbeit der Zukunft – Industrie 4.0* (Stuttgart: Fraunhofer-Institut für Arbeitswirtschaft und Organisation).

Srnicek, N. and A. Williams (2015) *Inventing the Future: Postcapitalism and a World Without Work* (London: Verso Books).

Taylor, P. (2013) *Performance Management and the New Workplace Tyranny. A Report for the Scottish Trade Union Congress* (Glasgow: University of Strathclyde).

Thompson, P. and B. Harley (2007) 'HRM and the Worker: Labor Process Perspectives', in *The Oxford Handbook of Human Resource Management* (Oxford: Oxford University Press), pp. 147–65.

Valenduc, G. and P. Vendramin (2016). *Work in the Digital Economy: Sorting the Old from the New* (Brussels: ETUI).

▶

Warhurst, C. and P. Thompson (1998) 'Hands, Hearts and Minds: Changing Work and Workers at the End of the Century', in P. Thompson and C. Warhurst (eds), *Workplaces of the Future* (London: Macmillan Education UK), pp. 1–24.

Wilson, H. J. (2013) 'Wearables in the Workplace', *Harvard Business Review*, 91, 23–25.

Wood, S. (ed.) (1982) *The Degradation of Work? Skill, Deskilling, and the Labour Process* (London: Hutchinson).

Robots and Virtualities – the Changing Face of Manufacturing Work

Industrie 4.0 in the Making – Discourse Patterns and the Rise of Digital Despotism

Sabine Pfeiffer

Introduction: *Industrie 4.0* – Technology or Discourse?

New technological developments – frequently referred to using umbrella terms such as the *Internet of Things* (IoT), *Industrial Internet* or more broader the *smart factory* – promise to change the realm of production and manufacturing. These new manufacturing concepts are today regarded by national governments and international economic institutions (e.g. the World Economic Forum – WEF) as a key factor for national competitiveness. The major economies are starting to develop programmes aimed at gaining a pole position in this race. In the USA, the Smart Manufacturing Leadership Coalition promotes the Industrial Internet (Hannah, 2015); the Chinese government has set up the Made in China 2025 programme (see Butollo and Lüthje, Chapter 3, in this volume). Both the Chinese and the US national programmes explicitly refer to Germany's *Industrie 4.0* approach as their main competitor.

At the moment, all these national programmes are at an early phase. We do not yet know how far they will transform the world of manufacturing work. It is important, however, to understand what the origins, aims and potential consequences of these programmes are. In this chapter I will answer this question using the case of the German *Industrie 4.0* strategy.

After its launch at the Hannover Trade Fair in 2011, *Industrie 4.0* was elevated to a central strategic goal for German economic and industrial policy. *Industrie 4.0* seemingly promises a glorious future:

> *Industrie 4.0* will address and *solve some of the challenges facing the world today* such as resource and energy efficiency, urban production and demographic change. … Smart assistance systems release workers from having to perform routine tasks, so that they can focus on creative, value-added activities. … Flexible work organisation will allow workers to combine their work, private lives and continuing professional development more effectively, thus promoting a better *work-life balance*. (Kagermann et al., 2013, p. 5; italics in original)

For the initiators of the debate, *Industrie 4.0* marks nothing less than the fourth industrial revolution, following the rise of the steam-engine-based factory system in the eighteenth century, the advent of electrification in the nineteenth century and the introduction of computers in factories in the twentieth century.

The debate about *Industrie 4.0* is premised on two assumptions. First, it is often assumed that *Industrie 4.0* arose in reaction to a new level of technological development. In future, it is anticipated that businesses will network their machines, warehouse systems and operating equipment as worldwide cyber-physical systems (CPS). This vision of an industrial Internet, concerns the digital networking of the physical elements in the production process, support services and logistics. All manipulable objects in the production process, once fitted with data transponders, will communicate their position and production status to the processing machines. The restrictions of traditional mass production can be overcome in the 'smart factories', which are built on these principles, as well as in the 'smart service world' that will emerge afterwards (cf. acatech, 2015). Customised production that is responsive to individual needs and is on demand only is one of the ideas put forward. Data volume will increase exponentially as a result of CPS. It is not only the elements moving through the production process which continuously generate status data but also all the sensors and activators of all the machines and plants involved. This data stream may one day be extended even to driverless systems delivering the finished product right to the customer's door. Further technical developments are also central to the *Industrie 4.0* scenarios under discussion, such as light, two-armed and adaptive robots, additive manufacturing or 3D printing and wearables like data glasses or smart gloves. All these technical capabilities, once combined with social media and mobile devices, could be integrated into the factory.

Assumptions are also made concerning the intellectual home of *Industrie 4.0* principally being Germany – with its economy still highly dominated by mechanical engineering and manufacturing – in order to retain a competitive advantage in a global market. In the German economy, the mechanical engineering sector employs more than one million people working in thousands of mostly small and medium-sized enterprises (SME) that develop, produce and maintain complex machinery used around the world for producing and processing goods of all kinds: from food to cars, from packaging to electronics. The VDMA (Verband Deutscher Maschinen und Anlagenbau) – the German industrial association representing this sector – describes the German mechanical engineering industry as a global leader in 25 of 31 subsectors.[1]

In this contribution, I will argue that both assumptions are mistaken, or at least problematic, and that they overlook both the actual aims of *Industrie 4.0* and its actual origins. Drawing on discourse analysis, this article examines the concept's strategies and its actors. In doing so, it goes beyond the now quite extensive reach and the buzz that surrounds *Industrie 4.0* and focuses on the core documents in which this concept was developed.

Based on discourse analysis, I develop a new interpretation of the *Industrie 4.0* concept as part of a newly emerging global production regime. I base my argument on Michael Burawoy's work. First, his empirical approach of a rigorous ethnology of work seems more necessary than ever if we are to comprehend ongoing changes. Second, his theoretical perspective on the enduring significance of the 'politics of production' (Burawoy, 1985) takes on an unexpected new relevance. This article follows in Burawoy's footsteps, not with his ethnographic attention to actual manufacturing work, but with what Burawoy himself – albeit rather self-critically – has referred to as something that he has 'so readily missed': 'the importance of global capitalism and its dynamics, or the changing economic interventions of the state, or the way institutions sow the seeds of their own destruction' (Burawoy, 2013, p. 533).

Tomorrow's reality emerges from the outcome of today's decisions and is shaped by powerful economic and political actors. This chapter discusses these actors and their intentions. Following this short introduction, the next section reviews the origins of the *Industrie 4.0* concept, its actors and the intentions pursued with the concept; the strategies that helped in gaining political support for the concept; and potential consequences for workers. This section shows that the discourse is far more concerned with economics than technology. Based on this critical discourse analysis, and theoretically informed by Michael Burawoy's *Politics of Production*, the third section elucidates my central argument that *Industrie 4.0* (or, rather, that which is discussed in Germany under this name) represents an intentional effort to force the establishment of a *global production regime*.

A Global Strategic Discourse

Origins: The Rediscovery of Manufacturing's Strategic Economic Significance

Let us begin with an initial look at the origins of the *Industrie 4.0* discourse. While the discourse seemingly focuses on technical matters and national competitiveness, I will demonstrate that its original motivations lay more strongly within economic rather than technological concerns and that they were more strongly influenced by the international strategic environment than by national economic policies. The pervasive presence of *Industrie 4.0* talk during 2015 was, in fact, not caused by German society having reached a new stage of technological development. Instead, it was first and foremost the result of professionally managed *agenda setting*.

At first sight, the *Industrie 4.0* discourse led by politicians and economic leaders as well as by unions and scientists seems to be specifically German: the expectation that *Industrie 4.0* would generate immense growth is closely linked to the strong performance of German mechanical engineering in export and innovation. *Industrie 4.0* scripts assign companies in this sector a leading role as infrastructure providers. Germany's competitive advantages and the still relatively high share of added value in industrial production brought about a favoured view of *Industrie 4.0* as it was filtered through the lens of national interest. Key actors were keen to see the global networking of manufacturing become a reality so that it would generate positive economic effects for the German economy. With a view towards global competition, especially with the USA and China, *Industrie 4.0* has even been characterised as 'the question that will decide the fate of German manufacturing' (Finanznachrichten, 2015). Yet, while the specific concept may have been a German invention, its underlying ideas are part of an ongoing international debate.

Between 2009 and 2010 major consulting firms argued in a number of studies for a renewed strengthening of the sector of mechanical engineering, expressing concern over the stalling competitiveness of established industrial economies (Germany, Japan, USA) relative to emerging ones, especially in Asia. Key messages were established accordingly:

- In 2009, an elaborate comparison of the complexity of national economies (Hidalgo and Hausmann, 2009) ranked Germany at the top of 129 countries. Deloitte created the Shift Index (Hagel et al., 2009a), which combined, probably for the first time, many of the factors characterising the national *Industrie 4.0* discourse. The strategy called for the creation of a global 'flow of knowledge', based on digital infrastructures and even greater market liberalisation. Economic and political actors were advised to cooperate in realising these goals on so-called platforms (2009b, pp. 6–14).
- In 2010, Germany was ranked 8th on the Global Manufacturing Competitiveness Index (Deloitte, 2010). Although Germany remains technically advanced, Chinese manufacturers had clearly caught up by then, even outcompeting their German rivals in wind and solar power technology. High labour costs and bureaucratic barriers for start-ups were cited as obstacles. Germany was also ranked 13th on the Enabling Trade Index in 2010, a strong enough position to make it 'best performer' among the large national economies (WEF, 2010, p. 24).

Influenced by these studies and their strategic recommendations, three initiatives were launched during the WEF in January 2011: a task force, the 'Future of Manufacturing' project and the Global Agenda Council on Advanced Manufacturing (WEF, 2012, p. 5). These new initiatives included corporate representatives from Volkswagen, Bosch and Daimler. Siegfried Russwurm of Siemens AG was part of this group and would later become one of the German *Plattform Industrie 4.0*'s spokespersons once it was established in 2013. As one of the first measures agreed upon, the WEF promoted a 'data-driven narrative' in support of 'the strategic use of public policy as an enabler of economic development' (WEF, 2012). Just three months later, in April 2011, the term *Industrie 4.0* was introduced at the Hanover Trade Fair. Since then, the debate has not stopped; in fact, the term has spread further still, into day-to-day communication. From the European level to national levels, politics fulfils precisely the role it has been assigned by the WEF: it has become an exemplary enabler. All the major corporate consultancies have also incorporated the narrative in the way that it was initiated and under-pinned with data by the WEF, and they have continued to build on it with their own data and further elaborations. The plan forged in Davos is bearing fruit.

This has meant that, somewhat ironically, the same consultancies that had previously joined the vanguard in recommending intentional de-industrialisation were now pointing to the industrial sector not only as the centre of the value chain but also as the essential prerequisite for preserving 'high-quality services' in national or regional economies (Blanchet et al., 2014). Entirely transparently and without any ambiguity, Roland Berger Strategy Consultants proposed in a study of how to create an *Industrie 4.0* 'ecosystem' (2014, p. 20) a roadmap that centred on its promotion as a European idea, as well as on the basis that any required infrastructures for flourishing start-ups would be provided by the legislative powers. European and national-level politicians were of course the ones appealed to.

The *Industrie 4.0* discourse in Germany demonstrates in an exemplary manner just how much resonance these initiatives have found. Little doubt remains over how dutifully the political actors attend to their part of the plan. For this observation, one does not need to assume a causal influence 'from above' to guide the dynamics of national public discourses and ensure their success. Instead, the coming together of diverse personal alliances, the influence of corporate consultancies and the economy-driven world view shared over the years by politicians and corporate leaders fully suffices to ensure that reality remains consistent with the master plan. *Industrie 4.0* received its discursive legitimacy not primarily from the rise of new technical possibilities but rather from economic 'exigencies' as identified by economic elites. From today's vantage point, we can observe that Germany was neither the inventor of nor the protagonist in a narrative brought into motion by other actors intent on reinventing the world of industrial production.

'Marketing': Fuelling False Hopes for a New Source of Unlimited Growth

An important reason for *Industrie 4.0*'s rapid success in gaining political support lay in its promise of substantial potential growth. Some analysts dared to predict that *Industrie 4.0* would result in 78 billion euros' worth of economic growth for Germany by 2025 (Bauer et al., 2014). This figure sounds incredible, and in politics many were only too eager to accept it. However, a recent systematic comparison of studies that assess the potential impact of *Industrie 4.0* has criticised this and similar predictions for a lack of methodological rigour, and it has argued that while *Industrie 4.0* was indeed likely to promote economic growth, the investments necessary for doing so were most likely to cancel out any overall growth effect (Wischmann et al., 2015). The concept's advocates had apparently overlooked a detail that every entry-level manager would have been aware of: for any calculation of profit to be correct, the investment costs have to be subtracted from revenue.

Nonetheless, the overoptimistic predictions that intended to cast *Industrie 4.0* in a positive light were not intentionally duplicitous; they present merely another example of a pervasive flaw in business-school thinking, referred to as 'the capitalist's dilemma'. In a thus titled article (Christensen and Bever, 2014), the economists take their own colleagues to task and argue against promoting innovation at any cost. Instead, they urge their colleagues to differentiate between 'innovations that create new markets' and 'efficiency innovations'. Most *Industrie 4.0* scenarios link growth projections to an increased flexibility of production with assumed productivity gains. This, however, presents just another form of efficiency innovation, which in the long term is considered unsustainable from Christensen and van Bever's perspective. Greater efficiency, they argue, serves only to eliminate jobs (or to prevent the necessity to create new jobs from arising) and to generate additional capital. Yet, corporations already possess more capital than they would want to invest. The authors estimate that corporations are currently sitting on more than 1.6 trillion dollars in unused capital – money, so the authors suggest, that would be better invested in innovations geared towards the creation of markets.

Another important promise of *Industrie 4.0* also proves to be illusionary. The inventors of the German term claim that *Industrie 4.0* 'will address and solve some of the challenges facing the world today such as resource and energy efficiency' (Kagermann et al., 2013, p. 5) and thus will bring environmental advantages. Certainly, insofar as *Industrie 4.0* means on-demand-only production, fewer natural resources would be wasted. Yet, a convincing reason for doubting the concept's green credentials can be found on the assembly lines of every major automobile manufacturer. Even on these assembly lines, designed for high-volume production, every automobile can be individually identified from the point of its creation onwards and can thus be fitted with individualised options at every point along the line. Thus, a production in series is by no means the same as rolling out identical products 'en masse'. The state of today's data networks and assembly line technologies is so advanced that it already enables companies to produce individual automobiles after receiving just one specific order from a customer. There is no doubt that the technology associated with *Industrie 4.0* would improve the capabilities of such a production regime. Yet, as long as the logic of unlimited growth remains dominant, the new capabilities of self-directed CPS will not be employed to improve environmental outcomes. It will serve only to heighten what Klaus Dörre (2009) calls the dual crisis of economy and ecology.

If we assume that the growth promises of *Industrie 4.0* were to be realised, it is hard to imagine how they could benefit the environment. A prognosis provided by the corporate consultancy McKinsey estimated that the IoT would lead to over 11 trillion dollars per year (!) in additional growth between now and 2025 (Manyika et al., 2015). However, this calculation assumes a price for rare earth elements – essential for many IoT components – already far too low from an environmental perspective, and in addition, the study also assumes a reduction of 30 to 70 per cent in the price for other essential components such as micro-electromechanical sensors (ibid.). The consequences of such a dramatic fall in prices of the tide of global electronic garbage, which already grew globally by 42 million tonnes during 2014 alone, are difficult to fathom.

Consequences: The Global Reorganisation of Work

What are the potential consequences of *Industrie 4.0* for labour? For years now, jobs have been replaced by automated systems in a continual process of labour rationalisation. In the 1980s, armies of typesetters and analogue print workers were swept aside by new printing technologies. And who today remembers shop-floor secretaries? Or the fact that 'bank teller' was once synonymous with secure employment? Or the days when more humans than robots worked on Germany's automotive assembly lines? These and other profound changes in the organisation of work have occurred relatively unnoticed. The issue of technology-driven unemployment only returned to the public agenda because of new, *Industrie 4.0* production technologies. It is not without reason that these technologies are considered to have the potential to completely transform productive labour as we know it. Intelligent algorithms and big data could replace qualified knowledge workers, at least partially, and inexpensive light robots are likely to be used in production environments that have so far resisted automation. Incidentally, if the driverless car ever becomes a reality, it will dramatically change all economic activities dependent on package delivery and small-scale transportation.

In light of the potential magnitude of these changes, it comes as no surprise that numerous studies address the effects of automation on job elimination, which, most certainly, can also mean the elimination of *all* jobs in any given production environment through the replacement of human workers by intelligent things (Collins, 2013; Frey and Osborne, 2013, 2015; Brynjolfson and McAfee, 2014; Pistono, 2014; Pupo, 2014). Studies like the popular one by Carl Benedikt Frey and Michael

A. Osborne's (2013) assume that practically every single human task on a machine is simple and routine and thus easily replaced by these new automation options. Although their methodological approach underestimates the complexity and diversity of production work (Pfeiffer and Suphan, 2015), the fear of major job losses has even the WEF asking whether 'capitalism need[s] some Marxism to survive the Fourth Industrial Revolution' (Bendell, 2016). While contemplating a potential large-scale transformation of labour, one should not overlook the fact that current prognoses concerning these new technologies' possible effects on jobs often stand diametrically opposed to one another. Although some authors emphasise the potential creation of new high-skill jobs, others warn of massive job destruction due to increasing automation.

Putting these objections aside for the moment, however, a narrow focus on individual technical options, on current methods of effecting a division of labour or on assignment of job roles and tasks, does not address the heart of the matter. Current visions of a future with globally networked economic actors reconceptualise the world of work anew on a far larger scale, with the management of all global value chains being central to such new conceptions. These visions are intended to secure new structures free from local connections, regional expertise and labour-market-specific configurations. They are intended to create globally standardised, networked production and service structures that enable the flexible and self-directed collaboration of fixed and variable capital.

A report issued in 2012 by the WEF, The Future of Manufacturing Opportunities, illustrates these visions well, citing several case studies in support of its recommendations and demonstrating their feasibility. The central case study used by the WEF is Intel's Copy EXACTLY! strategy (WEF, 2012, p. 24); the unorthodox orthography was chosen by Intel, with the upper-case letters and exclamation mark intended to convey the expression of a purposeful underlying 'paradigm shift'. At first glance, it seems odd that the WEF would use a strategy pioneered in the 1980s (McDonald, 1998). A closer investigation of the original project is worthwhile, however, to gain insight into the perspective of the Intel managers who invented and implemented it. In doing so, we are in a better position to understand the future of work as imagined by the actors of today's *Industrie 4.0*. Intel's core idea, addressing the problem of how to best expand manufacturing capacity globally, was to build multiple exact copies of already existing manufacturing lines in different sites around the world. 'Stated in its simplest form, everything which might affect the process, or how it is to run, is to be copied down to the finest detail, unless it is … *physically impossible* to do so' (McDonald, 1998, p. 2). As it transpired, nearly nothing *material* proved impossible to replicate – right down to the smallest details, such as the colour of assembly workers' gloves.

The problems that Intel encountered in trying to establish an exact replica of an American factory at European sites were *immaterial*: 'Making a philosophical statement is obviously much easier than implementing it within a large team of R&D and manufacturing engineers' (McDonald, 1998, p. 3). Intel's European technicians and engineers, headstrong and better trained than their American colleagues, resented the directive to merely copy an American production line. This order offended their professional integrity, which placed a high value on continual improvement. An analysis of the project concluded with a quote of a surprised American Intel manager's observation that European educational systems train graduates to think independently, which meant that the order to copy felt to them like an order to 'cheat' (ibid.). This impasse led to a process of corporate learning. To neutralise any opposition rooted in their European employees' professional identities, Intel eventually established a four-stage implementation system that made concessions to local creativity and still created assembly lines that exactly copied American production lines.

What is noteworthy of Intel's implementation process is that the headstrong European engineers' regionally rooted skills were neither played down in their significance nor technically substituted. The solution lay in 'taming' those regional and unique aspects of engineering knowledge during the copying phase. Later, once the line was up and running, the copying phase ended and the regional expertise of the European engineers was reactivated and indeed rewarded considerably. Ideas for improvement that proved effective in one plant were implemented in all similar facilities worldwide (they had to be implemented within one week!). Thus, identical production facilities worldwide meant not only that benefits of engineering know-how were no longer limited to local plants but also that the total sum of actual production improvements worldwide increased without an overall increase in technician numbers. 'In effect, the number of engineers per process step or per area for improvement is increased, as is the number of improvement ideas generated' (McDonald, 1998, p. 5). The system extracts the innovative capacity of local engineers from specific regional environments, thus increasing their effectiveness while guaranteeing a particularly high production flexibility: 'With three sites running the exact same process, products were easily transferred back and forth with no re-qualification…. Using free capacity at another site has also solved manufacturing bottlenecks' (ibid.).

Copy EXACTLY! was initially established purely as a strategy of one company to optimise its trans-local production methods. For the WEF, it presents both an example and an instructive blueprint for utilising today's new technologies. The underlying goal is to optimise process efficiency by making production less dependent on local and situation-specific knowledge: in the case of a medium-sized company, for example, an algorithm-based optimisation of its 'milk runs' (the intra-logistical routes for delivering parts to machines on the factory floor) is outsourced to a service contractor's data server. Other possibilities include instances when maintenance-relevant data from numerous sensors and activators in a complex production facility is analysed using big data in order to prevent malfunction. Examples include occasions when a technology such as 3D printing is used to shorten the time from prototype to series production. These are all illustrative of an entirely novel, flexible and globally managed division of labour. Once it expands through techniques such as crowdsourcing or crowdworking and is applied in different markets such as 'sharing' or 'platform' economies, new and highly varied constellations will emerge to combine value creation and value realisation, offline and online, as well as commodity and commons in entirely new manners (cf. Pfeiffer, 2013).

The success of strategies like Copy EXACTLY! is questioned within the research literature, because the local adaptation of global standards often contradicts local interests or identities (cf. Collinson, 1994; Henning, 2002; Brunsson, 2002; Thursfield, 2015). On the other hand, especially automotive companies show a surprisingly high readiness to break with local traditions and to adapt global standard production systems (Jürgens and Krzywdzinski, 2016).

It remains yet to be seen what work will actually look like in the *Industrie 4.0* factories. At this moment in time, *Industrie 4.0* is a discourse, a campaign, meant to change the way we work. The demands that this model places on the workers' willingness to cooperate with management are high, and thus it is not surprising that an increasing number of authors (cf. Malone, 2004; Sattelberger at al., 2015) emphasise the need to develop democratic and participatory forms of business governance. The interaction between humans and machines is considered to be of particular relevance for *Industrie 4.0*, the implication being that companies have to obtain the workers' acceptance before any changes are introduced. Official documents identify human knowledge – and with it, human work – to be key. However, the considerations of what constitutes useful knowledge and thus human work are in the midst of rapid change. Many observers agree that fast-developing digital infrastructure in combination with years of deregulatory politics create a second-order effect: 'They unleash a flood of knowledge flows on a global scale that become more diverse and richer with each passing year' (Hagel and Brown, 2012, p. 28). In this context, the knowledge required for corporations to make decisions is assumed to be in constant flux. Companies cannot afford to merely preserve already acquired knowledge but need to adopt a strategy of continuous knowledge acquisition: 'Now, there is an opportunity to learn faster and drive more rapid performance improvement than ever before by harnessing these knowledge flows' (ibid., p. 28). 'Knowledge flow' becomes the abstract metaphor for hiring or firing humans, and in this context, it is again presented as an argument for deregulating labour relations.

Of course, the concepts for the global organisation of value chains discussed under *Industrie 4.0* are not merely a repetition of Copy EXACTLY! Compared with the earlier engineering concept, the new discourse places a much stronger emphasis on decentralisation. Bosch manager Siegfried Dais is an important voice in the ongoing discussion who echoes the views of many others with his claim that we are on the cusp of an 'elemental paradigm shift', quite unlike the automation concepts of the past, such as the computer-integrated manufacturing (CIM) of the 1980s (2014, p. 630). Dais advocates replacing older production models, based on central planning and robust but rigid value chains, with models based on decentralised self-management and the ad hoc organisation of value-creating networks (ibid., p. 613). In Dias' estimation, we need to create an 'architecture and rules for a value-creating network that links millions of decision points globally, is secure and robust, and is characterised by high availability' (ibid., p. 633).

At one point, Dais affirms that 'the pace of production will be a human pace.' Yet, despite all the emphasis on decentralisation, we should be sceptical about such claims. If the employment of human labour is described at once as both highly flexible and dependent on expertise needed *in a certain span of time* (ibid., p. 614), the author appears to be merely paying lip service to individuals' ability to influence the pace of production. Note, for example, that the German logistics companies have argued that logistics can make use of the new technologies only if production sites in future adapt and accept shorter response times. 'The whole thing begins with the fact that the best location for a system can no longer be determined on a long-term basis due to the ever more volatile production and trade environments. There is no such thing as the ideal production location, sometimes for many years. The logistics network and its nodes must be continuously adjusted to circumstances. Thus, the logistics nodes of the future will have to be moveable' (Hompel, 2014, p. 615). Consultancies have described

Industrie 4.0 as a system in which humans and intelligent machines increasingly meld into a 'blended workforce' and in which technology is not just a set of physical tools but the 'newest employee' and should be considered as such or, better still, as a 'partner in a new collaborative workforce' (Accenture, 2015, pp. 88–9). The WEF employs nearly identical definitions, also favouring the term 'blended workforce'. It characterises 'digital labour' in a manner that no longer distinguishes between variable and fixed capital, between (wo)man and machine. 'Digital labour' is a specific reference to the use of digital technologies which take over work once done by humans: 'smart sensors, machines (for example, robots) or intelligent systems that can do parts of the jobs that only humans used to do' (WEF, 2015, p. 28).

What remains puzzling in the *Industrie 4.0* discourse is exactly how all these changes will make human work more autonomous and decentralised, as its proponents repeatedly claim. If humans, machines and intelligent systems are to be transformed into a globally networked, digital–human blended workforce (ibid., p. 7) with individual components that are universally deployable in a highly efficient, self-directed collaborative production system, how will its human components be free to concentrate on the 'more human elements of their jobs like creative problem-solving and collaboration' (ibid., p. 17)?

Industrie 4.0: Global Production Regimes and Digital Despotism

In the previous section, I developed an analysis of the *Industrie 4.0* discourse in order to identify its main goals, the key approaches for legitimising these changes and the potential consequences for workers and for work itself. I have tried to show that the changes of the labour process are not mere outcomes of technological innovation but that they follow an ideological script written by powerful economic actors. This empirical observation needs, however, the framing of a theoretical approach able to link the micro level of production work with the macro level of global politics of production. Thus I would like to propose an interpretation of this discourse based on Michael Burawoy's analysis of the interdependence of economics, politics and reproduction as developed in his *Politics of Production* (Burawoy, 1985).

Disregarding issues and behaviours inseparable from the physical production process allowed Burawoy to focus on the sociopolitical aspects of the production process, which, while extraneous to it, have nonetheless become integral to diverse forms of production. His interest was

directed, first, at the political and ideological effects of different organisational forms of work and, second, at how political and ideological
production systems (*apparatuses of production*) regulate industrial relations on multiple levels all the way down to the factory floor. These
apparatuses of production influence equally the actions of management
and employees and are reproduced daily through corporate practices.
Together, these are what Burawoy calls the 'factory regime' (1985, p. 8).

Burawoy confirms the centrality of production, but he differentiates
further into labour processes and political apparatuses. The labour process is defined narrowly as the coordination of tasks and interactive relationships necessary for the transformation of raw materials into useful
products. The political apparatuses of production are defined as the institutions, formed by political agreement, that structure the production of
goods and services in a social context. For Burawoy, a production system
consists of the interaction of the labour process and the political apparatuses of production (1985, p. 87). It should be evident that his approach
stands apart from the kind of economic reductionism that even in texts
critical of industrial relations tends to underestimate the role of state
institutions and their historical links with corporations. At the same
time, he critiques the idea that the historical progression of different
phases of economic and social development is ultimately determined by
economic exigencies. Addressing himself to the Marxist-inspired works
of Harry Braverman on Taylorism, he rejects the distinction between
'hand work' and 'mind work' as misleading and even more strongly
criticises as arbitrary the analytical separation of the labour process in
'subjective' and 'objective' factors. Instead, Burawoy points to the constitutive nexus of economics, politics and ideology – visible throughout the
production process right down to the factory floor:

> Any work context involves an economic dimension (production of
> things), a political dimension (production of social relations), and
> an ideological dimension (production of an experience of those rela-
> tions). These three dimensions are inseparable. Moreover, they are
> all 'objective' in as much as they are independent of the particular
> people who come to work, of the particular agents of production.
> (Burawoy, 1985, p. 39)

With this set of analytical tools, Burawoy examines capitalist and
state-socialist production regimes. Burawoy observed a whole range
of forms of control linked to different phases of the development of
capitalist societies, leading him to differentiate analytically between
'patriarchal', 'paternalistic', 'bureaucratic' and 'market' despotism.

He characterised the period from the 1980s onward as a 'hegemonic despotism', based on the analysis of five dimensions: (a) the forms of *control* of concrete labour; (b) the forms of coordination in the national and global *division of labour*; (c) the *industrial relations* in and outside the factory; (d) the role of *technology*; and (e) the role of the *state*.

Burawoy's analysis enables us to develop a deeper understanding of what has happened over the past three decades. What once was a hegemonic despotism is poised to become a *digital despotism*. Table 1 contrasts key dimensions of Burawoy's hegemonic despotism with preliminary reflections on the contours of a digital form of despotism, as they derive from my discourse analysis in this chapter.

Table 2.1 From hegemonic to digital despotism

Dimensions of despotism	Burawoy's hegemonic despotism	Sketches of digital despotism
Control	Mixture of 'brutal coercion' across global manufacturing locations and 'silent submission' in core industrial countries.	Brutal coercion *and* silent submission in both global manufacturing locations and core industrial countries. These are supplemented by increasingly important *digitalised* silent coercion.
Coordinating the division of labour	Part time work is 'orchestrated by specialised agencies'.	Work down to microtasks is orchestrated by digitised agencies on demand and over global value chains.
Industrial relations	'Separation of relations *of* production from relations *in* production, mystifying the former while effectively subordinating workers to the latter'.	Deregulation of work and discrediting the role of industrial relations; negation of concrete production and of work.
Role of technology	'Artefacts of advancement' become 'instruments of atomisation', not 'potential instruments of collective solidarity'.	'*Digitalised* artefacts of advancement' become 'instruments of atomisation' *and* instruments of control, and not 'potential instruments of collective solidarity'. This applies not only to the world of work but also to the *life-world*.
Institutional relationship between apparatuses of factory and of state	Indirect intervention of state in factory regime (ibid., p. 13), setting conditions for the reproduction of labour.	National states serving the needs of a global market by deregulating industrial relations and providing the infrastructure for digital technology.

Source: Author, based on Burawoy (1985, pp. 256–64).

First, Burawoy characterises the hegemonic despotism by the duality of brutal coercion of labour in developing countries and silent submission of labour in Western industrial countries. This duality has persisted and continues even today. The working conditions at Foxconn, a Taiwanese corporation that uses sites on mainland China to profit from the structures of post-communist state oppression (Chan et al., 2013), illustrate how the digital despotism relies on brutal coercion. Furthermore, in Western countries, we observe silent submission to precarious working conditions and long working hours (see Wright in this volume).

Second, regarding the coordination of labour, Burawoy emphasises the 'growth of part-time and temporary work … orchestrated by specialised agencies' as part of the hegemonic despotism. In today's digital despotism, the instruments to coordinate precarious labour have become even more sophisticated and rely, for instance, on digital crowdwork platforms.

Third, Burawoy points to the new strategies of union bashing and concession bargaining or of a straightforward fight against unionisation as part of the hegemonic despotism. Given the available 'sticks' of offshoring threats, management no longer needs the 'carrot' of collective bargaining and interest representation. In the digital despotism, this trend seems to persist. Human labour, robots and algorithms are addressed without any distinction as 'digital labour'. There is no recognition of the need for collective bargaining or a specific human labour voice.

Fourth, Burawoy emphasises the role of technology. He argues that technology in the labour process is not neutral, but always bears the marks of a certain form of control. Computers at the workplace are, for instance, tools for a bureaucratic control regime. He describes how certain 'artefacts of advancement' (meaning in his time telephones and cars) will become 'instruments of atomisation', although they also have the potential to act as 'instruments of collective solidarity' (1985, p. 265). I argue that the use of technology in the digital despotism makes it possible to intensify the control of the labour process developed earlier. It combines bureaucratic control (computers), physical control (machinery, assembly lines) and bodily control (wearables like data glasses and smart textiles to control and track individual behaviour).

Finally, Burawoy stresses the role of what he calls 'the political apparatuses of production', which strongly influence labour relations and factory regimes. The discourse analysis presented in this chapter seems to suggest, however, that the state is undergoing a major change in the period of digital despotism. The economic actors are trying to reduce the influence of the state on the economy and to make it a mere provider of the digital infrastructure for the global factory regime. One reason for this transformation is the creation of a global digital labour market which reduces the reliance of capital on specific national state apparatuses to create consent in the workforce.

As this short discussion shows, I do not suggest that the digital despotism represents a completely new phase of capitalist development. It instead seems to be the outcome of an evolution of Burawoy's hegemonic despotism in a new geopolitical situation after the fall of state socialism which makes use of the technological innovations available in this phase.

Conclusions

In this article, I have argued *first* that the catchphrase *Industrie 4.0* stands for a discourse conceived and propagated by globally networked economic as well as transnationally operating political actors. International institutions such as the WEF and global consulting agencies have played an important role in developing the basis for the *Industrie 4.0* discourse, even before the German government's decision to make it an official policy.

Second, this discourse is fuelled by a rediscovered economic interest in realising the potential for value creation in industrial production. This renewed interest emerged after the financial crisis of 2008 as global actors sought new foundations for economic growth. The fact that at the current stage of development any economic benefits of *Industrie 4.0* are, however, only speculative does not prevent companies, industrial associations and consultancies from promising incredible growth opportunities to governments so as to gain political support.

Third, I interpret *Industrie 4.0* as a blueprint for a new global production regime that would seek to regulate all global material and financial flows with the help of digital infrastructures. A central prerequisite of this vision is a labour process in which the material means of production, such as human labour power, are entirely flexible and globalised. Building on Burawoy's approach – which connected the dots between economic, political and individual corporate organisations 30 years ago – I call this regime 'digital despotism', and I argue that this is fruitful even though Burawoy originally intended to describe very different work contexts.

Given the extensive number of powerful actors participating in the *Industrie 4.0* campaign, ranging from the most important global corporations to national governments and global institutions like the WEF, it is almost certain that *Industrie 4.0* will have a long-term impact on the manufacturing sector and its workers. Similar to all the other technological leaps in the history of capitalist development, the government, industrial associations and companies paint a positive picture of how the technology will transform and upskill work. Burawoy (1985) commented on similar discussions in his time by pointing to the fact that most technological advances since the Industrial Revolution have been 'frustrated by the capitalist effort to reconstitute and even deepen the division of labour in all of its worst aspects'(p. 53).

Nevertheless, we should not lose sight of the fact that *Industrie 4.0* is simply one face of digital despotism. While the current managerial literature celebrates the 'democratic firm' and 'participatory decision making', our society is busy perfecting the collection of enormous amounts of data on all aspects of individuals' work-relevant activities, both as employees and consumers. Is the digitally augmented hollowing-out not only of privacy but also of labour rights and the democratic potential of industrial relations not also a new form of despotism? The key actors on the global scale frame their recommendation for economic reforms and new production concepts as a global long-term strategy. Let the experts from Deloitte have the last word, again with a quote from the 2012 WEF paper:

> To understand the future of manufacturing, we need to explore a much broader set of dynamics that are reshaping the global business economy. These powerful forces have been playing out for decades and will continue to unfold over many decades ahead. ... We call these forces and the trends they set in motion the 'Big Shift' (Hagel and Brown, 2012, p. 28).

Industrie 4.0, as this contribution argues, is not only a central element of this 'big shift' but, furthermore, the manifestation of a development towards a digital form of despotism.

Note

1 http://www.vdma.org/article/-/articleview/6656392

REFERENCES

acatech (2015) *Smart Service Welt. Recommendations for the Strategic Initiative Web-based Services for Businesses. Final Report* (Berlin: National Academy of Science and Engineering). http://www.acatech.de/fileadmin/user_upload/ Baumstruktur_nach_Website/Acatech/root/de/Projekte/Laufende_Projekte/ Smart_Service_Welt/Smart_Service_Welt_2015/BerichtSmartService2015_ LANGVERSION_en.pdf, date accessed 27 June 2016.

Accenture (2015) *Digital Business Era: Stretch Your Boundaries* (Phoenix: Accenture Technology Labs). https://www.accenture.com/t20151117T010853__w__/ nl-en/_acnmedia/Accenture/Conversion-Assets/Microsites/Documents11/ Accenture-Technology-Vision-2015.pdf#zoom=50, date accessed 27 June 2016.

Bauer, W., S. Schlund, D. Marrenbach and O. Ganschar (2014) *Industrie 4.0 – Volkswirtschaftliches Potenzial für Deutschland* (Berlin: Bitkom). https://www. bitkom.org/Publikationen/2014/Studien/Studie-Industrie-4-0-Volkswirtschaft liches-Potenzial-fuer-Deutschland/Studie-Industrie-40.pdf, date accessed 27 June 2016.

Bendell, J. (2016) 'Does capitalism need some Marxism to survive the Fourth Industrial Revolution?', https://www.weforum.org/agenda/2016/06/could-capit alism-need-some-marxism-to-survive-the-4th-industrial-revolution/, date accessed 27 June 2016.

Blanchet, M., T. Rinn, G. von Thaden and G. de Thieulloy (2014) *Industry 4.0. The New Industrial Revolution. How Europe Will Succeed* (München: Roland Berger Strategy Consultants). http://www.rolandberger.de/media/pdf/Roland_ Berger_TAB_Industry_4_0_20140403.pdf, date accessed 27 June 2016.

Brunsson, N. (2002) 'Standardization and Uniformity' in N. Brunsson and B. Jacobsson (eds) *A World of Standards* (Oxford: University Press), pp. 138–50.

Brynjolfson, E. and A. McAfee (2014) *The Second Machine Age: Work, Progress, and Prosperity in a Time of Brilliant Technologies* (New York, London: Norton).

Burawoy, M. (1985) *The Politics of Production* (London: Verso).

Burawoy, M. (2013) 'Ethnographic fallacies: reflections on labour studies in the era of market fundamentalism', *Work, Employment & Society*, 27, 3, 526–36.

Butollo, F. and B. Lüthje (this volume) '"Made in China 2025": Intelligent Manufacturing and Work' in K. Briken, S. Chillas, M. Krzywdzinski and A. Marks (eds) *The New Digital Workplace* (London: Palgrave Macmillan).

Chan, J., N. Pun and M. Selden (2013) 'The politics of global production: Apple, Foxconn and China's new working class', *New Technology, Work and Employment*, 28, 2, 100–15.

Christensen, C. M. and D. van Bever (2014) 'The Capitalist's Dilemma', *Harvard Business Review*, 92, 6, 60–68.

Collins, R. (2013) 'The end of middle class work: No more escapes' in I. Wallerstein, R. Collins, G. Derlugian and C. Calhoun (eds) *Does Capitalism Have a Future?* (Oxford, New York: Oxford University Press), pp. 37–70.

Collinson D. (1994) 'Strategies of resistance: power, knowledge and subjectivity in the workplace' in J. Jermier, D. Knights and W. Nord (eds) *Resistance and Power in Organizations* (London: Routledge), pp. 25–68.

▶

Dais, S. (2014) 'Industrie 4.0 – Anstoß, Vision, Vorgehen' in T. Bauernhansl, M. ten Hompel and B. Vogel-Heuser (eds) *Industrie 4.0 in Produktion, Automatisierung und Logistik. Anwendung Technologien Migration* (Wiesbaden: Springer Vieweg), pp. 625–34.

Deloitte (2010) *Global Manufacturing Competitiveness Index 2010*, http://www2. deloitte.com/content/dam/Deloitte/global/Documents/Manufacturing/ gx_2010%20Global%20Manufacturing%20Competitiveness%20 Index_06_28_10.pdf, date accessed 11 July 2016.

Dörre, K. (2009) 'The New Landnahme: Dynamics and Limits of Financial Market Capitalism' in K. Dörre, S. Lessenich and H. Rosa (eds) *Sociology, Capitalism, Critique* (London, New York: Verso), pp. 11–66.

Finanznachrichten (2015) 'Kaeser: Industrie 4.0 ist Schicksalsfrage der deutschen Industrie', http://www.finanznachrichten.de/nachrichten-2015-04/3337131 4-kaeser-industrie-4-0-ist-schicksalsfrage-der-deutschen-industrie-003.htm, date accessed 20 June 2016.

Frey, C. B. and M. A. Osborne (2013) *The Future of Employment: How Susceptible are Jobs to Computerisation?* (Oxford: Oxford Martin School). http://www. oxfordmartin.ox.ac.uk/publications/view/1314, date accessed 31 March 2014, date accessed 27 June 2016.

Frey, C. B. and M. A. Osborne (2015) *Technology at Work. The Future of Innovation and Employment* (Oxford: Oxford Marin School). http://www.oxfordmartin. ox.ac.uk/publications/view/1900, date accessed 27 June 2016.

Hagel, J. I. and J. S. Brown (2012) 'Essay – The Big Shift and Manufacturing' in World Economic Forum (ed.) *The Future of Manufacturing: Opportunities to Drive Economic Growth* (Davos: World Economic Forum), pp. 28–9.

Hagel, J. I., J. S. Brown and L. Davison (2009a) *Measuring the Forces of Long-Term Change. The 2009 Shift Index* (Ann Arbor, MI: Deloitte).

Hagel, J. I., J. S. Brown and L. Davison (2009b) *The Big Shift. Why It Matters* (Ann Arbor, MI: Deloitte Center for the Edge). http://www.johnseelybrown.com/ bigshiftwhyitmatters.pdf, date accessed 27 June 2016.

Hannah, M. (2015) 'Industry 4.0: Turning The Vision Into Reality', *Manufacturing Business Technology*, http://www.mbtmag.com/articles/2015/01/industry-4 0-turning-vision-reality, date accessed 30 August 2016.

Henning, R. (2002) 'Selling Standards', in N. Brunsson and B. Jacobsson (eds) *A World of Standards* (Oxford: Oxford University Press), pp. 114–24.

Hidalgo, C. A. and R. Hausmann (2009) 'The building blocks of economic complexity'. *PNAS – Proceedings of the National Academy of Sciences of the United States of America*, 106, 26, 10570–5.

Hompel, M. ten (2014) 'Logistik 4.0' in T. Bauernhansl, M. ten Hompel and B. Vogel-Heuse (eds) *Industrie 4.0 in Produktion. Automatisierung und Logistik. Anwendung Technologien Migration* (Wiesbaden: Springer Vieweg), pp. 615–34.

Jürgens, U. and M. Krzywdzinski (2016) *New Worlds of Work. Varieties of Work in Car Factories in the BRIC Countries* (Oxford, New York: Oxford University Press).

Kagermann, H., W. Wahlster and J. Helbig (2013) *Recommendations for implementing the strategic initiative INDUSTRIE 4.0. Final report of the Industrie 4.0*

Working Group (Frankfurt am Main: Plattform 4.0). http://www.acatech.de/fileadmin/user_upload/Baumstruktur_nach_Website/Acatech/root/de/Material_fuer_Sonderseiten/Industrie_4.0/Final_report__Industrie_4.0_accessible.pdf, date accessed 27 June 2016.

Malone, T. W. (2004) *The Future of Work: How the New Order of Business Will Shape Your Organization, Your Management Style and Your Life* (Boston, MA: Harvard Business).

Manyika, J., M. Chui, P. Bisson, J. Woetzel, R. Dobbs, J. Bughin, et al. (2015) *The Internet of Things: Mapping the Value Beyond the Hype* (San Francisco, CA: McKinsey & Company). https://www.mckinsey.de/sites/mck_files/files/unlocking_the_potential_of_the_internet_of_things_full_report.pdf, date accessed 27 June 2016.

McDonald, C. J. (1998) 'The Evolution of Intel's Copy EXACTLY! Technology Transfer Method', *Intel Technology Journal*, 2, 1–6.

Pfeiffer, S. (2013) 'Web, Value and Labour', *Work Organisation, Labour and Globalisation*, 7, 1, 12–30.

Pfeiffer, S. (2014) 'Digital Labour and the Use-value of Human Work. On the Importance of Labouring Capacity for understanding Digital Capitalism', *tripleC, Journal for a Global Sustainable Information Society*, 12, 2, 599–619.

Pfeiffer, S. and A. Suphan (2015) *The Labouring Capacity Index: Living Labouring Capacity and Experience as Resources on the Road to Industry 4.0* (Stuttgart: University of Hohenheim, Chair of Sociology). http://www.sabine-pfeiffer.de/files/downloads/2015-Pfeiffer-Suphan-EN.pdf, date accessed 27 June 2016.

Pistono, F. (2014) *Robots Will Steal Your Job but That's Ok. How To Survive the Economic Collapse and be Happy* (Los Angeles: Federico Pistono).

Pupo, A. (2014) 'Cognitivity Everywhere: The Omnipresence of Intelligent Machines and the Possible Social Impacts', *World Future Review*, 6, 2, 114–19.

Sattelberger, T., I. Welpe and A. Boes (2015) *Das demokratische Unternehmen. Neue Arbeits und Führungskulturen im Zeitalter digitaler Wirtschaft* (Stuttgart: Haufe).

Thursfield, D. (2015) 'Resistance to Teamworking in a UK Research and Development Laboratory', *Work, Employment & Society* 29, 6, 989–1006.

WEF (2010) The Global Enabling Trade Report 2010 (Davos: World Economic Forum). http://www3.weforum.org/docs/WEF_GlobalEnablingTrade_Report_2010.pdf, date accessed 20 June 2016.

WEF (2012) *The Future of Manufacturing Opportunities to Drive Economic Growth* (Davos: World Economic Forum).

WEF (2015) The Future of Manufacturing: Driving Capabilities, Enabling Investments (Davos: World Economic Forum). http://www3.weforum.org/docs/Media/GAC14/Future_of_Manufacturing_Driving_Capabilities.pdf, date accessed 27 June 2016.

Wischmann, S., L. Wangler and A. Botthof (2015) *Industrie 4.0. Volks- und betriebswirtschaftliche Faktoren für den Standort Deutschland. Eine Studie im Rahmen der Begleitforschung zum Technologieprogramm AUTONOMIK für Industrie 4.0* (Berlin: BMWi). http://www.autonomik40.de/_media/Studie_AUTONOMIK_fuer_Industrie_4.0_Volks-_und_BetriebswirtschaftlicheFaktoren_fuer_den_Standort_Deutschland.pdf, date accessed 27 June 2016.

Wright, A. (this volume) 'Understanding Self-Exploitation in the Digital Games Sector', in K. Briken, S. Chillas, M. Krzywdzinski and A. Marks (eds) *The New Digital Workplace* (London: Palgrave Macmillan).

'Made in China 2025': Intelligent Manufacturing and Work[1]

Florian Butollo and Boy Lüthje

In the wake of its rise to a global manufacturing power, China has become an important player acting as a testing ground in the present drive to rejuvenate the world economy through a new paradigm of capitalist production under the mantra of digital production, intelligent manufacturing or *Industrie 4.0*. In 2015 the Chinese government presented a masterplan for China's transition to the age of digital manufacturing entitled 'Made in China 2025' (MiC 2025), for which Germany's *Industrie 4.0* concept serves as point of reference. This project has gained much attention in international media and industry circles, since it proposes the large-scale robotisation of manufacturing and, therefore, offers golden growth potentials for providers of advanced automation equipment. However, the strategic implications as well as the shortcomings of *MiC 2025* have not been well understood, especially with regard to the transformation of working conditions and labour markets in China's emerging 'digital capitalism'.

This chapter will analyse China's advanced manufacturing strategy under the present conditions of the Chinese and the global economy, characterised by slower growth in emerging economies (in China labelled 'the new normal') and continuing instability as heritage of the financial crisis of 2008–9. We will examine *Made in China 2025* and the related 'Internet Plus' strategy for advanced information networks in the context of socioeconomic rebalancing in the wake of the global financial and economic crisis of 2008–9 and the resulting problems of industrial development. Continuing weakness in basic technologies, innovation bound to domestic mid-technology mass markets and mounting overcapacity in industries that had been driven by heavy investment in infrastructure and real estate are expressions of these problems. The major obstacles to socioeconomic rebalancing, however, are in the continuing instability of wage incomes and increasing social inequality, triggered by the persistence of low-wage production models in most industrial sectors (Lüthje and McNally, 2015). A sustainable path of innovation-driven economic development would require fundamental changes in work systems, labour market regulation, professional education and industrial relations. A socially and environmentally sustainable paradigm shift in industrial development, therefore, would call for substantial reform in basic institutions of socioeconomic regulation, rather than the present policies of rebalancing without institutional change (Lüthje, 2017 forthcoming).

The chapter will give an overview of major trends and develop an analytical framework for further research, based on empirical studies of global production networks, industrial upgrading, economic rebalancing and industrial relations in China in recent years. We propose to look at the emerging new forms of digital production as a sociotechnical transformation that, in the long term, may result in a new paradigm of manufacturing organisation. The driving force of this development is not digital technologies as such, but often complex economic, social and political power relations, emerging from the existing regimes of accumulation and modes of regulation in national and global contexts. To better understand socioeconomic conditions of this process in China, we refer to the concept of Sino-capitalism (McNally, 2013) and to our own analysis of regimes of accumulation in Chinese core industries in the perspective of regulation theory (Lüthje, 2017 forthcoming) and of regimes of production based on labour process theory (Lüthje, Luo and Zhang, 2013). We will try to (1) explain the basic economic and social parameters of the present drive to develop advanced manufacturing; (2) analyse the key strategies of *Made in China 2025* and the complex constellation of private and state actors governing its implementation; (3) trace basic pathways of restructuring along the different production regimes in core manufacturing industries; (4) examine key projects of manufacturing automation and their impact on work at firm and shop-floor level; and (5) discuss preliminary conclusions concerning labour standards in the age of digital manufacturing.

Understanding China's Trajectory

The hype in international and Chinese media about the digital revolution in manufacturing does not help much in understanding the motivation for China's ambitious drive for advanced manufacturing. Techno-determinist conceptions of the 'fourth industrial revolution', as in the German *Industrie*

4.0 debate, may provide good selling points for digital manufacturing equipment (Kaeser, 2014) but obscure the driving forces behind the changing faces of manufacturing both in advanced and in emerging economies. A more realistic approach may be to look at 'intelligent manufacturing' (zhineng zhizao (智能制造), the term mostly used in China) as a newly emerging sociotechnological paradigm of manufacturing organisation, similar perhaps to the lean production concepts of the 1980s and 1990s. In this perspective, intelligent manufacturing constitutes a reaction to the specific problems of innovation and social organisation of the capitalist process of production under existing practices, embodied in the currently dominant models of lean and flexible production and the related globalisation of value chains. The process of reshaping production is highly open and contingent on conflicting economic, social and political interests and forces.

In the wake of the massive globalisation of manufacturing since the 1990s, the economic and social contradictions of post-Fordist production models are felt particularly in emerging economies like China, which became the industrial workshops of today's world economy. As has been widely analysed in the literature on global commodity chains (Gereffi and Korzeniewicz, 1994), value chains (Sturgeon and Kawakami 2011) or production networks (Borrus et al., 2000; Henderson et al., 2002; Lüthje, Hürtgen et al., 2013), the massive shift of relatively advanced industrial production capacity to a small number of developing countries has been intimately intertwined with the vertical disintegration of production embodied in the various manifestations of modularised production and innovation, such as the Toyota model in the automotive industry (Womack et al., 1990), Wintelism in the IT sector (Borrus and Zysman, 1997) or the retailer-led production models in the shoe industry and the textile and garment industry (Bair, 2002).

This sea change in the localisation of global production activities has resulted in the enormous growth of manufacturing in newly industrialising countries, substantial industrial upgrading through the creation of relatively developed supplier networks and the relocation of innovative activities in the context of global design networks (Ernst, 2006). However, the integration into global production networks remained limited in its potential for indigenous innovation, and it had also increased social polarisation, since world-market-oriented production at the lower and middle tiers of global production networks relies on large-scale forces of cheap labour, provided mostly by migrant workers (Lüthje et al., 2013). The working conditions in most of these sectors continue to make negative headlines and have led to disastrous events, such as the wave of suicides at electronics maker Foxconn in China in 2010 or the more recent collapse of the Rana Plaza manufacturing building in Bangladesh.

The economic, innovative and social limits of this form of world-market integration have come to the surface with the end of the China boom (Hung, 2016) and the transition to slower growth rates, known in China as the 'new normal'. The massive effort to rebalance the Chinese economy in the wake of the 2008–9 global financial and economic crisis has fuelled the rapid growth of the domestic market with significantly increased roles for Chinese brand-name firms and suppliers. But this growth has been driven mainly by heavy fixed-capital investment in infrastructure, housing and related supply industries. Despite rising wages and consumer spending, the share of consumption as a proportion of GDP has remained at the same low levels since the late 1990s (Hung, 2016, p. 235 ff.). Fixed-capital investment can no longer prevent slowing economic growth; over-accumulation of capital is mounting; and the continuing instability of urban wage incomes due to the lack of collective bargaining and other institutional safeguards (Lüthje, et al., 2013) keeps China's wage-earning middle classes fragile (*Financial Times*, 2014).

China's trajectory of manufacturing modernisation under the auspices of post-Fordist production models has contributed to the contradictions of the present accumulation regime (Lüthje, 2017 forthcoming). In the wake of global production networks, state-of-the-art production systems have been implemented in core manufacturing industries and supported structural overcapacity. The automobile industry, dominated by joint ventures between Chinese state-owned enterprises (SOEs) and multinational carmakers mainly producing for the domestic market, represents a most visible example. Following a lengthy period of restructuring of state-owned carmakers in the 1990s, multinational companies implemented state-of-the art production systems in most factories, especially in many of the greenfield plants erected since 2008–9. This has led to skyrocketing productivity growth for several years, accompanied by rising wages for workers in core assembly plants. However, indigenous innovation has remained weak, since Chinese state-owned carmakers rely on reaping profits from making and selling foreign-branded cars rather than developing their own products and brand names. At the same time, production networks (as well as wages and working conditions) remain highly segmented between joint ventures and car suppliers, especially at the lower end of production systems. Since there is little indigenous development of new product concepts, there has not been much room to reconfigure manufacturing systems around the needs of the Chinese market, especially in the field of new energy vehicles and mobility systems (Lüthje and Tian, 2015).

In export-oriented industries dominated by private and foreign capital, production models are different, but the weakness in indigenous innovation in manufacturing systems has been comparable. In the IT industry, cutting-edge production systems have been introduced by major contract manufacturers under their strategy to offer highly standardised manufacturing services in factories around the world. In recent years this has resulted in the proliferation of large-scale factories and industrial parks in export production areas, accompanied by the rapid construction of similar manufacturing bases in Central and Western China. The emerging new brand-name companies in the Chinese IT industry, led by Huawei, Lenovo, ZTE, Xiaomi and so on, have used this manufacturing infrastructure to successfully imitate 'factory-less' production under the 'Wintel'-model (Lüthje and Butollo, 2016). The exploitation of highly developed modularised manufacturing (and low-wage workers) has significantly facilitated the rise of Chinese brand-name companies, but most of their products are still made from foreign-branded, imported core components in foreign-owned and overseas Chinese-owned factories. Manufacturing of basic components, namely semiconductors, has remained relatively weak (Ernst, 2017 forthcoming). Also, as we will explain in more detail below, the technological and organisational level of manufacturing among indigenous Chinese electronic firms that own manufacturing facilities has remained relatively low, lagging behind global contract manufacturers.

Under these conditions, China's manufacturing sector is no longer playing the role of a productivity driver that compensates for weaker productivity in most other sectors of the Chinese economy: construction and services in particular. This is reflected in the protracted slowdown of macro-level productivity in China since 2010, when the annual growth in GDP per worker started to drop from previous levels of 10–12 per cent to under 4 per cent in 2015/16, according to data from The Conference Board and the *Financial Times* (2016). We argue that the relative slowdown in manufacturing modernisation itself is a result of the world-market-led restructuring of recent years – that is, the import of advanced manufacturing systems with the simultaneous employment of large numbers of low-wage workers in global production networks. Like in the global arena, hopes for the rejuvenation of China's growth model are heavily pinned on automation. The Chinese government, therefore, has declared 'innovation-driven development' the number-one priority of economic policies under the 'new normal'.

MiC 2025 –Strategies and Actors

Against this background, *MiC 2025* is a masterplan for industrial development and transformation, put forward with reference to new technological paradigms in advanced manufacturing. Compared to Germany's *Industrie 4.0*, *MiC 2025* is much broader and not restricted to a technology-focused vision of 'cyber-physical systems'. Rather, it is a strategic concept of industrial development and transformation in the broader context of socioeconomic rebalancing. It focuses on developing core technologies through fundamental research, on the one hand, and on sectoral and trans-sectoral restructuring of chains of production and technology, on the other: patterns that are similar to Japan's industrial policy in the 1960s and 1970s (Okimoto, 1989; Johnson et al., 1989) or older concepts of industrial chains in France or other European nations with strong traditions of state-led industrial development. Unlike previous approaches to industrial policy in China (and different from Japan and South Korea), the concept does not bet on the creation of national champions from restructured SOEs, a strategy that had failed in industries such as automotive, telecommunications equipment and others (Chin, 2010; Pawlicki, 2015). It instead picks up on the relatively successful development of strong Chinese players in mid- and high-technology markets that emerged 'from the sidelines' in industries such as solar systems, wind turbines, LED, household appliances or, most prominently, telecommunications and advanced information technologies (Ernst and Naughton, 2008; Brandt and Thun, 2010; Nahm and Steinfeld, 2014; Butollo, 2014).

This orientation on creating strong Chinese-led production networks and value chains is also reflected in the emphasis given to advanced communication infrastructures, as outlined in the Internet Plus strategy. This concept, proposed simultaneously and in coordination with *MiC 2025*, represents another industrial masterplan to develop the high-capacity data infrastructure needed for digital manufacturing and the comprehensive integration of material and non-material production processes in Internet-based communication networks, known as the 'Internet of Things' (IoT). In contrast to Germany and some other advanced industrial nations, China does have a comprehensive and relatively coherent plan for the development of public infrastructure in this area. At the same time, the language of those programmes signals a shift from older conceptions of 'indigenous innovation' with a focus on building Chinese brand-name companies and core technologies (Liu et al., 2007) to value-chain-oriented concepts of development. Non-state-owned enterprises of all kinds play a key role in *MiC 2025*, a remarkable step beyond the traditional strategy of positioning SOEs as technology leaders while strengthening market forces (Lüthje et al., 2013).

MiC 2025 reflects the insight of the Chinese leadership that a purely export-driven model of innovation (climbing the ladder from OEM to ODM and to OBM) has exhausted its potentials for China's further industrial development (Ernst, 2017 forthcoming). The strategy moves away from approaches of hooking into global value chains (GVCs) of certain flagship companies or industrial sectors (as proposed by GVC theories; cf. Gereffi and Fernandez-Stark, 2016) towards the development of a relatively integrated system of China-based globalised networks of production and innovation led by Chinese companies and industries. This historic change of perspectives has been made clear by the Chinese leadership, but it is not well understood in Western discussions. In a remarkable speech to provincial-level party cadres, for instance, President Xi Jinping explained China's success story of world-market-oriented production and constant upgrading within global supply chains, but he also gave a pointed analysis of why this strategy will no longer support economic growth, social stability and the country's quest for global leadership. Under the dominance of imperialism and colonialism, and later the global split between capitalism and socialism, so his argument went, China was excluded from the first, second and third industrial revolutions. Reform and opening to the world market since 1978 gave China a role as the biggest manufacturing power, which would now enable the country to play a leading role in the impending industrial revolution of the twenty-first century (Xi, 2016).

Like most other national industrial policies in China, *MiC 2025* is a top-down concept, made by engineers and leading science agencies and put forward in terms of technological evolutionism. The Chinese Academy of Sciences and engineering departments of major universities and of the Ministry of Industry and Information Technology (MIIT) and the Ministry of Research and Technology are the main proponents of such a technocratic vision of China's role as a strong manufacturing nation. The underlying technological determinism is reflected in the prominent and frequent reference given to the German *Industrie 4.0* debate and in a large number of publications proposing this approach as a model for China (e.g. Wang, 2015; Xia and Zhao, 2015). Measured against this yardstick, the official policy documents give a relatively clear analysis of China's present competitive advantages and disadvantages, including existing problems of developing core components, such as in the chip industry (cf. Ernst, 2014). In order to move away from the global factory model, advanced manufacturing know-how created in China becomes a critical element for Chinese-led global production networks. However, the concept does not openly address the deeper roots of China's difficulties to integrate indigenous innovation in technologies and products on the one hand and manufacturing on the other. Nor is there a vision of how to overcome the path dependencies of the former growth model, which are rooted in ownership structures and power relations. In the field of new energy vehicles, for example, the government documents lay out a complex scenario of product development and integrated supply chains, but there is no strategic approach on how to institutionalise regulation of the car industry in order to curb the triple alliance between Chinese auto holdings, their government shareholders and global carmakers in joint ventures—an alliance that aims at expanding the production of foreign-branded conventional cars to maximise profits by exploiting low-wage work along their supply chains. Similarly, with regard to the IT industry, the disconnect between the relatively successful product innovation on the part of Chinese IT brand-name firms, on the one hand, and the lack of innovation in manufacturing (along with the related forms of neo-Taylorist work organisation), on the other, is not even mentioned as a policy problem (Lüthje and McNally, 2015; for extensive analysis, see Lüthje, 2017 forthcoming).

Not only does this lack of strategic analysis in the relevant government documents as well as in the accompanying literature in academic and party media (e.g. Bi and Ma, 2013) reflect the continuing priority of economic growth and competitiveness over socially and ecologically sustainable development. It also points to the institutional weakness of labour and environmental standards and of the representation of workers and relevant communities within China's political system. Although *MiC 2025* is supposed to have a major impact on work and labour markets, the trade unions, the Ministry of Labour and Social Security and the labour bureaus at provincial and local levels did not participate in its drafting. New automation technologies are promoted in the name of combating the notorious labour shortages in key manufacturing industries (*jiqi huan ren* – robot replaces man), but there are no assessments of the mid- and long-term impacts on the labour market and on skill development from the Chinese government or by relevant research institutions (Ernst, 2016 forthcoming). In short, the present discourse does not address the negative impact of neo-Taylorist rationalisation strategies over the recent two decades on the development of work standards and workforce education. *MiC 2025* is symptomatic of the continuing weakness of corporatist regulation in the Chinese political system (McNally, 2013), and in industrial relations in particular (Taylor et al., 2003).

Regimes of Production and Trajectories of Automation

The selection of enterprises that are singled out as pilot projects by the MIIT differs from what Western observers would expect of such a programme. For 2015, 94 projects were listed under the Intelligent Manufacturing Special Project of *Made in China 2025*; for 2016, there were 64 (MIIT, 2015, 2016). The list of participants is an across-the-board selection of manufacturing companies and research institutes from all parts of China, including companies from fields such as dairy production, traditional Chinese medicine pharmaceutics, shipbuilding and steel production. It does emphasise providers of IT, robotics and industrial services, but the selection demonstrates the ambitions of a comprehensive programme of generating product- and process-related upgrading. The heterogeneity of actors indicates that there is no one-size-fits-all path of 'intelligent manufacturing'. Prior research has highlighted that Chinese industry is characterised by diverging regimes of production with marked differences regarding their production models (including their position in global production networks), production technologies, employment policies and labour relations (for a systematic introduction, see Lüthje, Luo and Zhang, 2013). The implementation of 'intelligent manufacturing' must be analysed in the context of the resulting path dependencies. Based on existing analysis of production regimes and rationalisation strategies of the relevant industrial sectors in China, one can trace the following scenario.

Large SOEs and joint ventures have mostly *state-bureaucratic* or *corporate-bureaucratic* production regimes, which mirror the heritage of the traditional socialist management system or its complicated marriage with the work systems of large multinational corporations in joint ventures. Such industrial core companies have undergone considerable transformation, during which highly modern production systems were introduced. The automobile industry, for example, has seen the accelerated introduction of state-of-the art production equipment and Japanese and Western models of lean production (Zhang, 2008, 2015; Lüthje and Tian, 2015). Some carmakers have introduced relatively comprehensive professional education and training for higher-skilled workers (Jürgens and Krzywdzinski, 2015). Car companies do not figure prominently among the participants in *MiC 2025*, but they are seen as the role models for advanced automation in China, especially with regard to the deployment of robots. Most automakers introduce strategies of intelligent manufacturing, but as a gradual improvement of existing methods. The emphasis is on advanced systems of lean or modular production, such as Toyota's second-generation production system (TPS2), Honda's SSS or Volkswagen's MQB/MQL, which are typically introduced in greenfield plants in relatively new locations of car manufacturing (2015–16 field research data).

Among the newer privately or semi-privately owned Chinese industrial enterprises, in technology-intensive industries such as IT and telecommunications, household appliances, the solar panel and wind turbine industries or certain segments of the auto industry, *corporate high-performance* regimes of production prevail. Companies have adapted flexible employment and performance-related wage systems typically from US, Taiwanese or Korean companies. Most of the rising stars of Chinese brand-name firms are in this category. As far as they have not relied on foreign or overseas Chinese contract manufacturers, such companies have grown on the basis of relatively simple and labour-intensive manufacturing systems that often mirror the labour practices of *classic low-wage regimes* at the low end of global production networks. They are most sharply exposed to the limits of low-wage manufacturing and continuing labour shortages among semi-skilled workers, of which there seemed to be unlimited supply. Efforts for automation are coupled with a catch-up on basic methods of lean production. A typical example are large Chinese TV makers participating in *MiC 2025*. One of the leading companies that we studied is now implementing automated assembly equipment for printed circuit boards (known as surface-mount technology, SMT) that has been industry standard for over 20 years. Led by a group of newly hired Korean manufacturing managers, the company is developing an enterprise resource-management system modelled after the practices of a major US-based electronics contract manufacturer with a heavy presence in the region (2016 field research data).

Under regimes of *flexible mass production*, epitomised by the large global contract manufacturers in electronics such as Foxconn, the automation drive is much less radical than is often suggested by recent media reports. Foxconn's announcement in 2012 of the installation of 1 million robots within one year (Se, 2015) has not materialised, and the company is far from its vision to become a major producer of industrial robots. Automation is directed mostly at the elimination of bottlenecks of semi-skilled workers in certain manufacturing processes and of labour insubordination, for which the contract manufacturers are notorious. The general level of automation is relatively high already, since most factories follow the globally standardised EMSs (electronics manufacturing services) model and the quality requirements of first-tier brand-name customers (Lüthje, Hürtgen et al., 2013). So far, there has been no breakthrough to new levels of automation, since manual labour seems to be more suited to a large range of tasks in electronics assembly, especially in final assembly and the configuration of customer-specific orders (2015–16 field research data).

At companies in labour-intensive low-tech industries, the mainstay of *classic low-wage* regimes of production, rising labour costs are particularly pressing since their business strategies rest on the extensive use of cheap labour and other resources. Intelligent manufacturing here is equated with the introduction of standard automation equipment, which has become affordable due to the lower cost of robots and the emergence of Chinese service providers that adjust automation equipment to the specific needs of local enterprises. The economics of automation are directed strictly at the reduction of costs, with return on investment in robot equipment expected within very short periods, usually one or two years. Automation is focused on single operations that require a certain amount of experience under mostly harsh conditions, for which workers are increasingly scarce. Industrial robots thereby often eliminate the tasks of relatively skilled migrant workers in, for example, textile and garment manufacturing, consumer household goods of all kinds, furniture and lower-tier automotive suppliers as part of their automation strategies (2015–16 field research data).

Although this overview seems to reveal highly diverging strategies and trajectories along regimes of production, the heavy emphasis on cutting costs and on automation is a common feature. Our preliminary mapping of the field suggests that most of the technological and organisational changes promoted under *MiC 2025* do not aim at comprehensively 'networked' and 'digitalised' manufacturing. Most of the automation projects we have studied so far entailed not 'cyber-physical systems' but basic or advanced automation, which would correspond to the stages of industry '2.0' or '3.0' in the lingo of the German *Industrie 4.0* discussion. Apart from the deployment of industrial robots, the most important element of the current rationalisation drive seems to be the introduction of comprehensive systems of lean production and the corresponding enterprise resource-management systems. Against this background, the strategy of 'robot replaces man' appears to be the least common denominator for describing changes at the workplace, and therefore provides a handy political slogan for Chinese policy makers and the media. The promise of sweeping changes with short-term cost reductions seems to be particularly suited to mobilise cash-strapped small and medium enterprises at the middle and lower ends of supply chains to invest in automation equipment and to promote the goals of provincial and local governments to reach ambitious but often unrealistic returns in their industrial development plans.

Contours of Advanced Manufacturing at the Shop Floor

China's leading companies in the home appliances industry have emerged as prominent examples of industrial enterprises that pioneer the path of 'intelligent manufacturing'. Two of those enterprises were the subject of our investigations in 2016. They aggressively promote their efforts to build 'interconnected factories' with reference to the international discourse on innovation and manufacturing in the digital age, including the German *Industrie 4.0* concept. These facilities are seen as flagship projects in the context of *MiC 2025*. Both companies also represent role models of indigenous innovation since they emerged as two of the largest makers of home appliances worldwide. They developed successful brand names, quality production and supply-chain management under their own direction. One of the companies is a former SOE (company A), the other an enterprise formerly owned by a village collective that became private after a management buyout (company B). Key to their strategies has been the production of large volumes of household equipment for the domestic market, partially by taking advantage of foreign technological inputs which were obtained through joint ventures. The companies were able to position themselves as viable alternatives to more expensive, imported products and thereby entered a path of continuous growth and product improvement. As a result of this successful upgrading trajectory, one of the companies emerged as a well-known brand on export markets and acquired factories in Europe and the US; the other is striving to become a major player in manufacturing automation equipment and recently acquired a leading robot maker from Germany.

Our investigation focused on the most advanced air conditioner factories of both companies.[2] The *production models* of both companies in the area of air conditioning systems are similar. They rely on a network of in-house assembly plants in several locations across China that deliver the relatively heavy products to regional markets. Both companies maintain large networks of external suppliers, mostly located in regional proximity. Supply-chain coordination has been based on relatively traditional methods (telephone and email communication), but seems to be highly flexible and efficient. The most visible change related to intelligent manufacturing is the extensive integration of those factories into advanced networks of digitalised supply-chain management and new models of web-based marketing and sales. This includes a relatively sophisticated system of web-based product configuration by the consumer (C2B), publicised extensively through exhibitions, video clips and elaborate websites. Furthermore, both companies create environments for smart home appliances which can be controlled by smart phones or tablet computers and are linked to a user community whose data is collected and analysed.

Comprehensive networking of this kind requires extensive internal control of manufacturing data. Both companies have implemented 'big data' systems, managed from large control rooms in the respective factories. In company A's lead factory, more than 12,000 sensors generate about 4 million data units per day, displaying the position and physical properties of the components. The production process is thus monitored in real time through a virtual image, which can be used to adjust the production flow and to spot disruptions. As soon as a customer's order has been paid, it is sent to the factory, where the sequence of production is set in accordance with real-time demand and in coordination with the supplier network. The customer is able to monitor the state of their order throughout the whole process and is provided with real-time videos of the production process – although not of an individual order. In order to shorten delivery cycles, the supply chain is sped up and consolidated. The number of supply modules was reduced from 300 to 77 pieces, all of which can be delivered within 12 hours. The management of company A boasts that this will reduce supplier delivery times to 24 hours from 72 hours under the existing system.

Despite such comprehensive efforts, the variety of products was limited at the time of our investigation. At company A, the share of customised products made up 5 per cent of the production volume, and the bulk of products comprised standardised models. At company B, the factory produced about 20 different configurations of air conditioners on the same assembly lines. But there were no products configured to orders of single customers, rather batches of 5–10 products or more of the same variety, following the orders of retail distributors. In both cases, the product portfolio consists of a small number of standardised cases that differ from each other in a limited number of specifications and components. The main field of customisation concerns the shell of the indoor units, which is provided by a supplier that prints the designs upon them.

With regard to *work organisation and working conditions* automation through the widespread use of assembly robots was the most prominent feature of 'intelligent manufacturing'. In both companies, automation focused on the production of evaporators and condensers and the final assembly of the outdoor units of the air conditioning sets. These components are considered technological key elements, since the quality of the materials and the welding are crucial for the functioning and the durability of an air conditioner. Work in these manufacturing divisions is usually relatively skilled (welding) and physically demanding since it involves the processing of heavy parts of sheet and stamped metal. In these areas, large numbers of robots replaced workers in cutting, welding and assembly. Elimination of strenuous work and quality control were cited as the main reasons for automation, since robots guarantee the uniformity of processes and the safe handling of the heavy units. Job reductions were substantial. Company B publicly announced that it would eliminate 68 per cent of the roughly 50,000 workers in its six air conditioning assembly plants between 2011 and 2018. In the case of the surveyed factory, about 50 per cent of roughly 3,000 jobs were eliminated at the time of the investigation.

In the assembly department of the indoor units, a different picture prevails. This segment contains mainly light, mostly manual assembly work of parts and components with a higher degree of product variation. The degree of automation and the use of heavy equipment is much lower than it is in the assembly of outdoor units. Traditionally, the production process involves a high proportion of manual assembly work by using electric screwdrivers. Standardised products were assembled on a short production line of five to six steps where workers passed on the sets after manually adding and fixing certain components or the outer shell. In this 'intelligent manufacturing' section, the customised share of the products, namely those that implied specific wishes by customers, is higher. Parts were pulled out of the regular production chain to single work stations, where individual workers undertook up to 30 steps to assemble the devices. Each step was indicated to them by 3D symbols on a screen. All in all, automation thus remains limited to standardised production processes, whereas the flexible assembly of customised products remains the prerogative of manual workers.

In terms of skill requirements, automation has different implications in the two main sections of the assembly process. In outdoor-unit assembly, there clearly is a trend of further standardisation and intensification of work. The remaining assembly staff works in between the automated assembly sections in segments of five to ten workers. Work speed seems to be completely controlled by the complex machinery; there are no visible pockets of manual work in which workers could influence their work speed. The machinery is controlled by technicians and engineers, many of them from the equipment supplier. Line workers are not involved in setting up and maintaining the machinery. In indoor-unit assembly, customising products requires a certain work experience and is executed by workers who have learned to assemble various types of models on the regular production line. However, upskilling remains limited since the use of 3D guidance for every production step is designed to simplify the cognitive element of this work.

The production regime at both companies is generally characterised by *labour relations* in which trade unions and protection of labour standards are weak. Both companies generally accept labour laws; we could not find major violations, especially with regard to working hours. Trade unions exist in both companies, but they appear to be weak. In company A, the role of the trade union is rooted in the historic practice of a state-owned enterprise, in which the union and the party organisation have a comprehensive presence. In company B, there are no such traditions. According to the district trade union, trade union elections, as requested by a recent guideline of the provincial government, have not yet taken place in the factory. In both companies, there are no collective negotiations on wages and working conditions and, therefore, no contractual safeguards for workers regarding technological or organisational changes at the workplace. Wages are determined individually and fixed in each worker's personal labour contract, as common in China. Hourly wages prevail in outdoor-unit assembly, whereas piece-rate incentives are used in indoor-unit assembly. In the case of company A, the workers at the new, 3D-led flexible configuration workstations could earn more than their colleagues at the standard production line, depending on their output. The work performance of each individual worker is shown on a screen. Digital monitoring of the production process is also used to control work performance and to trace the source of failures.

Conclusion: Labour Standards and Decent Work in the Age of Digital Manufacturing

In this article we offered an understanding of China's trajectory into advanced manufacturing driven by the productivity slowdown in the present models of globalised production networks and the need to restructure the economic and social growth model of China's emergent capitalism. As a masterplan for China's industrial transformation, *MiC 2025* reflects the global and domestic constraints of the dominant accumulation regime and spells out a strategic scenario of restructuring manufacturing technologies and value chains with the goal of acquiring a leading position for Chinese brand-name firms and technology providers in domestic and global production networks. The underlying strategic shift in industrial and technology policies away from focusing on large SOEs as flagship companies towards a network-oriented approach, in which non-state-owned newcomer firms play key strategic roles, has been missed by most foreign observers. The dynamics of innovation, therefore, are not so much in the deployment of robots and other advanced automation equipment on the shop floor but in the accelerated reconfiguration of value chains.

The broad spectrum of industrial actors involved in *MiC 2025* results in a variety of highly different scenarios of industrial automation and robotisation, commonly seen as the core of this effort, and specific trajectories of change along regimes of production in various sectors and subsectors. In most industries, catching up on existing automation technologies, digital enterprise management systems and schemes of lean production dominate the agenda, rather than the large-scale deployment of advanced robots and digital networks. Our analysis of two key 'interconnected factories' reveals how such pathways of manufacturing automation are based on advanced but mostly standard technologies and are linked to innovative strategies of network-based consumer relations and supply-chain management. On the side of work, however, massive cost-cutting through automation is the key element, and there are no changes to the existing neo-Taylorist forms of work organisation.

From these observations, one may conclude that digital manufacturing in China is characterised by organisational innovations that entail a recombination of technology- and labour-intensive elements of the production process, based on the existing patterns of (mostly neo-Taylorist) rationalisation (Butollo, 2014; Lüthje, Hürtgen et al., 2013). This proposition, which surely requires further empirical evidence, differs from technology-centric visions such as the frequently voiced expectation of China's factories becoming 'staffless' or Western studies that focus on theoretical possibilities of substituting workers through robots (Frey and Osbourne, 2013). One may ask whether this recombination actually entails a new paradigm of manufacturing organisation rather than a catch-up in manufacturing technologies with little or no upgrading of work. The answer, however, cannot be given from a shop-floor perspective, but has to consider the larger environment of restructuring of value chains.

In this field, China's innovative potentials are tremendous. The reconfiguration of value chains is driven by the rapidly unfolding large-scale infrastructures of electronic commerce, in which China has now assumed a leading position in the global economy. We assume that this development will profoundly change the hitherto existing structure of production networks and value chains. The leading players of China's emerging 'network capitalism' (Lüthje, 2017 forthcoming), particularly internet giants Ali Baba, Baidu and Tencent, are assuming the position of the new intermediaries connecting factories, suppliers and sales channels. They thereby assume the role of system integrators of future models of digital manufacturing. The drive among Chinese brand-name manufacturing firms to develop new Internet-related business models and supply chains, such as in our examples above, can also be seen as a strategic move to maintain control over strategic market interfaces vis-à-vis the leading e-commerce platforms.

The Chinese case highlights the complex technological, organisational and social interactions in this transformation process and its specific character as a large-scale restructuring of production. At the same time, the importance of human work in its existing forms and of the regulation of the wage relation becomes visible. The pathway of rationalisation in Chinese factories, obviously, cannot be understood without their labour regimes based on weak contractual regulations of the wage-labour nexus (Boyer, 2017 forthcoming) and the massive use of low-wage migrant labour. The 'digital revolution' in manufacturing, therefore, reiterates the importance of bringing the labour process back into the research on global production networks and value chains (Lüthje et al., 2013; cf. Gereffi and Fernandez-Stark, 2016). The combination of neo-Taylorism on the shop floor and highly innovative networking in supply chains, distribution and consumer relations may emerge as the most characteristic element of 'intelligent manufacturing Made in China', with potentially heavy influence on the pathways of restructuring in the global context.

Politically, our analysis confirms the importance of labour standards and stronger links between the growth of productivity and wages as a problem of economic regulation, social organisation and public policy. The blatant absence of these topics from public discussions and policies in China and the failure of the official trade unions to address these issues in the political arena and at the shop-floor reveal the urgency of institutional reforms in labour policies. At the shop floor, the massive drives to automate and restructure production confront Chinese workers and trade unions with the day-to-day issues of technological change at the workplace under the condition of a lack of legal, contractual safeguards for workers and a lack of viable representation of employee interests. The magnitude of the problem and the potentially massive impact of automation on China's labour markets (especially for migrant workers) raise fundamental questions of social stability and point to the need to advance China's labour reforms from the protection of individual rights to the institutionalisation of collective labour rights (Chang, 2015).

As in developed industrial countries, the question of labour standards has to be addressed as part and parcel of the challenge to upgrade industrial production in the age of digital manufacturing. Sustainable industrial development calls for an integrated mode of development in which innovative technologies can support the creation of decent work and well-paid jobs. Fortunately, industrial relations are in motion in China, at least in some economically relevant regions. Guangdong province, China's largest manufacturing region and a laboratory for experiments with advanced manufacturing, has recently enacted significant changes to its labour relations model by admitting democratic elections of trade unions, collective bargaining and democratic workplace representation at workplace and company level. Frequent labour unrest under the conditions of notorious labour shortages was a main driver of this significant social innovation. *Made in China 2025* may promise that 'robot replaces man', but it will certainly not end the social problems of regulating industrial relations.

Notes

1 The authors wish to thank the members of our research team, Mrs. Gao Jing, M.A., Mr. Xu Hui, M.A., Dr. Luo Siqi, Lin Haibin, M.A., and Mrs Tian Miao, M.A., for their excellent assistance and comments. Empirical research comprised 15 visits to factories of relevant industries and about 50 in-depth interviews with managers, industry experts, government officials, and trade unions. The research was supported by the Volkswagen Group China.

2 Our approach to investigate regimes of production along basic parameters of production models, work organisation, working conditions and industrial relations follows the methodology laid out in Lüthje et al., 2013.

REFERENCES

Bair, J. (2002) 'Beyond the Maquila Model? NAFTA and the Mexican Apparel Industry', *Industry and Innovation*, 9, 3, 203–25.

Bi, D. and S. Ma (2013) 'Xin gongye geming weizhe shenme' (Where goes the new industrial revolution)? *Xuexi Shibao* (Study Times), 2013, No. 7.

Borrus, M. and J. Zysman (1997) *Wintelism and the Changing Terms of Global Competition. Prototype of the Future?* (BRIE Working Paper 96B). Berkeley, CA: Berkeley Roundtable on the International Economy.

Borrus, M., D. Ernst and S. Haggard (eds) (2000) *International Production Networks in Asia: Rivalry or Riches?* (Abingdon: Routledge).

Boyer, R. (ed.) (2017 forthcoming) *China Analyzed by Regulation Theory* (Beijing: China Social Science Press (in Chinese)).

Brandt, L. and E. Thun (2010) *The Fight For the Middle: Upgrading, Competition, and Industrial Development in China* (University of Toronto, Department of Economics: Working Paper 395).

Butollo, F. (2014), *The End of Cheap Labour? Industrial Transformation and 'Social Upgrading' in China* (Frankfurt and New York: Campus).

Chang, K. (2015) *Role of Trade Unions in Labor Relations Governance*, keynote speech at the 7th Annual Industrial Relations Conference, School of Labor Relations and Human Resources, 28–29 November 2015 (Beijing: Renmin University).

Chin, G. (2010) *China's Automotive Modernization. The Party-State and Multinational Corporations* (Basingstoke and New York: Palgrave Macmillan).

Ernst, D. (2006) *Upgrading through Innovation in a Small Network Economy: Insights from Taiwan's IT Industry* (Paper presented at workshop High Tech Regions 2.0 – Sustainability and Reinvention, Stanford University, November 13–14).

Ernst, D. (2014) *From Catching Up to Forging Ahead? China's Prospects in Semiconductors* (East-West Center Working Papers: Innovation and economic growth series, No. 1).

Ernst, D. (2017 forthcoming) 'Advanced Manufacturing and China's Future for Jobs', in E. Paus (ed.) *The New Technological Revolution: What Future for Jobs and Livelihoods?* (Ithaca, NY: Cornell University Press).

▶

Ernst, D. and B. Naughton (2008) 'China's Emerging Industrial Economy. Insights from the IT Industry' in C. A. McNally (ed.) *China's Emergent Political Economy. Capitalism in the Dragon's Lair* (London: Routledge).

Financial Times (2014) 'The Fragile Middle – Slowdown Puts 1bn Middle Class at Risk. FT Analysis Questions Durability of March Out of Poverty in Emerging Markets', 13 April 2014.

Financial Times (2016) 'The Productivity Puzzle That Baffles the World's Economies', 30 May 2016.

Frey, C.B. and M. A. Osbourne (2013) *The Future of Employment: How Susceptible are Jobs to Computerisation* (Oxford: University of Oxford).

Gereffi, G. and K. Fernandez-Stark (2016) *Global Value Chain Analysis: A Primer* (Raleigh, NC: Duke University Center for Globalization, Governance and Competitiveness).

Gereffi, G. and M. Korzeniewicz (eds) (1994) *Commodity Chains and Global Capitalism* (Santa Barbara: ABC-CLIO).

Henderson, J., P. Dicken, M. Hess, N. Coe and H. W.-C. Yeung (2002) 'Global Production Networks and the Analysis of Economic Development', *Review of International Political Economy*, 9, 3, 436–64.

Hung, H. F. (2016) *The China Boom: Why China Will not Rule the World* (New York and Chichester: Columbia University Press).

Johnson, C., L. Tyson and J. Zysman (eds) (1989) *Politics and Productivity: How Japan's Development Strategy Works* (New York: Harper).

Jürgens, U. and M. Krzywdzinski (2015) 'Competence Development on the Shop Floor and Industrial Upgrading. Case Studies of Auto Makers in China', *The International Journal of Human Resource Management*, 26, 9, 1204–25.

Kaeser, J. (2014) '"Gongye 4.0" shidai ruhe jinxing chanye shengji? Zhuanfang deguo ximenzi gongsi zongcai Kaige ("Industry 4.0" – how does it affect industrial upgrading? An interview with Siemens CEO Joe Kaeser)', *Nanfang Ribao*, 16 July 2014.

Liu, X., B. Lüthje and P. Pawlicki (2007) 'China: Nationales Innovationssystem und marktwirtschaftliche Transformation', in F. Gerlach and A. Ziegler (eds) *Innovationspolitik: Wie kann Deutschland von anderen lernen?* (Marburg: Schüren Verlag), pp. 222–49.

Lüthje, B. (2017 forthcoming) 'Regimes of Accumulation and Modes of Regulation in China's Emergent Capitalism' in R. Boyer (ed.) *China Analyzed by Regulation Theory* (Beijing: China Social Science Press (in Chinese)).

Lüthje, B. and F. Butollo (2016) 'Why the Foxconn Model Doesn't Die. Production Networks and Labour Relations in the IT Industry in South China', *Globalizations*, 13, 6. http://dx.doi.org/10.1080/14747731.2016.1203132

Lüthje, B., S. Hürtgen, P. Pawlicki and M. Sproll (2013) *From Silicon Valley to Shenzhen: Global Production and Work in the IT Industry* (Landham, MD: Rowman & Littlefield).

Lüthje, B., S. Luo and H. Zhang (2013) *Beyond the Iron Rice Bowl: Regimes of Production and Industrial Relations in China* (Frankfurt and New York: Campus).

Lüthje, B. and C. A. McNally (2015) *China's Hidden Obstacles to Socioeconomic Rebalancing.* (Asia Pacific Issue No. 120).

Lüthje, B., C. A. McNally and T. ten Brink (2013) 'Rebalancing China's Emergent Capitalism: State Power, Economic Liberalization and Social Upgrading', *Journal of Current Chinese Affairs*, 42, 4, 3–16.

Lüthje, B. and M. Tian (2015) 'China's Automotive Industry: Structural Impediments to Socioeconomic Rebalancing', *International Journal of Automotive Technology and Management*, 15, 3, 244–67.

McNally, C. A. (2013) 'Refurbishing State Capitalism: A Policy Analysis of Efforts to Rebalance China's Political Economy', *Journal of Current Chinese Affairs*, 4, 45–71.

MIIT (Ministry of Industry and Information Technology of the People's Republic of China) (2015) *Gongyibu gongbu 94 ge zhineng zhizao zhuanxiang xiangmu* (MIIT publicly noticed 94 project cases for intelligent manufacturing). http://www.miit.gov.cn, June 3, 2015.

MIIT (2016) *Gongyibu gongbu 64 ge zhineng zhizao zhuanxiang xiangmu* (MIIT publicly noticed 64 project cases for intelligent manufacturing). http://www.miit.gov.cn, date accessed 17 June 2016.

Nahm, J. and E. S. Steinfeld (2014) 'Scale-up Nation: China's Specialization in Innovative Manufacturing', *World Development*, 54, 288–300.

Okimoto, D. I. (1989) *Between MITI and the Market: Japanese Industrial Policy for High Technology* (Palo Alto: Stanford University Press).

Pawlicki, P. (2015) *The Development of Chinese Telecom Equipment Companies and China's Industrial Policies – Adaptability and Unintended Consequences* (Unpublished Research Report. Goethe University Africa's Asian Options (AFRASO) Research Program).

Se, B. (2015) 'Manufacturing Tomorrow. Introducing Industry 4.0.' *German Chamber Ticker*, 1, 14–17.

Sturgeon, T. and M. Kawakami (2011) 'Global Value Chains in the Electronics Industry: Characteristics, Crisis, and Upgrading Opportunities for Firms from Developing Countries', *International Journal of Technological Learning, Innovation and Development*, 1, 4, 120–47.

Taylor, B., K. Chang Kai and Q. Li (2003) *Industrial Relations in China* (Cheltenham: Edward Elgar).

Wang, X. (2015) *Gongye 4.0: Tongxiang weilai de deguo zhizao 2025* (Industry 4.0: Towards the future Made in Germany 2025). Beijing: China Machine Press.

Womack, J. P., D. T. Jones and D. Roos (1990) *The Machine that Changed the World* (New York: Rawson Associates).

Xi, J. (2016) *Zai sheng bu ji zhuyao lingdao ganbu xuexi guanche dang de shiba jie wu zhongquanhui jingshen zhuanti yantao banshang de jianghua*, speech at leading provincial cadres studies meeting to promote the spirit of the 5th central committee meeting of the 18th party congress (Beijing: Xinhua).

Xia, Y. and S. Zhao (2015) *Gongye 4.0. Zhengcai fasheng de weilai* (Industry 4.0: The future taking place in the present) (Beijing: China Machine Press).

Zhang, L. (2008) 'Lean Production and Labor Controls in the Chinese Automobile Industry in An Age of Globalization', *International Labor and Working Class History*, 73, 24–44.

Zhang, L. (2015) *Inside China's Automobile Factories: The Politics of Labor and Worker Resistance* (New York: Cambridge University Press).

Virtual Temptations: Reorganising Work under Conditions of Digitisation, Virtualisation and Informatisation

Mascha Will-Zocholl

Digitisation and its consequences has moved to the centre of debates concerning the changes and challenges of contemporary work. Talking of 'digital capitalism' (Schiller, 2001) or even a 'digital revolution' (Rifkin, 2011) means comparing the dimension of these changes to those of the industrial revolution. Indeed, digitisation can be seen as a qualitative step to earlier developments. The products of labour are digitised (and informatised), which in turn makes them available in an undefined quantity, anywhere and at any time. The spread of the Internet has created a worldwide 'information space' (Boes and Kämpf, 2007), which enables information, models and data to be utilised at various times and in different places. This may give credence to the idea that (the) time and place (of work) no longer matter. New topologies of work are emerging, including new forms of communication and cooperation, new platform-based business models, new modes of work (like cloud and crowd working) and, at least, a new global division of labour. Recent research indicates that these digital practices are more contradictory than they initially appeared to be in the popular narratives. The local embeddedness of work and workers remains significant. However, the spatial relations within and between organisations are changing (e.g. Massey, 2005; Flecker and Meil, 2010; Mayer-Ahuja, 2011; Roth-Ebner, 2016). In the past, global strategies of reorganisation affected mainly production processes and simple service work. Yet, current impulses for informatisation shift the focus towards high-skilled work as sites of reorganisation and rationalisation in a digital world of work (see for example Levy and Murnane, 2005; Boes and Kämpf, 2010; Schmiede and Will-Zocholl, 2011; Pfeiffer, 2015).

An 'anything goes' attitude marks recent discussions on the possibilities and consequences of digitisation. 'Techno euphoria' and 'management utopias' arise – despite an earlier belief that such technology-focused perspectives had been overcome by the late 1980s (Bijker and Pinch, 2002). Management expects to gain more control and transparency over employees, to realise an increasing flexibility in working time and place, to generate cost savings and to accelerate the whole work process. Further, knowledge, skills and cheaper hiring costs of an emerging global workforce shall be used – also with respect to what is often called 'knowledge work'. In the face of ongoing and anticipated possibilities and changes, it is necessary to evaluate whether these lures of the virtual will in fact come true: what are the limitations of digitisation and virtualisation? Which challenges will emerge, and for which ones might strategies be needed? Is it really true that place no longer matters? To contribute to the current debate, this chapter will take into account research conducted into automotive engineering. The field of automotive engineering is particularly interesting because here digitisation and virtualisation, where physical prototypes are substituted by virtual ones, enable the availability of data, information and computer-aided design (CAD) models resulting in a range of consequences, ultimately leading to physical, usable products (cars). The progress made in this field can be considered as a forerunner for future developments elsewhere. In the automotive product-development process, ideas of distributing work across the world play an increasingly important role. The notion of 'placelessness' (Flecker and Schönauer, 2016) is enacted in visions of global engineering – 24-hour engineering around the world. The virtual seems to offer all the benefits of an efficient reorganisation of work. It begins to blur possible boundaries such as the significance of place or a dependency on 'tacit knowledge' (Polanyi, 1967) or 'experience-based work' (Böhle, 1994). Respectively, the use of even more technology, both tools and systems, tries to overcome any issues that arise in the process. With the virtualisation of objects, the material link to places and people loosens. The goal of reorganising work flexibly across space and time seems within reach. Under these conditions, Bailey et al. (2012), with reference to automotive engineering, identified the 'lure of the virtual' in the relationship between the possibilities of virtual models and the real products in use. This chapter argues that this is only one lure among several. Further, it explores the implications and limitations of digitisation and virtualisation that can be found in automotive engineering. This contribution thus aims to critically remark on the promised benefits of digitisation and virtualisation to offer an in-depth insight into how these processes occur in practice and which antagonisms may therefore emerge.

First of all, the terms informatisation, digitisation and virtualisation – often used interchangeably – are introduced. This is necessary so as to be able to analyse detailed changes without subsuming everything under the term 'technology' while remaining open to specific outcomes. Which relations are inherent, and what is their specific meaning? The next section focuses on the new topologies of work in automotive engineering. Following this, the case studies are introduced, and the findings of the research are presented. Finally, the contradictions and consequences of current developments are discussed.

Informatisation, Digitisation and Virtualisation

Informatisation is often used interchangeably with computerisation or digitisation, or even more generally, with ICT's ubiquitous pervasion of all spheres of society. This ubiquitous spread marks, without doubt, a new phase in the informatisation process and of the economy as encapsulated in the concept of 'informational capitalism' (Castells, 1996). It is necessary to take a closer look at the concept of informatisation in order to fully comprehend its denotation. The beginning of the informatisation process goes back to long before the invention of personal computers (PCs). Informatisation, understood as the historical process of developing information techniques, reached an important stage with the dissemination of double-entry bookkeeping in the Middle Ages (by the end of the 15th century). Generally, informatisation characterises a process of the systematic production and use of information, with the goal of gaining further information and by doing so reaching an intersubjective, exchangeable form of knowledge (Boes and Kämpf, 2007). The informatisation process is closely connected to the development of capitalist societies, enabling the rationalisation of the use of information in large companies. This leads to a 'structural duplication' of the material working process (Schmiede, 1996; Schmiede, 2006). These abstractions are today implemented in the form of management ratios or IT systems to facilitate the control and governance of complex organisations. Over time, information and knowledge have gained further importance; they have never been considered as important as they are today. From this perspective, informatisation is to be understood as a meta-process of information handling within a capitalist economy and cannot be reduced to the use of computers, smart phones or 'the cloud'.

Digitisation can thus be understood as a special phase in the informatisation process. It describes the transformation of analogue information into digital (e.g. the telephone signal) and the emergence of digital representations (e.g. software). Digital and digitised data enables first of all the transmission process of data and information (pictures, among other things) from place A to place B. Secondly, it allows for an arbitrary amount of data and information and an arbitrary number of models to be transmitted. This enables the separation between humans and the phenomena that are represented.[1] Digitisation thus means the separation of material and non-material objects of labour. Yet this doesn't imply severing the relationship between physical and digital entities, as we will discover later on. Digitisation also marks the coming together of the computer as machine and medium (Esposito, 1993). These events can be considered as a new phase of informatisation (Boes and Kämpf, 2007).

Virtualisation marks a particular form of digitisation. In general, 'virtual' means something that is 'very close to something without actually being it',[2] something that also, quite possibly, actually exists. The virtual is specific in that it offers functionalities that allow for proceeding as if an actual physical entity had been used. In terms of automotive engineering, this means taking a virtual prototype for test simulations – or, in software engineering, to use virtual drives, which are cloud-based instead of the ones physically located inside the computer. Furthermore, virtualisation signifies the generation of digital representations or effects that stand in for physical entities (objects, processes or people). Thus, these digital representations substitute for the functionalities (acting as a functional substitute) of physical objects or are used in such a way as non-virtual ones would be. This discussion extends beyond Bailey et al.'s (2012) definition, in which they proposed that virtual entities only substitute for physical entities. Yet, the example of software given above demonstrates that this limitation falls short. Those representations do not possess a 'real' as assumed, but instead the 'real' is in fact an information produced technologically on a spatio-temporal basis (Hubig, 2013). This indicates a more complex understanding of reality and virtual reality. Hubig (2013) introduces the formal differentiation of 'virtual reality' and 'virtual actualities' to describe the references between reality, virtuality and actuality (p. 7).

The differentiation between digital and virtual can be explained with an example of automotive (and other fields of) engineering: CAD software – by now in 3D – represents models with the support of a computer. These models are digital and form the basis for inventing virtual prototypes and digital mock-ups. These in turn enable the representation of an automobile's material characteristics, offering the opportunity to simulate functionalities (e.g. the wind flow of a chassis).

New Topologies of Work in Automotive Engineering

The spread of web-enabled devices and the formation of a global ICT infrastructure accelerates the new phase of informatisation. These developments are going hand in hand with a new spatial dimension of informatisation, as expressed in the thesis of an 'information space' (Baukrowitz and Boes, 1996; Boes and Kämpf, 2007). According to the aforementioned authors, in this concept, a worldwide information space acts as a space of production, in which value is generated. Whether the information space is constituted as one singular worldwide space, as emphasised by the authors, or as working spaces in the sense of Lefebvre's (2005) 'social space', constituted through the practices of people working together inside the information space, or whether many information spaces are created by people working together, may be a subject for discussion. This discussion would involve space becoming more independent of actual places and the relationship between time, distance and proximity changes,[3] using technologies that enable a shrinking of geographical distances. The development and use of airplanes marked an important step for the geographical understanding of 'space' and in terms of national borders: space in terms of a social space that emerges through social practice and enabled the thinking of a more abstract type of space that goes beyond geographical, national or constructed borders.[4] Adopting such an approach is necessary in order to adequately conceptualise how the information space transforms today's understanding of work, place and space. The further that digitalisation and virtualisation processes proceed, the more strongly concepts of reorganisation focus on an arbitrary distribution of work: anytime, anywhere. This assumption is based on digitised work objects, virtually available work products and the potential substitution of physical ones. This chapter argues that the connection between knowledge, people and places has so far been underestimated.

The spatial reorganisation of work became the focus of attention quite a number of years ago with debates around teleworking in the aftermath of the 1973 oil crisis. Meanwhile organisations without boundaries, time- and location-independent work and the emergence of a global workforce (also in terms of knowledge work) arose (Marchington et al., 2004). Reorganising work through the information space implies more cooperation, more competition and an increasingly global division of labour in various fields of work. Outsourcing marked an important stage in debates about the effects of organisational detachment away from the traditional company. IT or call centre services were central for this stage of relocating work, following on from the earlier globalisation of production work. Today, even more fields of work are affected, such as medical (Noronha and D'Cruz, 2008) or legal services. This is also true for automotive engineering, which changed from locally, very tightly connected organisational forms to much more globally organised ones today.

The general changes in the automotive industry's product and model strategies affect the product-development process. A standardisation of products (and procedures) accompany the informatisation of automotive engineering. In order to reduce costs and save time, carmakers and suppliers try to use as many single components, systems and even platforms across as many models as possible (the so-called common component principle). Common components are part of a modularisation strategy that will lead to a construction kit used to develop and build every new model. These are based on common platforms[5] shared by the same car segment or car class, sometimes even across different brands and manufacturers.[6] These standardisation processes are part of the lean management strategies that had begun to affect the automotive industry in the aftermath of Toyota's success in the 1990s. The discourse on core competencies led, in a first step, to an increase in the outsourcing of production tasks and was followed by a reduction in the scope of engineering. This has happened to a considerable degree during the last decade: the research study introduces the example of a motor with 256 components in which only four of these were engineered and produced by the original equipment manufacturer (OEM) itself (Will-Zocholl, 2011). More and more engineering units are outsourced to nearshore and offshore subsidiaries, to suppliers or to engineering service providers. Global and local engineering networks emerge (Schamp, Rentmeister and Lo, 2004) and lead to increasing international investments. In 2015, 53 per cent of R&D expenditures of car manufacturers based in Germany were actually spent in Germany. This means nearly every other euro was spent abroad (VDA, 2015).

The outsourcing of engineering is to a large extent based on the digitisation and virtualisation of data and models and is a prerequisite to work together in the information space. Previously, engineering was organised primarily centrally, in one location or region. Today, we are facing different types of outsourcing: (a) to an engineering service supplier, often in connection with leased workers or a system supplier; (b) to low-cost locations nearshore and offshore; and (c) to a company-wide network of almost equal subsidiaries. In the course of engineering outsourcing, 'collaborative engineering' has become a popular working method in and across multinational and national companies; 'global engineering' is supposed to be the next step forward in the future of engineering. The vision of 24-hour engineering rotating with the time zones around the world is premised on expanding technological possibilities. Engineers would be able to cooperate worldwide, working nonstop on the same components. This concept suggests that engineering is becoming spatially and temporally flexible; this idea is rather optimistic and does not reflect the real challenges that are part of its implementation (Anderl and Völz, 2009; Downey and Beddoes, 2014). The anticipated advantages seem obvious: mobilising a global engineering workforce would reduce costs and save time as well as expand the use of common components. The expectations linked with these visions obstruct the view on discrepancies that may appear in practice. The following section first directs a spotlight onto the automotive industry itself, discussing the digitisation of engineering and the subsequent changes for the work of product-development engineers.

Changes in Engineering Work

The automotive industry is one of the industries that generates the most revenue while also being one of the most employment intensive industrial sectors in Germany. It has benefited from an increase in worldwide sales while the Western European markets have remained static (cf. Ernst and Young, 2013; VDA, 2015). The range of companies active in the German automotive industry is vast, and the industry benefits from the small and medium enterprises that employ more than 80 per cent of the employees and create 75 per cent of the total value (VDA, 2013). Market conditions in the German automotive industry have so far remained robust, despite the Volkswagen emissions scandal and the challenges of new mobility concepts and new players entering the market in the context of electro-mobility and self-driving cars.

Three types of companies can be identified in the automotive sector: original equipment manufacturers (OEMs), who provide the car brands and most of the production plants; different kinds of supplier companies (either specialised in producing a single product or complete systems, e.g. climate control) and engineering service companies providing engineering services and/or an engineering workforce (for hire). The success of the German automotive industry is based on a high capacity

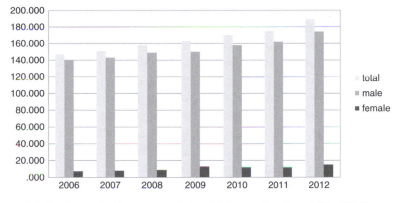

Figure 4.1 Engineers in the segment of vehicle construction (VDI, 2015)*

[1] Based on the Mikrozensus Germany (VDI 2016). The statistical definition of engineers employed in the automotive industry is not unique as the automotive industry itself is defined differently across the official statistics, the inter-trade organisation VDA or the engineers association VDI. Thus, the figures provided here are an approximation.

for innovation, with more than 40 per cent of global innovations invented by German car companies (Bratzel and Tellermann, 2013). The principle R&D centres of OEMs and suppliers are based in Germany. The amount of money invested in R&D activities grew by more than 250 per cent during the past 20 years and is still rising. Compared to R&D expenditure across the German manufacturing industry as a whole, the automotive industry's proportion is very high at almost a third (VDA, 2015). The increasing R&D activities during the past decade have been followed by rising employment figures for engineers or equivalent (Figure 4.1).

The amount of engineers (or equivalent) employed in the vehicle construction sector rose by 2012 to 189,000. According to the VDA, more than 90,000 work in R&D in the automotive industry; this amount has remained stable when compared to earlier figures (Will-Zocholl, 2011; VDA, 2015).

In the course of informatisation, engineering work has changed, particularly due to digitisation and virtualisation. How did this occur? The beginning of these newer developments can be identified with the introduction of CAD software in the late 1980s. For this, first vast work stations, later desktop PCs and today mainly laptops were used. Prior to the introduction of work stations, engineering was strongly locally based at a single site where engineers met to work together on drawing boards. The drawings had to be stored and physically exchanged; team work was possible only on site. These drawings were more than just ink strokes on paper: they were also a communication medium. Meeting around the drawing boards fostered the emergence of new ideas and design improvements. The logic of work changed with the introduction of CAD systems in the way that Böhle and Millkau (1988) described: at the drawing board, the thinking started with the overall big picture, and details were developed afterwards. Working with CAD meant starting with the details and composing the big picture out of numerous individual pieces. Today's 3D CAD models and product data management systems reinforce this development. The 3D CAD models are used to create so-called digital mock-ups (DMUs): digital versions of the latter components to combine them into a digital version of the complete car. These virtual prototypes allow the development of production tools long before the actual production plant is built. Finally, it is possible to simulate in advance not only the functionality of the car but also the whole production process, including all relevant areas like manufacturing, controlling, logistics, finance and even marketing (Anderl, 2006). 3D CAD models, and even the analogue ones, are broken down to itemised bills of materials. In today's digitised form, these are implemented in specialised software such as SAP automotive. The bill of materials tags the informatisation of engineering just as the introduction of double-entry bookkeeping marked an important step in the general informatisation process. On the basis of the digitised bill of materials and CAD models, product data management (PDM) systems were developed, changing the entire engineering process. Instead of a step-by-step process where one engineering phase followed another, simultaneous engineering processes are established, with parallel, overlapping and iterative engineering phases (Eigner and Stelzer, 2009). This shortens a single engineering cycle (down to the current average of seven years), while the need for staff has risen. The entire engineering process also changed in the course of virtualisation. Clearance to produce the tools needed for the manufacturing process is now given before a new model is tested with physical prototypes. Previously consecutive engineering steps have now changed their order (Schulte-Frankenfeld et al., 2007). The digitally-based global reorganisation of engineering leads at the same time to an increasing need for cooperation, on site and across different locations and suppliers. Over the past decades, the scope of engineering in the production sector, in the ways that it had been previously done, was reduced. Thus, systems suppliers and engineering service companies have gained importance in the whole engineering process, assuming ever more tasks outsourced by the OEMs.

The study evaluated a number of further tendencies of changes in engineering work, such as increasing time and cost pressures due to the incrementally saturated markets in Europe and North America. The coordination of new tasks and standards requires a higher degree of self-organisation so as to adequately address the increased demands for documentation and coordination, a higher communication effort and a shift from creative tasks to administrative work (as a consequence of more documentation and IT-based requirements). We have termed the latest change the 'enucleation' of engineering work (Schmiede and Will-Zocholl, 2011). Additionally, engineers face the dilemma of gaining more responsibility in the course of a globalising vehicle construction sector, on the one hand, and less autonomy to address these develop- ments, on the other hand. Standardisation tendencies due to the use of IT systems and the division of labour arise while experiences of insecu- rity are on the rise in the companies that offshore and outsource their work (Vester et al., 2007; Will-Zocholl, 2011). These changes amplify with the ongoing digitalisation and virtualisation. Further standardisa- tion and globalisation also ensues.

In general, the manner in which virtualisation is addressed depends on the respective, and often high, expectation of the company's man- agement. It expects globalisation (through product standardisation and a global workforce) to save money, to accelerate the development of new models and to explore new markets. Furthermore, transparency should increase to enable more control and controllability. To reach this aim, management tends to opt for the temptation of the virtual, ignoring antagonisms that arise either in the work process or at organisational level, or these are explained away. The following section introduces three dimensions to these antagonisms. These are based on four case studies, which were conducted between 2006 and 2013.

The Temptation of the Virtual – Case Study Results

Case studies with engineers in the automotive industry were conducted to gain further insight into these antagonisms. Following a short intro- duction to the companies in the case studies, this section illustrates the engineers' subjective perspectives on changes in work (Table 4.1).

The OEMs under study are trying to drastically cut their engineering costs per car project. Due to new players in engineering, especially in the emerging markets of China and India, they are still seeking 'the' strat- egy to do so. For MassCar this is more relevant than for PremCar, since the latter's margins are lower as a consequence of a combination of high engineering costs and lower selling prices. MassCar follows an interna- tional engineering strategy that integrates all captive engineering centres

Table 4.1 Companies in the case studies[1]

Case study	Type and size of business	Type of service value chains and central dynamics
MassCar	American-based original equipment manufacturer	Global engineering network characterised by competition, subsidiary in India
PremCar	German premium car OEM selling two brands worldwide	Central engineering site in Germany, a small extent of direct offshoring to a subsidiary in India
FirstTier1	A large German based system supplier	German location for the headquarters of engineering activities, subsidiaries based across the world. The German location faces intensified outsourcing to nearshore locations in Eastern Europe
FirstTier2	A medium-sized German system supplier	Centrally organised engineering at German site, outsourcing of standardised work to an Eastern European subsidiary

[1]Four case studies were conducted during two research projects (funded by the German Research Foundation, DFG, and the German Federal Ministry of Education and Research, BMBF), lasting from November 2006 until July 2013. More than 45 qualitative interviews form the basis of this analysis of the case studies (Pongratz and Trinczek, 2010).

in the four engineering regions of the world. Every car development project has a 'home base' for engineering, while all the regions are involved in creating new models. As a consequence, an intellectual property agency has to be engaged to account and invoice for the performance of any individual engineering site. All engineering centres are competing with each other to be commissioned with new car projects. Global standardisation of processes takes centre stage in the restructuring effort. The global management board decides which processes should be standardised globally and which processes must be adapted locally. Staff at the German location describe these processes as Americanisation rather than globalisation. Besides the core strategy of jointly working across the globe within the company, the suppliers and engineering service companies are located nearby or within reach, mostly in Germany.

PremCar pursues an engineering strategy concentrated in a German engineering R&D centre. They prefer working with suppliers and engineering service providers located nearby, both in Germany and Austria. The components to build their brand identity are realised in their German R&D centre. Their organisational structure has remained very centralised and hierarchical, even though car projects are organised in a project matrix. PremCar has also tried to standardise processes but is not as consistent as MassCar. Their focus rests on avoiding doing things twice. Both MassCar and PremCar outsource their engineering to a high degree. While MassCar has the opportunity to distribute work among captive engineering centres around the world, including Korea, India and China, PremCar relies almost entirely on its partners along the value chain as well as an engineering centre in India. Both engage suppliers and engineering service companies to engineer projects as well as modules or components. They highly value the physical presence of their partners. This is the reason why many suppliers or engineering service companies have subsidiaries located near the OEMs or send resident engineers to them. Temporary employment in engineering also plays an important role, especially for the system supplier (FirstTier). The strategies of the two OEMs are aimed at reducing the overall engineering time and reducing engineering costs. However, whether they actually reduce costs is questionable, due to the additional costs for technological systems (e.g. videoconferencing), new software and data systems, higher travel expenses as well as solving communication problems occurring in intra- and inter-organisational project teams (cf. Will-Zocholl, 2011).

Three dimensions have emerged during this study: (a) the relationship between virtual and physical prototypes, (b) the standardisation of processes and knowledge and (c) fragile cooperation. In these areas, the development currently encounters limitations, with respect to the technology itself, the restricted perspective of management and technical experts as well as the qualifications of people working on the project. These will be discussed in turn.

The Relationship between Physical and Virtual Models

Informatisation processes, especially virtualisation, raise questions over how the relationship between information and knowledge-based processes and material entities is configured. These novel questions need to be addressed. The detailed representation of components and even whole cars is suggestive of actually being the vehicle itself. This is evidently the reason why management overestimates the potential of virtualisation in the product-development process (Bailey et al., 2012; Will-Zocholl, 2016). The extent to which these potentials are in fact underestimated shows up in practice. In one case, this happened during the cooperation with off-site locations. The example of FirstTier1 demonstrates that the need for competencies was underestimated and that in fact more support was needed. At FirstTier1, part of the vehicle testing was outsourced to a nearshore location in Eastern Europe.

This was facilitated by a simulation based on virtual prototypes which allowed for testing without an actual car (that this was only possibly up to a certain extent will become clear in the discussion below). The near-shore site took over in first-step simulations with the virtual prototype, yet the necessity soon arose to use physical prototypes to validate the virtual testing. This led to the following situation, as a project engineer illustrated:

> We are building up the road-test division. One thing is that you need test tracks over there…. You can't use the prototype systems on the road immediately – that could be dangerous. … Therefore we need a test track there. But we also need the car there. And prototypes are especially very expensive and therefore rare. … They are extremely rare, so we have to share one with the customer and other departments – it's not only us with our ESP-System – we have to share these vehicles here and then with [Eastern European Subsidiary], too. … Therefore I can't easily say: 'Either I will do it here or there.' On the level of road testing there is no legwork in this sense. (FirstTier1)

This example shows the unintended consequences of the outsourcing to a supposedly cheaper location. On the one hand, the location was established to reduce engineering costs, especially HR costs in Germany; on the other hand, new expenses arose to exchange prototypes throughout Europe. The transportation costs are high because prototypes cannot be driven on public roads. The availability of digital data and virtual prototypes allows for engineering work to be divided into smaller, more arbitrary pieces than before. Routine work like simulations and calculations are separated out and distributed among several individuals (and different locations). Doing so, however, would underestimate the existing linkages between physical and virtual prototypes. Not everything that can be simulated can be transferred one to one onto the physical prototypes. Problems arising from this have led to OEMs facing an increase in product recalls during the last decade (CAM, 2015).

These results confirm those of Bailey et al. (2012), who found in their study of the US automotive industry that management overestimated the possibilities of virtual models and simulations in the production process (p. 1485). The same is true for universities, which adopt these visions optimistically and instruct students that the digitisation of labour products and their availability in the information space will lead to a placeless reorganisation of work and to the models in use being applicable in a uniform manner across the globe (cf. Hubig, 2015). Accelerated technological development, such as available Internet speeds and just-in-time data, reinforced these expectations. Engineers on the operative level with experience in both the virtual and physical world are able to provide a much more realistic picture. They describe how the material side persists and remains important, while the models are being virtualised. Today's virtual models possess the ability for functionality testing (e.g. crash tests) while making the tempting proposition of appearing to be real. Used as substitutes for physical prototypes they are nonetheless *not* actual substitutes but remain an abstraction of a real car. These abstractions rely on mathematical models and theoretical assumptions. These models' appearance reflects probabilities under certain conditions, not the real product. Compared to earlier models used to construct physical prototypes, such as matchstick models, the virtual ones appear far more concrete and 'real'.

In the process of informatisation, qualifications and competencies develop in divergent ways. Processes of specialisation lead to a further drifting apart of the physical and virtual world. Engineers without any experience of physical prototypes do not possess the competence to transfer the results of the virtual into the physical world. They take results for granted without reflecting strongly enough on the relationship between virtuality and reality. The synthesis of binding the virtual to the material quality is a necessary but not sufficient condition to construct new components (in an adequate manner). Thus it is not possible to work with only virtual representations without having experienced physical entities.

The linkages between physical and virtual prototypes indicates that product development in the automotive industry is more strongly locally bound than commonly understood by management. They point to an inability to transfer all relevant previous knowledge (specifically the one relating to drawings and drawing boards) into the information space.

Standardisation of Processes and Knowledge

Virtualisation goes hand in hand with globalisation and standardisation, as the empirical case study findings demonstrate. The aim of dividing production work into arbitrary pieces to further the division of labour leads to a standardisation of work. Management is the driving force to control and organise distributed processes, preferably globally. In order to achieve such control and organisation, processes were standardised across the globe. This section traces some of the problems arising in the course of this development.

Under conditions of standardisation and globalisation, more attention is devoted to the processes of production while the product itself slides out of view. The engineers confronted with these developments are sceptical of the strategy's likely success, as the following quote shows:

> It is less about the product itself but about the processes. And behind every process there are people tracking this process – so to say, controlling the project engineers as to whether they always follow the processes. This is not always good for the product because it sometimes gets neglected. That's a problem which we see in this whole reorganisation: too many processes. (MassCarP5)

The increasing focus on processes is closely connected to an increased reach of documentation tasks, in addition to extensive legal requirements. Before processes become standardised, a substantial description is needed to eliminate the existing single steps and to assess the potential for standardisation. Among the companies in the case studies, MassCar's German locations were affected the most. Up until the time of our study (2006–13), documentation played a minor role, with engineering strongly organised around the notion of a 'working capacity' (Pfeiffer, 2004) which utilised the experiential knowledge of every single engineer. In Germany, engineers usually hold the same employment position for a long time, working under the same remit. Under these conditions, documenting every single step is not as important as it is in more mobile environments, such as in the United States, where the documentation effort has always been higher since positions are filled more often with new staff who have to find out how existing processes and procedures are organised. Therefore, the central engineering unit in the United States sets out 'to harmonise', as the standardisation is named, processes across the world. Even PremCar, with its very central engineering organisation, is affected by standardisation, as are its suppliers. The situation at the suppliers differs from the carmakers insofar as they are forced to standardise processes to demonstrate their trustworthiness and reliability. In the minds of the engineers and their own perception of their role and position, these developments are not without consequences. Increasing documentation and an intensified division of labour may lead to a shift in engineering work from 'creative work' to 'administration work' (Will-Zocholl, 2011).

However, the analysis indicates that the outcomes of standardised processes that ought to lead to the same result still differ despite detailed documentation and instruction. Huge databases and new ICT systems were implemented to standardise work processes further still. Yet, the fact that many different local software versions are used and that the assimilation has so far failed demonstrates how difficult this strategy proves to be. A MassCar project engineer illustrates this issue:

> Yes, with the effort to document, the accuracy has increased compared to previous projects. In doing so, they try to globalise the whole thing, i.e. an American folder and documentation system should be the same as the one here, [...] It is a huge challenge because the underlying systems are not the same and must be assimilated. (MassCarP7)

Moreover, the standardisation of processes and documentation does not automatically lead to uniformity. The codification of knowledge is pursued regardless in order to enhance the division of labour. That is, the transformation of 'tacit knowledge' (Polanyi, 1967) or 'working knowledge' (Harper, 1987) into an organisationally useful form is pursued. The goal is gaining a form of experiential knowledge (Böhle and Millkau, 1988; Böhle, 2003) independent of any knowledge held individually. However, this form of experiential knowledge cannot be extracted materially from people and easily put to the service of distributing knowledge-intensive work across the globe. This approach to gather experimental knowledge also ignores the fact that knowledge changes with every single transfer and with everyone participating in this process or incorporating knowledge. The idea of extracting knowledge from individuals is not entirely new, in fact it constitutes a crucial aim in the informatisation process. Yet, with the idea of distributed knowledge work, it re-emerges with renewed force. The problem of working practices not being identical across the globe remains to be resolved. Further, virtual representations and physically absent colleagues encourage a more open interpretation than what is provided for by the earlier drawing process. Thus, they can be interpreted in more diverse ways than before. Up until now, engineering work has been less standardised than that and has not led to the same results in different countries, as it is undertaken by different people. One crucial point in this is that engineers are trained differently across the different countries.

Nevertheless, the companies studied enforce their effort to standardise engineering. It is obvious that a certain amount of standardisation, such as in terms of routine work, is possible (and potentially desirable) in the view of the engineers interviewed. Yet, this does not imply the formulation of strict and narrow specifications; instead, a certain amount of freedom is necessary because not every single issue arising can be anticipated (even though management would like this to be the case).

In the view of a MassCar engineering manager, this would lead to 'robot work': for example, telling engineers in which corner of the digital paper to start with what brush stroke. And in the end, it would be a different draft anyway. This is not the only reason why engineers at low-cost sites have to spend a certain amount of time at the German locations to learn in person (face-to-face) and in the presence of physical prototypes from their German colleagues. It remains to be seen whether the issue of standardisation can be fundamentally resolved. Maybe changes in education and advanced training and adaptations in the engineers' experiential knowledge will alleviate this effect in future.

Fragile Cooperation

The virtualisation of engineering has led to a global division of labour. Combined with the older preference of reducing the scope of engineering, the need for cooperation has risen. The case studies reveal new forms of global cooperation in the engineering sector, which so far has not been too strongly affected by globalisation tendencies. To date, no fully functional mode of coordination has evolved. Globalisation strategies take place in the face of 'global engineering'. The degree of understanding and implementation of global engineering strategies differs across the case companies. They range from a worldwide strategy integrating all captive engineering centres with a subsequently emerging internal market (MassCar) to global sourcing strategies (FirstTier1) or using offshore locations and other suppliers/engineering services as prolonged workbenches to disperse standard work (PremCar). Furthermore, OEMs apply global engineering approaches so that their suppliers have to use offshore outsourcing to lower the price for their work and services. 'Follow-the-sun' is an approach to utilise the different time zones around the globe. This includes the distribution of routine work like testing, simulations and calculations to locations in subsequent time zones to save time (and money because the engineers based outside Germany are generally paid less). The different approaches adopted across the companies in the case studies show that they are still in the process of finding their own best approach. By using these forms of global cooperation, concerns over the standard of the distributed work arise, such as in relation to cross-cultural misunderstandings, language problems or difficulties in coordinating time (zones). These issues hide the fact that conflicts of interest often exist in competitive contexts. This occurs among different locations of the same company and between different companies. Outsourcing (in the companies in the case studies) has a disciplinary effect for the employees. Sometimes there is simply no choice not to outsource; the workload of every single engineer is so high that every opportunity to transfer tasks to somewhere else seems to be a solution. This view may change along the work process when problems over quality, language and mutual understanding arise. The likelihood of these matters arising also demonstrates why this model of work is not working. The effect of co-working in one location, such as teaching colleagues from abroad, exists in cases where significant threats would arise otherwise. The engineers are faced with contradictory positions in this current reorganisation and the challenges that arise from active resistance, boycott and resignation, which so far have not been resolved.

A further challenge to global cooperation lies in a legal, and continually worsening, problem of the data-driven economy: the question of intellectual property rights. At MassCar these problems arose during a global platform project. The captive engineering centres were not merely part of a global company but competing with each other so as to gain new projects and responsibilities in worldwide projects. This situation originated with the common component model adopted by MassCar. In order to facilitate the joint working of the different locations and to share relevant knowledge, a central institution was charged with the oversight of intellectual property rights. This institution's roles were to ensure that rights on data, ideas and components were applied and then to calculate the price for exchanging knowledge connected to these rights. Yet, this development solved the dilemma of the German engineers at MassCar in only a limited sense. Currently, relevant data is exchanged, but only as little as possible. The competing forces among locations remain active because in every new project single sites compete over competencies, knowledge and 'head count'. The German site is convinced that they are disadvantaged because of the high staffing costs in Germany. Thus they try to do the work with a smaller number of engineers.

Until now, the companies in the case studies have tried to resolve problems of cooperation with classic strategies, none of which contribute to the goal of reducing travel (in fact, the opposite is the case) or to effectively reorganising work. Two examples are as follows: the first one relies on the engineering of a mid-sized vehicle at MassCars. An engineering process was designed with the involvement of all captive engineering locations to use the platform for their local brands in future. The global team could use video and telephone conferences as well as virtual team conferences based on specialist software to organise their communication. Yet, they had enormous difficulties in addressing any of the emerging problems. One of the engineers involved recounts the following:

> We had a global process, we had a telephone conference once a week, lasting two to three hours and people were not able to reach agreement. Sometimes, when the fronts were hardening, they couldn't even talk reasonably to each other. Then we said: 'Ok. We will have a four-day workshop.' … After four days of workshopping they emerged and resolved 80 per cent of the problems they had not been able to solve throughout a whole year. (MassCarS1a).

The company seeks a combination of local and distributed methods of global cooperation. So far, however, they have not succeeded. Another platform project proceeded so poorly that they decided to base everyone involved for two years at the German engineering centre. The examples show that distributed work is dependent on a number of prerequisites, aside from any technological possibilities it may offer. The issues of trust under conditions of competition, in particular, and the complexity of ICT-mediated communication are considerably underestimated (Schilcher et al., 2011). At PremCar, they conducted an experiment to develop a concept car for an automotive fair: everyone involved in the development was located in a project room (one huge hall) around the car. The offices were located around the physical prototype in the centre of the building so that everybody could see anybody walking around or working on the model. This spatial organisation provided the engineers with short distances to meet others to discuss problems, disagreements or similar. The result of this engineering process was considered a success, and the work seemed to be comparatively efficient.

Concurrently, management also looked at the product-development process for serial cars. Here, the whole development process was too complex with too many people involved to organise them in a similar way. However, they attempted to create a maximum spatial proximity for project teams (inside the same building, on the same floor, etc.). This was also true for engineers of suppliers and engineering service companies, who were hosted on the company site close to others working on the same projects.

Engineering has become more global than previously anticipated. The introduction of modularisation and platform principles went hand in hand with processes of digitisation and virtualisation, leading to a globalisation 'through the back door'.[7] This means that the idea of using common components and platforms in various models and brands (belonging to one company as well as across companies) enforced a global reorganisation of engineering. The opportunities of digitisation and virtualisation intensify the international division of labour. Therefore, one cannot speak of one global engineering strategy but of different ways in which globalisation opportunities are perceived. These processes are components of an enforced reorganisation of work through the information space. Their range and timescale is dependent upon the respective company. At the same time, the results demonstrate that strategies on the basis of which conflicts can be resolved remain absent. Furthermore, it becomes apparent that if engineering work is to be reorganised globally beyond the principles of prolonged workbenches, it will be necessary to do more than merely use virtual team spaces (e.g. TeamCenter Software) or semantic connotations of digital models (Völz, 2011).

Conclusion

The options of using virtual models in product development are tempting. One of the managers interviewed saw the future of engineering work completely transferred to the virtualised world of *Second Life*. The views of those who experience the implications of digitisation and virtualisation in their everyday practice indicate that upholding these visions is more difficult, contradictory and challenging than expected. Three antagonisms have been identified, among these virtual temptations.

First, the relationship between virtual and physical models and overestimating simulation was underestimated (Hubig, 2015). The exposure to virtual prototypes and to test results based on virtual prototypes and virtual testing remains problematic. Virtual models – even if they appear to be real – are more abstract than the models used previously in the product-development process. This abstraction could be seen as a limitation of virtual models: they are not a complete substitute for physical prototypes. A stronger reason is that employees' experience with physical models is important so as to develop the working capacity needed provide the translation or interpretation of those simulations. This cannot be stressed highly enough. A challenge to be solved for future work in the information space.

Second, fragile global cooperation has been emphasised instead of the frictionless organisation of a single piece. The companies under study display the difficulties that arise in a context of the simultaneous necessity to cooperate and compete, what Nalebuff and Brandenburger (1997) called 'coopetition'. Further, shifting work into the information space is by no means something that takes place effortlessly. Commonly, standard solutions were used to address these problems, such as face-to-face workshops or international teams being based at one location for a period of time as seen in the examples of MassCar or PremCar. It has been shown that approaches already exist to organise global cooperation but that there still remains potential to create new ones. Also, the importance of trust is far more strongly visible in global ICT-mediated cooperation than before (Schilcher et al., 2011).

Third, standardisation of work in the course of an intensifying division of labour takes the place of increased autonomy and creative, self-determined work. The standardisation of tasks and processes is a reaction to the reinforced global division of labour and leads to a rationalisation of engineering work. This is particularly apparent when looking at the scope of changes in engineering work (Will-Zocholl, 2011). The relationship between globalisation and standardisation is reciprocal. On the one hand, standardisation enables a global division of labour by dividing work into individual pieces for processing; on the other hand, globalisation enforces standardisation to adjust processes across the globe. Until now, there have been attempts to address standards by increasing documentation and the use of ICT systems. In doing so, it becomes obvious that automotive engineering – in contrast to software engineering – can be standardised to only a limited degree. Existing solutions to address this problem with even more standardisation have so far not succeeded.

Current developments illustrate that processes for useful strategies to adopt virtualisation are still in the making. The need for configurations inside the companies, for example in education and advanced training, is strongly apparent. For researchers studying the world of work, it is important to identify these antagonisms, options and problems in the current debate on digitisation and the implications of technology on work, in order to be able to take a stance and to contribute to existing debates – not least, so as not to leave the interpretative authority over ongoing changes in the hands of the techno-sciences and the visions of the stars of Silicon Valley.

Notes

1 The understanding of what is meant by representations of phenomena can be explored further with reference to semioticians like Saussure (1916) and Frege (1892), as Bailey et al. (2012) did (p. 1486). Yet, this seems insufficient if we want to explore the social implications of digitisation.
2 Taken from the Merriam-Webster Learning Dictionary, see http://www.merriam-webster.com/dictionary/virtual.

3 As emphasised in Giddens's (1984) concept of 'time-space distanciation' or Harvey's (1989) 'time-space compression'.

4 This issue is discussed and described as 'spatial turn' or 'topological turn' in contemporary cultural studies and sociology (Bachmann-Medick, 2016; Massey, 2005).

5 A car platform consists of material entities like common components but also of common efforts, depending on design and construction.

6 This is the case for the 2009 model of Vauxhall Corsa and Fiat Punto, for example.

7 While being dependent on the 'bureaucratisation through the back door' as argued by Jörg Flecker and Pamela Meil (2010).

REFERENCES

Anderl, R. (2006) 'Produktentwicklung in der Automobilindustrie', in A. Baukrowitz, T. Berker, A. Boes, S. Pfeiffer, R. Schmiede and M. Will (eds), *Informatisierung der Arbeit – Gesellschaft im Umbruch* (Berlin: edition sigma), pp. 37–52.

Anderl, R. and D. Völz (2009) 'Global Engineering', in K. Robertson-von Trotha (ed.), *Schlüsselqualifikationen für Studium, Beruf und Gesellschaft* (Karlsruhe: Universitätsverlag)

Bachmann-Medick, D. (2016) *Cultural Turns: New Orientations in the Study of Culture* (Berlin and Boston, MA: De Gruyter).

Bailey, D. E., P. M. Leonardi and S. R. Barley (2012) 'The Lure of the Virtual', *Organization Science*, 23, 5, 1485–504.

Baukrowitz, A. and A. Boes (1996) 'Arbeit in der "Informationsgesellschaft"', in R. Schmiede (ed.), *Virtuelle Arbeitswelten. Arbeit, Produktion und Subjekt in der 'Informationsgesellschaft'* (Berlin: edition sigma), pp. 129–58.

Bijker, W. E., and T. J. Pinch (2002) 'SCOT Answers, Other Questions. A Reply to Nick Clayton', in *Technology and Culture*, 43, 361–68.

Boes, A. and T. Kämpf (2007) 'The Nexus of Informatisation and Internationalisation – A New Stage in the Internationalisation of Labour in Globalised Working Environments', *Work Organisation, Labour and Globalisation* 1, 2, 193–208.

Boes, A. and T. Kämpf (2010) 'Offshoring and the New Insecurities: Towards New Types of "White Collar Consciousness" in Germany in Globalised Working Environments', *Work Organisation, Labour and Globalisation*, 4, 1, 104–19.

Böhle, F. (1994) 'Relevance of experience-based work in modern processes', *AI & Society. Journal of Human Centred Systems and Machine Intelligence*, 8, 3, 207–15.

Böhle, F. (2003) ,Wissenschaft und Erfahrungswissen. Erscheinungsformen, Voraussetzungen und Folgen einer Pluralisierung des Wissens', in Stefan Böschen, Ingo Schulz-Schaeffer (eds), *Wissenschaft in der Wissensgesellschaft* (Wiesbaden: Westdeutscher Verlag), pp. 143–77.

Böhle, F. and B. Milkau (1988) *Vom Handrad zum Bildschirm* (Frankfurt am Main and New York: Campus).

Bratzel, S. and R. Tellermann (2013) Die Innovationen der globalen Automobilkonzerne, working paper May 2013. (Bergisch Gladbach).

▶

Brynjolfsson, E. and A. McAfee (2014) *The Second Machine Age: Work, Progress, Prosperity in a Time of Brilliant Technologies* (New York: W. W. Norton & Company).

Castells, M. (1996) *The Rise of the Network Society: The Information Age: Economy, Society and Culture I.* (Cambridge, MA, and Oxford: Blackwell).

Center of Automotive Management (CAM) (2015) *Automotive Performance 2015* (Bergisch-Gladbach: CAM).

Downey, G. L. and K. Beddoes (eds) (2010) *What is Global Engineering Education For? The Making of International Educators, Part 1* (London: Morgan and Claypool).

Eigner, M. and R. Stelzer (2009) *Product Lifecycle Management. Ein Leitfaden für Product Development und Life Cycle Management* (Berlin: Springer).

Ernst and Young (2013) European Automotive Survey 2013. Eschborn.

Esposito, E. (1993) 'Der Computer als Medium und Maschine', *Zeitschrift für Soziologie*, 22, 5, 338–54.

Flecker, J. and P. Meil (2010) 'Organisational restructuring and emerging service value chains – implications for work and employment', *Work, Employment and Society*, 24, 4, 1–19

Flecker, J. and A. Schönauer (2016) 'The Production of "Placelessness": Digital Service Work in Global Value Chains', in J. Flecker (ed.), *Space, Place and Global Digital Work* (London: Palgrave MacMillan), pp. 11–30.

Frege, G. (1892) 'Über Sinn und Bedeutung', *Zeitschrift für Philosophie und philosophische Kritik*, 100, 25–50.

Giddens, A. (1984) *The Constitution of Society: Outline of the Theory of Structuration* (Cambridge: Polity Press).

Harper, D. (1987) *Working Knowledge. Skill and Community in a Small Shop* (Chicago, IL: University of Chicago Press).

Harvey, D. (1989) *The Condition of Postmodernity: An Enquiry into the Origins of Cultural Change* (Oxford: Blackwell).

Hubig, C. (2013) *Virtualisierung der Technik – Virtualisierung der Lebenswelt. Neue Herausforderungen für eine Technikethik als Ermöglichungsethik*. http://www.philosophie.tu-darmstadt.de/media/institut_fuer_philosophie/diesunddas/hubig/downloadshubig/virtualisierung_der_technik_virtualisierung_der_lebenswelt.pdf, date accessed 2 February 2016.

Hubig, C. (2015) 'Simulationen wovon und Simulationen wofür – Virtual Realities und Virtual Actualities als Herausforderungen pragmatischer Wahrheitstheorie', talk at the SAS Workshop, 12 October 2015, Stuttgart, Germany.

Lefebvre, H. (1991) *The Production of Space* (New York: Wiley and Sons).

Levy, F. and R. J. Murnane (2005) *The New Division of Labor: How Computers are Creating the Next Job Market* (Princeton: University Press).

Marchington, M., D. Grimshaw, J. Rubery and H. Willmott (2004) *Fragmenting Work. Blurring Boundaries and Disordering Hierarchies* (Oxford: Oxford University Press).

Massey, D. B. (2005) *For Space* (London: Sage).

Mayer-Ahuja, N. (2014) *Everywhere is becoming the same? Regulating IT-work between India and Germany* (New Delhi and Hyderabad: Social Science Press).

▶

Nalebuff, A. M. and B. J. Brandenburger (1997) *Co-opetition* (New York: Crown Business).

Noronha, E. and P. D'Cruz (2008) 'Seeking the future: After-hours telecommuters in Indias's medical transcription industry', *Labour and Management in Development*, 8, 15–26.

Pfeiffer, S. (2004) *Arbeitsvermögen* (Wiesbaden: Springer).

Polanyi, M. (1967) *The Tacit Dimension* (Chicago, IL: University of Chicago Press).

Pongratz, H.-J. and R. Trinczek (eds) (2010) *Industriesoziologische Fallstudien. Entwicklungspotenziale einer Forschungsstrategie* (Berlin: edition sigma).

Rifkin, J. (2011) *The Third Industrial Revolution. How Lateral Power is Transforming Energy, The Economy, and The World* (Basingstoke and New York: Palgrave Macmillan).

Roth-Ebner, C. (2016) 'Spatial Phenomena of Mediatised Work', in J. Flecker (ed.), *Space, Place and Global Digital Work* (London: Palgrave Macmillan), pp. 227–45.

Saussure, F. (1916) 'Course de linguistique générale', edited by C. Bally and A. Sechehaye. (Lausanne and Paris: Payot).

Schamp, E. W., B. Rentmeister and V. Lo (2004) 'Dimensions of Proximity in Knowledge-based Networks: The Cases of Investment Banking and Automobile Design', *European Planning Studies*, 5, 1, 607–24.

Schilcher, C., A.-K. Poth, S. Sauer, K.-P. Stiefel and M. C. Will-Zocholl (2011) 'Trust in International Teams. Cultural, Spatial and Organizational Issues', *Journal of Business Research*, 11, 4, 29–38.

Schiller, D. (2000) *Digital Capitalism. Networking the Global Market System* (Cambridge, MA: MIT Press).

Schmiede, R. (1996) 'Informatisierung und gesellschaftliche Arbeit', in Schmiede, R. (ed.), Virtuelle Arbeitswelten. Arbeit, Produktion und Subjekt in der "Informationsgesellschaft" (Berlin: edition sigma), pp. 107–128.

Schmiede, R. (2006) 'Knowledge, Work and Subject in Informational Capitalism', in J. Berleur, M. I. Nurminen and J. Impagliazzo (eds), *Social Informatics – An Information Society for All?* (Wiesbaden and Heidelberg: Springer Science and Business Media), pp. 333–54.

Schmiede, R. and M. C. Will-Zocholl (2011) 'Engineers Work on the Move. Challenges in Automotive Engineering in a Globalized World', *Engineering Studies*, 3, 2, 1–21.

Schulte-Frankenfeld, N., M. Brass and A. Pieck (2007) 'Methoden und Prozesse zur Kostensenkung. Ein Status der Wandlungen im Fahrzeugentwicklungsprozess durch CAE-Methoden', in Dynamore GmbH (ed.), Proceedings of the 6th LS-DYNA Anwenderforum 2007 Frankenthal, Germany, and Karlsruhe, Germany, pp. 13–28.

VDI (2016) MonitorING-Datenbank. https://www.vdi.de/wirtschaft-politik/arbeitsmarkt/monitoring-datenbank/, date accessed 10 November 2016.

Verband der deutschen Automobilindustrie (VDA) (2013) Jahresbericht 2013 (Frankfurt: VDA).

Verband der deutschen Automobilindustrie (VDA) (2015) Jahresbericht 2015 (Frankfurt: VDA).

▶

▶

Verband deutscher Ingenieurinnen und Ingenieure (VDI) (2015) monitor-ING-Datenbank. https://www.vdi.de/wirtschaft-politik/arbeitsmarkt/monitoring-datenbank/, date accessed 5 September 2016.

Vester, M., C. Teiwes-Kügler and A. Lange-Vester (2007) *Die neuen Arbeitnehmer: zunehmende Kompetenzen – wachsende Unsicherheit* (Hamburg: VSA).

Völz, D. (2011) *Semantische Annotationen zur rechnergestützten kooperativen Produktentwicklung* (Aachen: Shaker).

Will-Zocholl, M. C. (2016) 'New Topologies of Work. Informatisation, Virtualisation and Globalisation in Automotive Engineering', in J. Flecker, Jörg (ed.), *Space, Place and Global Digital Work* (London: Palgrave MacMillan), pp. 31–52.

Will-Zocholl, M. C. (2011) *Wissensarbeit in der Automobilindustrie. Topologie der Reorganisation von Ingenieursarbeit in der globalen Produktentwicklung* (Berlin: edition sigma).

Clouds, Crowds, and Big Data – Changing Regimes of Control, Changing Forms of Resistance and Misbehaviour

On Call for One's Online Reputation – Control and Time in Creative Crowdwork

Philip Schörpf, Jörg Flecker and Annika Schönauer

Introduction

Work in creative occupations is often viewed as requiring subjective contributions, leaving relatively high levels of autonomy to the workers and offering opportunities for self-expression. It is therefore difficult for management to apply direct forms of control, and managers frequently need to resort to indirect, normative and hegemonic control. What is more, in many creative industries the proportion of self-employed workers is exceptionally high. Self-employment adds to the image of creative work as autonomous and focused on the creative process. However, a core problem for self-employed creative workers is to secure continuous employment and sufficient income. Reputation in local creative milieus and concessions in particular with regard to time and payment are key in the efforts of project acquisition.

In recent years, Internet platforms acting as intermediaries between clients and creative workers have become more and more important. Many of them are specialised in creative work or even in particular creative industries. Commissioning work and working over crowdworking platforms create a triangular relationship between the client, the platform and the worker. This brings additional features into self-employment in creative occupations – with wide variations in the degree of actual creativity in work. Crucially, the design of platforms provides standardised opportunities for clients to post jobs and for workers to offer their services. In addition, platforms provide standardised ways to implement and carry out a project, to settle the payment and to handle disputes. Platforms also include tools to measure and display workers' online reputations, which is crucial to their possibilities to acquire orders.

The structures and rules of Internet platforms add to the power asymmetry between clients and workers in crowded markets for creative services. The dependency of workers on the platform becomes particularly salient, in relation to temporal aspects of creative self-employment. In this contribution, we argue that the triangular relationship and the platform design exacerbate these pressures for constant availability, short reaction times and irregular and at times extremely long working hours. Based on empirical work on crowdworking in creative occupations in Austria, we describe the temporal aspects of work and show how the specific forms of control contribute to this time use.

Control, Digitisation and Time in Creative Occupations

Work in creative occupations is often presented as a model of the project-based and freelance economy (Boltanski and Chiapello, 2003; Manske and Schnell, 2010) and a field of labour in which great importance is attributed to self-expression, authenticity and reputation (Huws, 2010). As a consequence, flexible and temporary cooperation often go hand in hand with relatively high levels of autonomy at work. By definition, creative work is not amenable to direct control by supervisors or to control through organisational and technical structures. Workers' discretion is required so that companies may benefit from workers' ingenuity and creativity. Generally, within an internalised employment relationship, the indeterminacy of labour may be overcome also by indirect forms of control aiming at eliciting workers' effort through target setting; paying bonuses; promising employment stability and advancement; addressing normative orientations; influencing workers' beliefs, norms and values; or creating corporate identities (Friedman, 1977; Edwards, 1979; Thompson, 1989; Marks and Thompson, 2010; Sturdy et al., 2010).

Creative workers, such as musicians, in fact 'self-manage their own creativity' (Thompson et al., 2007) within the framework set by production and business managers who control the access to resources and to the market. In addition, creative work seems to be particularly amenable to normative control because of the special relationship to work: The attachment to the content of work is usually rather high, as it provides opportunities for self-expression and the products 'may still be experienced as in some sense owned' (Huws, 2010, p. 510). The desire for public recognition and the search for opportunities to build up a personal reputation are part of workers' perspectives and thus enter into the bargaining process with the employer (ibid., p. 510). Although these industries and occupations are generally termed 'creative', the question remains to what extent workers are actually required or allowed to bring in their creativity. Workers frequently complain that their artistic aspirations cannot be fulfilled in their jobs in the creative industries due to customer demands, time pressures, standardisation or low pay (Schörpf et al., 2017).

However, in many creative industries, the internalised employment relationship seems to be the exception rather than the rule in that many workers are self-employed. Project-based and freelance work are typical of film, graphic design, architecture, music, advertisement and other creative sectors forcing people into self-employment (Banks and Hesmondhalgh, 2009; Manske and Schnell, 2010; Gill, 2010; Schiek and Apitzsch, 2013; Siebert and Wilson 2013). Given the widespread absence of an employment contract, one might assume that the issue of managerial control is not relevant. For several reasons, however, we argue otherwise. First, self-employment may include working for only one customer at least for a certain period of time. This blurs the boundaries between freelancing and dependent employment. Second, even in more independent freelancing, there is a problem of 'indeterminacy of outcome' (Thompson et al., 2007). The customers or cooperation partners want to ensure smooth cooperation or the timely delivery and the appropriateness of the contribution or product they ordered. In the creative industries, reputation is of particular importance for being able to continuously find work on a project basis (Blair, 2001; Boltanski and Chiapello, 2003; Townley et al., 2009; Barnes et al., 2015). As a consequence, workers' behaviour is strongly influenced by their concerns for their reputation and therefore reputation is at the core of control strategies.

Creative occupations both use and develop new technologies in particular in the area of information technology which has profoundly changed creative occupations. For the past two decades the computer has emerged as a universal work tool. Major new fields of work have emerged for creative occupations due to the spread of broadband Internet access, the digitalisation of content and multimedia applications. In particular, transitions from 'old' to 'new' media or the use of video for communication and documentation have changed work in the relevant occupational fields. What is more, the Internet offers and creates a 'global information space' (Boes and Pfeiffer, 2006, S. 25) which provides easy access to information and allows new ways of distributed working. ICTs enable outsourcing and relocation (Huws, 2013), facilitate cooperation over long distances and allow the digital delivery of immaterial products, helping to overcome restrictions of transport (Holts, 2013) and making room for new business models such as e-commerce and crowdworking platforms.

Crowdsourcing means outsourcing, usually over an Internet platform, of projects or tasks to an undefined group of potential contractors (Howe, 2006; Hammon and Hippner, 2012). The numbers for crowdsourcing platforms, posted tasks as well as people looking for jobs are steadily increasing (Frei, 2009; Barnes et al., 2015). Workers are formally self-employed, have no formal work contract, get no regular wages, work with their own means of production and bear economic risk. As freelancing is widespread in many creative occupations, addressing an undefined and usually spatially dispersed group seems to be the important new feature. Obviously, the Internet, which allows for accessing a large number of recipients (Hammon and Hippner, 2012), and the services of the intermediary platforms are the key components of crowdsourcing. In addition, the call for tender, the project handling and the product delivery take place online. Companies and other clients benefit from increased flexibility and lower cost (Shepherd, 2012).

There is a triangular relationship between the worker, the intermediary (the platform) and the client. In principle, this is not new, because agency work also constitutes a triangular relationship and service work is often characterised by the influence of customers, who also play a part in the control over workers (Fuller and Smith, 1991; Korczynski et al., 2000; Gamble, 2007). While crowdsourcing resembles a multi-employer constellation (Marchington et al., 2005) or triangularised employment relationship (Helfen, 2014), the platforms deny the role of employer. And in contrast to service work in general, the client is often a principal rather than a customer.

In order to encourage clients to outsource work to the crowd and thus to waive possibilities of employees' supervision and control, the platforms offer tools for handling these higher levels of uncertainty (Felstiner, 2011). Interestingly, if work in creative occupations is being paid per hour and/or creative workers are being employed more or less continuously, not only does the issue of the indeterminacy of outcomes apply but so does that of the indeterminacy of labour. Crowdsourcing platforms provide various tools for managerial control through online surveillance of keystrokes or screenshots of work progress. These forms of direct control, however, do not seem to be appropriate for the kind of work and turn out to be time-consuming for the client. As in creative work in general, indirect form of control can be assumed to be much more relevant than online surveillance. One crucial aspect certainly is online reputation through platforms' rating systems and the rules for workers' profiles. Open-source communities are good examples of how gaining reputation both stimulates effort and controls behaviour in an environment where work is not motivated by income (Franck and Jungwirth, 2003).

More research is required into the nature of managerial control systems in crowdsourcing taking into account the design of the crowdsourcing platforms and the strategies of platform organisers: compensation schemes, trust building systems and features for voting, rating and commenting (Saxton et al., 2013). Temporal aspects play a particularly important role in this. First, the importance of the online reputation impacts on the time behaviour of workers, as response times and timely delivery are key criteria against which the workers are rated by clients. Second, platforms themselves monitor availability and response times and therefore control workers' behaviour in this respect. The platforms' influence on temporal aspects of crowdwork is supplemented by the clients' efforts to reduce the indeterminacy of labour or outcome through setting goals and milestones or demanding interim results. Temporalities of crowdworking are thus crucial to management and control.

Temporalities are also key aspects of the quality of work and life of workers in creative occupations. Not only crowdworkers but also self-employed workers in general face particular temporal demands and time restrictions. 'Portfolio work', such as working on different pieces of work for several different clients or employers, leads to pressurised work and high work intensity, and work–life balance suffers as a result (Clinton et al., 2006). The developments towards project-based work and the pervasive use of ICT, too, are often accompanied by a blurring of boundaries between paid work and other spheres of life, and they tend to change the perception of where and when it is normal to work (Vartiainen, 2006; Pfeiffer, 2012). The 'high speed society' (Rosa, 2005) seems to become reality as, due to digital communication tools, the speed of work and life further accelerates. In creative occupations the availability of workers via communication technology may lead to 'client colonisation' (Gold and Mustafa, 2013) in the sense of an intrusion into their privacy.

In this contribution, we present research findings on the temporalities of crowdworking in creative occupations in the context of management or control. While patterns of time use and increased time pressures are characteristics of self-employment in creative occupations, we argue that crowdworking and, in particular, the strategies and structures of Internet platforms as well as the structured relationship with clients have special impacts on crowdworkers. In the remainder of this contribution, we first present the method of our study and then briefly describe the findings on the characteristics of crowdsourcing platforms. This is followed by a detailed presentation of temporal aspects of creative crowdworking. Finally, in the conclusions, we will highlight the particularities of control and time use in crowdworking.

Methods

This chapter reports on 20 qualitative interviews, carried out between January and August 2015, whereof four were conducted with clients/employers (people who or companies that outsource creative tasks), three with experts in the field of creative crowdsourcing, three with crowdsourcing platform providers and ten with workers on crowdsourcing platforms (see Table 5.1). We focused on crowdworkers operating from Austria: nine respondents lived and worked in Austria at the time of the interview, and one respondent lived and worked in Romania. Most interviews were held face to face (15), while the remaining interviews were conducted over Skype/telephone. The interviews were between one hour and two and a half hours long (the average being 90 minutes), and we used a semi-structured interview guide. We were interested in how the respondents individually dealt with work and what experiences they made with crowdwork, in their working patterns, income situation or working time. All interviews were fully transcribed and interpreted using content analysis (Mayring, 2000). Interviews were coded systematically, and we built the codes in an inductive way from the interviews (in-vivo coding).

In addition, we mapped and in-depth analysed popular crowdsourcing platforms used for crowdsourcing creative tasks. Some of the mapped platforms are multi-purpose platforms (i.e. creative and non-creative tasks are offered, especially Elance, oDesk – consolidated and renamed as Upwork in 2015 – and Freelancer), other platforms focus on creative tasks exclusively (such as 99designs or voices). Participant observation was also undertaken through actively crowdsourcing a task via an online platform.

Table 5.1 Worker profiles

Name	Sex	Age	Services sold	Platform	Gross income/ month
Alfred	Male	34	Creative and administrative tasks	Freelancer	€ 1.000
Anna	Female	55	Voice over	Various, e.g. voices	€ 3.000
Bruce	Male	35	Coding	oDesk and others	N.A.
Carol	Female	35	Writing	N.A.	€ 1.400
Dragana	Female	32	Graphic design	99designs	€ 2.250
Joshi	Male	44	Video, graphic design, translations	Elance	€ 1.250
Johnny	Male	36	Graphic design	99designs	€ 90
Julia	Female	40	Graphic design	Freelancer, Elance	€ 590
Link	Male	30	Illustration	Elance, oDesk	> € 500
William	Male	31	3D Design	oDesk and others	€ 2.700

Internet Platforms as Crowdsourcing Intermediaries

Generally, two basic forms of crowdworking platforms for creative work can be distinguished: bid-based and contest-based platforms. On bid-based platforms clients who want to commission work online can place a job offer. Posting a project most often is free of charge; however, one can decide to have a project 'featured' for a fee, meaning that the project is highlighted prominently on a platform or is available to highly experienced workers only. The clients have to define a project according to their needs, for instance by using a template offered on the platform. It is necessary to list the requirements with as many details as possible, narrow down project duration and set a price. Workers have the possibility to apply for the projects by sending a short statement and linking their portfolio. However, they can also be invited for a job directly. Further details about the work and the terms might be discussed between client and worker. On contest-based platforms, clients can again post a briefing. Workers, however, do not submit a statement but already a finished or near-finished product. The client might choose a couple of the submissions and invite the workers into a final round. When the project ends, usually only the winning submissions (or submissions invited to the final round) are awarded payment. Both types of platforms might additionally offer shops where ready-made products can be sold for a fixed price. Platforms, bid- and contest-based alike, see themselves as intermediaries and only charge for the use of the matching service.

When a worker starts a profile on a crowdworking platform s/he might display professional and private information, such as country of origin, languages spoken or fields of work. This usually happens in a standardised way, often through a drop-down-menu or through ticking boxes. According to these selections, the workers receive information on jobs, and clients can find workers and decide to award tasks and projects. The platforms also allow workers to upload and present a portfolio. More importantly, most platforms provide information on the worker's activities, which might differ from one platform to another but generally include information such as total number of jobs, date of registration, last login, hours worked, hourly rate and so on. Often there are verifications of identity, telephone, payment or country of residence, which are necessary to indicate the workers' reliability. This profile information is complemented with statistics on repeated hiring for the same clients, availability per week, response time, rate of successful jobs or information on jobs done on time and budget. Moreover, some platforms have a badge and experience system, where workers might 'earn' achievements by completing specific tasks or having a certain level.

To provide proof of workers' competencies, platforms provide tests for a number of skills and topics. For this purpose, they use their own platform-specific testing procedures rather than well-established standard tests and categories, like the 'Test of English as a Foreign Language (TOEFL)', or the 'European Computer Driving Licence (ECDL)'. The workers are free to take tests, but if a worker starts a test s/he has to undertake it in a given amount of time. On some platforms these tests are charged. After completion, the results of the tests – measured in comparison to the average results of all workers – are published on the worker's profile page. Tests might encompass knowledge in areas such as language, numeracy or computer programmes.

On the platforms, workers' online reputations consist mainly of ratings and reviews. After a job or project is finalised, clients select an overall rating – often a grading with one to five stars – and possibly also assess the worker in several subcategories, such as quality, communication, timeliness, on budget and so on. These highly standardised means to assess workers stand in contrast to 'offline' reputation in creative professions or occupations in that they reduce the complexity of creative tasks and standardise the assessment. However, clients may, in addition, write a short review. Both the standardised ratings and the reviews are published on the worker's profile. For clients, ratings and reviews facilitate the selection process, on the one hand, and, on the other, turn out to be an effective tool for controlling and sanctioning a worker. Clients within our group of participants argued that ratings are the first thing they look at when awarding a job. Furthermore, platforms often allow a potential client to filter out crowdworkers with an average rating below a certain threshold.

Occasionally, crowdwork platforms monitor the communication between workers and clients or, if possible, the work progress. Our research indicated that this was a common procedure on a specialised platform for academic ghostwriting, where all communication was bound to the platform and thus can easily be accessed and read. This stands in contrast to other platforms, where chat logs are only accessed in cases of dispute resolution (according to the terms and conditions). Thereby the platform organisers know about the project details and the individual arrangements between worker and client and can prevent the client from making requests beyond the actual agreement. In addition, they can prevent bargaining outside the platform, and they can monitor whether their general terms and conditions are followed.

Autonomy, Control and Time Use in Creative Crowdworking

Temporal aspects of work appeared to be crucial in the crowdworkers' accounts of working and living conditions. The extent of control exercised over the workers most markedly shows in their autonomy – or lack thereof – regarding working time. What stands out for crowdworkers is the long periods of searching for online jobs, long working hours and high pressure with closing deadlines, a very irregular distribution of working time throughout the week, work during night-time and on weekends and high levels of availability, which all intensifies tendencies towards work patterns without boundaries.

In our interviews, we see that the period of acquisition and the period of doing the actual project work are characterised by different time constraints. Because crowdworkers frequently undertake acquisition while they carry out one or more projects, these periods usually overlap. In the following section, we first describe aspects of time related to the search for jobs and then discuss the time use during ongoing projects.

It's Acquisition Time

Long hours of searching for a job offer and the contribution required prior to the actual start of a project are endemic within crowdworking in creative occupations. In our research, participants often argued that it was common to spend considerable time searching for projects. Usually, workers spend a portion of their working day searching the platform(s) until they find a job that both matches their profile and meets their expectations. Finding work seems to be about timeliness more than anything else. Since a project might pop up at any time, workers might 'just sit at the computer, roaming the platform and wait' (Johnny) because the faster one reacts, the higher the chances of getting new projects.

> When you are the first who applies for a job and you have somewhat decent communication skills and your pricing is acceptable, you are contacted rather quickly. So, it's about quickness. People [the clients] are not waiting for long. (Joshi)

> If I don't confirm jobs on my mobile immediately, I wouldn't even get half the jobs I'm getting now. (Anna)

Being among the fastest to reply to an offer creates a situation where errors are more likely to occur. Job offers are only scanned briefly, and the creative workers have to decide in a short amount of time whether jobs are worth applying for. When both parties – workers and clients – agree on a project, they are bound and risk bad ratings and statistics if they withdraw. Another form of expedient jobs is called 'speedies', where workers have to deliver a product within a couple of hours after being awarded. This becomes challenging when clients and workers are in different time zones, because workers can apply for the job in the evening but they might be awarded only a couple of hours later, the period starting during night-time.

Yet, the whole process of preparing and sending applications for jobs can also be described as time-consuming. Especially when there is a high rejection rate, the application process can be tedious. Contest-based platforms usually provide information on how many competitions a worker participated in and how many of those s/he won. As people already submit a finished or near-finished project to such competitions, the periods of acquisition and actual project work blur with the high risk of not getting paid because only the winning submission is remunerated. Workers reported applying for dozens of contests every month, winning only one or two – if winning at all.

A worker aptly describes the situation giving the example of a contest he initiated.

> It's horrible! Once, I opened a contest myself and it's a horrible feeling. ... I made a contest for $100 for a logo, and that's a really low

price ... and in total I got 180 logos, meaning that with my $100 I triggered over 300 working hours and that hurts. In my opinion, these contests are an exploitation machinery. But I also participated in contests [as a worker], for a very simple reason, when starting fresh on a platform you won't get any jobs. You won't get any, because you don't have any ratings, no securities, no 5-star-rating. You have no chance. So you have to get, I don't know, 5 or 10 jobs with a good rating to get on the client's radar. (Alfred)

When working on contest-based platforms, workers emphasise their high involvement during the selection process as the client might demand immediate action from the worker. This makes it difficult not being available for clients during a contest. Thus, workers rely on clients' decisions, which limits their ability to define their own timing; they often simply follow the clients' schedules.

Workers also report that finding jobs may actually only take little time, such as when 'fitting' jobs are provided through the platform's selection process. However, this seems to happen only on more specialised platforms, and it may happen anytime during the day. After having found a job, organising work has to be undertaken, as clients and workers have to agree on terms or timetables or have to further specify the project. When working on more complex projects, there might be a video or telephone conference with the client. Interestingly, such activities prior to the actual work on a project are not regarded as part of the work. A worker told us:

Then we have a conference call, and ... the call lasts from 15 minutes to half an hour, depending on how extensive the job is. And afterwards I start to work, then the whole process starts. (Carol)

Overall, freelancers tend to spend a great deal of time looking for work; however, they cannot quantify the amount of time they usually spend during this process. For experienced individuals, this acquisition process becomes less time-consuming as workers gain an understanding about which projects are worth applying for. Workers learn to assess which jobs are likely to have too much competition and in which fields, at what prices and for what project length affords the best opportunities of success. The blending of work and free time and the importance of quick reactions are described by a worker when describing his routine in situations in which jobs are scarce and he needs to make ends meet. He describes his unorthodox way of finding and undertaking work as follows:

If the job situation is crappy and that happens from time to time, then I'll buy a six-pack, sit down at my computer at 10 p.m., gulp down the beer and accept everything. Everything and at any rate. ... When it is only about earning money, I contact the client right the second when a project is initiated. And I'm very straightforward, skipping the formalities, and sometimes it works. And, well, during a six-pack you can earn around $100 if you can manage yourself. (Alfred)

It's Project Time

Long Working Hours, High Time Pressure

People working on online platforms face an unstable job situation, with periods of few or no jobs contrasting with periods of excessive workloads. This results in excessive working hours over days or weeks, as a response to rigid time schedules during projects and rising pressure when deadlines are closing. Overall, the working time of the people interviewed varied between 20 hours and 60 or more hours per week. Though the effective working hours differed, incoming projects with a very short runtime (frequently 24 hours or less) put pressure on workers and led to long working days. Particularly over short time periods, working hours are regularly rising significantly, and one worker told us about his time schedule when deadlines are closing: 'When the shit hits the fan, I'm working all the time. That means about 16 or 17 hours every day for three or four days' (Alfred). Such excessive working days are no exception, as an artist in 3D design states:

Right now with a client I work 16 hours per day. I get up, brush my teeth, maybe take a shower, do some shopping and then 15, 16 hours. And the next day, it starts all over again. (William)

The clients set milestones and deadlines, which the workers consider rigid.

There are very rigid deadlines, you know exactly what to deliver. And you also know how long your 'contract' runs, in this case, until when you have to deliver the final product. (Carol)

And I knew I had to deliver within 24 hours, because you are getting penalty points [bad sub ratings] when you are not adhering to deadlines. So I worked 20 hours non-stop. I worked [from midnight] until

5 a.m., lied down, slept for three and a half hours, got up and cut from 9 a.m. until 9 p.m. Then I checked every audio file for another three hours. (Anna)

Nevertheless, crowdworkers argue that they find it difficult to estimate the length of a project. It is particularly problematic if clients demand multiple revisions, and workers find it difficult to reject these requests since they want to finish the project and need good ratings. Therefore, some projects which should only take a couple of hours might stretch indefinitely.

Long working hours become difficult to balance when crowdworking is undertaken in conjunction with other employment. One worker, who has to get up at 4 a.m. for his job in a supermarket, said that for an interesting job he 'stay[s] awake until there is no more work to be done' (Johnny), leading to nights without any sleep. Situations where workers had two or more jobs led up to 70 working hours per week and entailed cuts in the workers' private lives where time for the family was restricted to 'occasional Sundays' (Johnny). Another worker said that he tries to set a limit around 40 hours per week. So for 40 hours he tracks his working hours; however, after the limit is reached, he often keeps working if work remains to be done, and so effective working hours are likely to exceed 70 hours per week.

Work during the Night and on Weekends

It was very common for respondents to extend the working day into evenings and even nights. This was not always a result of long working hours but was also connected to an alternative working day. Some workers started to work around noon and from there worked in sessions of a couple of hours, with the last session starting after midnight. Others had to balance their creative online work with another job and hence had to squeeze in the online work, which most often meant working during night-time. Besides personal preferences and the balancing of different types of work, the strong dependence on jobs and on clients' demands made it hard to schedule working time in advance. One result of this client dependence was a shift in working hours, where working days started later (around noon) and lasted into the evening. This also made it very difficult to define work-free times, especially on weekends. For most crowdworkers in our sample, working on weekends was the norm rather than exception.

It's just my habit, I got used to working on weekends. (Dragana)

> For me, working on weekends is ok. I don't care if it's a work day or not. (Alfred)

> There are no weekends for me. (Anna)

For some workers it was a no-go to work on weekends, arguing that weekends have to be absolutely work-free. These individuals clearly defined when their work ended and when their weekends began; they also switched off their mobile devices and refrained from checking their emails and inboxes during the weekend. Other workers, however, were not able to be so strict about placing constraints on weekend working, either because they were not able to work during the week due to other responsibilities or because they argued that they had to work according to the client's needs. Among participants, the dependence on clients' requests was very high. One worker who had many clients in countries with different time zones said, 'You have to work when they [the clients] are there' (Julia).

Constant Availability

Working on online platforms actually means being on call – not only for the acquisition of new work but also during ongoing projects or relating to products offered in online shops. Being available in general and being available on short notice is seen as essential for crowdworkers. The communication usually runs over computers and mobile devices. Workers must regularly check their emails and messages, and this communication can be undertaken from anywhere and at any time. This is most pointedly reflected in workers' regularly checking their messages for clients' responses or requests. The morning routine of workers is usually to switch on their devices or computers to check new messages or emails right after waking up and prior to anything else.

> The first thing I do in the morning after getting up is switch on the computer, then I feed the cat and prepare breakfast. But then I'm curious, and I have to switch on my mobile, because maybe something [a request, project] rolled in during night-time. From Canada or America sometimes request come after midnight, and occasionally I'm not online anymore after midnight. (Anna)

Because clients and workers are often in different countries and thus operating in different time zones, waiting for responses can take up a lot of time. Availability is key, since clients expect the workers to be on call, and non-compliance could lead to poor ratings and impact on the workers' online reputations. Moreover, availability on many platforms is outlined on the workers profile via statistics, badges or experience levels.

The pressure to be constantly available also shows when workers discuss holidays or other travel. Especially problematic is the limited time to respond to clients, when selling ready-made work over the platforms. The pressure on workers often leads them to taking work away with them.

[Selling logos over the platform] is only a problem when I am travelling, because you cannot put a hold on my profile. I asked them to be clear. I wrote them once, asking, 'OK, I'm not going to be available for the next ten days. I will be on holiday. Is it possible to just stop everything that is happening there?' but they said 'no'. So basically, when you are selling the logo on the logo store and you don't respond within 24 hours, the platform will take over ... and you only get a portion of the money you are entitled to. (Dragana)

My daughter, who went to Greece with me said, 'Mum, please leave your mobile in the apartment', because I bought an Internet package for Greece, and it was impossible not to permanently check the mobile. (Anna)

When it comes to night work, some of our interviewees draw very clear boundaries.

I wake up around 7 a.m. and start my day. So whatever is happening overnight has to wait for me until the morning. I don't have sleepless nights. (Dragana)

When I'm offline in Skype, then my day's work is done. ... And clients usually don't have my phone number. These conflicting poles of being available all the time and the need to earn money are also always boundaries between work and free time, and they are blurring. If you don't draw boundaries for yourself, you are going mad. (Alfred)

Others are not as clear when defining work-free time.

"When my husband is around over the weekends I try to keep the weekend clear. But it happens regularly that on Saturday evening at 11 the mobile sounds and he asks 'well, what is it? Uzbekistan?', and he only laughs. And I excuse myself and run up [to the studio] and answer. I jump up, whether we watch a movie or whatever. Or I have to correct an audio recording because the client suddenly wants something different. Yea, that happens. That happens." Anna

Blurring Boundaries of Work

As a result of working at home, high levels of availability and the flexible working day, online workers often face difficulties drawing boundaries between paid work, domestic work and work-free time. A typical working day for Carol, an academic ghost-writer, for instance, starts with caring for her children and taking them to kindergarten. Afterwards, she has a couple of hours in the morning where she is able to undertake paid work. She is then only free to resume her online work after her children have gone to bed and she continues working until 10 p.m. This means a high organisational effort reconciling paid work, family work and leisure time – if any. Others face similar difficulties separating private and working life, as Link, an illustrator, explains:

> Well, I get up in the morning, grab breakfast and immediately start to work. During work I also do chores, like doing laundry or vacuum. And I also wash the dishes. And then I keep working until evening, until I go to bed, or rather shortly before going to bed. ... I don't think that I can switch off from work. Ever. But I'm trying to change that in the future. ... I would love to establish a routine, to work from morning to afternoon and to be able to switch off at six. (Link)

Online work can overlap with looking after children, domestic chores or social activities. Therefore, workers find it hard to structure their working day in a 9.00 to 5.00 manner. When people need to coordinate work with clients in different time zones, virtual meetings set cornerstones for the daily routine and private life is structured around work. For workers it is hard to draw clear lines between work and free time, either because of the discontinuous time structure or because free time might also be connected to the creative profession (or both). Workers describe the blending of work and non-work activities.

> Often I have to postpone meetings with friends, because I have a deadline and a competition is ending. That really bothers me. (Dragana)

However, the actual daily working time highly depends on the clients. People organise their working time around clients' needs. A crowdworker in design whose clients are mostly overseas described difficulties in organising social activities:

> During the week I really can't [meet friends], because ... this is the problem, you know, because in America most of the clients wake up at 4 o'clock in the afternoon, you know and this is morning in America, and they want to work, and that's why I stay up so long sometimes. ... And after that, during the week, I have no time to go out or something. And anyway, lately I don't have the power to do that. (Julia)

Another crowdworker, operating as a voice artist makes a similar observation:

> They are sending a message and an email at the same time. Then you log in via your mobile and you check the project if it suits. And then it's a job with a fixed price and only a couple of words to record. And when I'm out with a couple of friends, having a beer then I'll say 'folks, I've got to leave this moment: I've got to record 17 words.' (Anna)

While this can be detrimental to individuals, some workers are so involved in their work that they do not object to anti-social working hours. This makes it fairly simple to extend work into private life and keep working until late at night:

> For me, typically, work doesn't stop at 6 or 8 p.m. I keep coding because it's fun and it's my hobby. And then I'll go to bed sometime between midnight and 3 a.m. (Bruce)

Other freelancers note that it is common to keep working on projects for free if they are interested in the subject and project funds are exhausted. This means that although workers do not present the work they can do over platforms as highly creative, they nevertheless seem to find opportunities for self-expression that, in turn, bind them to the work and blur the client–worker relationship.

Conclusions

In this contribution, we describe the strategies and structures of crowdsourcing platforms for creative work and the temporal aspects of creative crowdworking. The design of the online platforms provides a framework within which clients offer tasks and workers present themselves and perform work. The platform's terms and conditions give a general framework defining its intermediary function. Commissioning work and carrying out work over the platform mean accepting the rules and structures set by the platform organisers.

When it comes to working time, crowdworking largely means giving up the very autonomy many invoke when explaining the advantages of freelancing and crowdworking. Daily and weekly work time is frequently distributed unequally, leading to several work sessions a day and to times of excessive amounts of work on the one hand and to time of little or no work load on the other. Working during the night, very early in the morning, on weekends and sometimes during holidays seems common for crowdworkers. Work time largely depends on the clients' expectations, and workers might not easily structure their working time according to their own needs. Some interviewees reported periods with extremely long working hours, limiting their life basically to work and sleep.

Yet, not all workers handle working time in a similar manner. Those who are better established as crowdworkers are seldom able to restrict their working time to an eight-hour day. In contrast, those who do not expect to make a living from crowdwork restrict work to the working week or limit the daily worktime – partly because of additional employment. However, all crowdworkers find it challenging, if not impossible, to limit and autonomously structure working time because they are mindful of missing out on lucrative projects, receiving unfavourable ratings and failing to attract follow-up opportunities.

So why do creative workers accept such constraints to their working and private lives? The question is especially pressing, as all our participants stressed the advantage of freelancing in terms of autonomy. However, for the benefit of autonomy, crowdworkers must accept intrusion into their time. We argue that this is not only due to their situation as freelancers but also because of the control triangle between platform, clients and workers.

The platform sets a framework of control which includes both control and surveillance of workers by the platform and tools for the clients to control workers. The required profile information, the statistics, the badge and experience systems, the templates, the tests and the possibility to rate workers are all designed to evoke particular behaviours. In relation to control, the badge and experience systems are important because they specify what workers should do or can achieve and what their priorities or goals should be. Besides providing proof of qualifications in an online environment, tests also imply normative control over crowdworkers. For example, on the platform Upwork, one can find the 'Upwork Readiness Test for Independent Contractors and Company Managers', and on Freelancer there is a test for 'Freelancer Orientation', where people are, for instance, asked how to handle clients, how to react when payment is delayed or when to contact customer support (and questions are very suggestive). We argue that such tests, together with the 'terms and conditions' on the one hand constitute a bureaucratic authority (Ouchi, 1979) and on the other act as bureaucratic control (Edwards, 1979).

There are also more direct forms of control found in creative crowdworking, as there are programmes to monitor that the workers and platforms are logging the communication between workers and clients. 'Of course they [the platform organisers] read everything. Certainly they don't want me to negotiate with the client privately' (Carol). This results in a Panopticon-like situation in which the potential presence of an overseer influences the workers' and clients' behaviour.

Tools for direct control, such as software programmes to monitor the work progress by registering keystrokes or screenshots, were infrequently adopted by clients and workers. Only one participant said that he had accepted it occasionally when he started as a crowdworker. In principle, such tools offer a solution to the client's problem of uncertainty whether the worker exclusively works on the client's project charged time (Felstiner, 2011). However, the application of these tools is too time-consuming for the clients, and workers were very reluctant to use such programmes, not wanting to have every working step monitored.

Consequently, clients influence the work process and workers' time use in three ways: First, they define the project and set a timetable and possibly a milestone at which workers have to deliver their products. Second, clients review the outcome and might demand revisions. And third, after a project is finalised, the clients may rate the worker and write a review. Ratings and reviews were identified by workers, clients and platform organisers as the most important tool for the workers' online reputation. Good ratings are obligatory for workers to be 'on the client's radar'. As one crowdworker describes, ratings are essential for getting jobs. At the start of a crowdworking career, without any projects to present and without an online reputation, acquiring ratings is considered to be even more crucial. A platform organiser suggested that, at the start of their career, crowdworkers, with a view to their ratings, should choose their projects carefully and should refrain from undertaking complex projects. Crowdworkers have to avoid poor ratings at all costs, and strategies for this frequently involve offering the clients multiple revisions, forfeiting payment or accepting reduced payment, tolerating disrespectful clients or investing a disproportionate amount of time into completing a project. A single bad rating can have a more significant impact at the start of someone's career.

Dissatisfied clients are put in a powerful position because they may demand a reduced price of the current project and not offer any follow-up jobs. In addition, a bad rating makes it much more difficult to acquire future jobs. On platforms there are ways to display workers according to their accumulated ratings, and some jobs are accessible only to workers with certain levels of ratings.

Overall, while working time and time autonomy of crowdworkers clearly demonstrates the characteristics of the self-employed in general and, in particular, the situation of 'connected freelancers' (Gold and Mustafa, 2013) or 'mediatised work' (Roth-Ebner, 2016), we would argue that crowdworking has specific consequences for workers. In addition to clients' setting tight deadlines and demanding constant availability, the platform design exacerbates these pressures when it comes to both the acquisition of projects and carrying out the work. Among other things, workers need to be quick to get a job, and their online availability and their reaction times are measured by the platforms. Not surprisingly, reputation is key to getting jobs since the creative industries are largely reputational economies. However, online reputation differs markedly from the reputation in local creative milieus in that is it standardised and one-dimensional. Surveillance and ratings, which are crucial for the online reputation, often include temporal aspects. As a consequence, workers' time use is strongly influenced by platforms, adding to the more general pressures facing self-employed workers in creative occupations.

REFERENCES

Banks, M. and D. Hesmondhalgh (2009) 'Looking for work in creative industries policy', *International Journal of Cultural Policy*, 15, 4, 415–30.

Barnes, S.-A., A. Green and M. Hoyos (2015) 'Crowdsourcing and work: Individual factors and circumstances influencing employability', *New Technology, Work and Employment*, 30, 1, 16–31.

Blair, H. (2001) 'You're Only as Good as Your Last Job: The Labour Process and Labour Market in the British Film Industry', *Work, Employment and Society*, 15, 1, 149–69.

Boes, A. and S. Pfeiffer (2006) 'Informatisierung der Arbeit – Gesellschaft im Umbruch. Eine Einführung', in A. Baukrowitz, T. Berker, A. Boes, S. Pfeiffer,

▶

R. Schmiede and A. Will (eds), *Informatisierung der Arbeit – Gesellschaft im Umbruch* (Berlin: edition sigma), pp. 19–36.

Boltanski, L. and È. Chiapello (2003) *Der neue Geist des Kapitalismus* (Konstanz: UVK).

Clinton, M., P. Totterdell and S. Wood (2006) 'A grounded theory of portfolio working: Experiencing the smallest of small businesses', *International Small Business Journal*, 24, 2,, 179–203.

Edwards, R. (1979) *Contested Terrain: The Transformation of the Workplace in the Twentieth Century* (New York: Basic Books).

Edwards, R. (1981) *Herrschaft im modernen Produktionsprozess* (Frankfurt a. M. and New York: Campus).

Felstiner, A. (2011) 'Working the Crowd: Employment and Labor Law in the Crowdsourcing Industry', *Berkeley Journal of Employment & Labor Law*, 32, 1, 143–203.

Flecker, J. and A. Schönauer (2016) 'The production of "placelessness" – digital service work in global value chains', in J. Flecker (ed.), *Space, Place and Global Digital Work* (London: Palgrave Macmillan), pp. 11–30.

Flecker, J., M. Pfadenhauer, T. Grenz and P. Schörpf (2016) 'Gesellschaftlicher Wandel im Zeitalter des Internet: Digitalisierung der Arbeit und Mediatisierung sozialer Welten', in *Gesellschaft im Wandel* (Reihe: University – Society – Industry. Beiträge zum lebensbegleitenden Lernen und Wissenstransfer (Wien: Uni Wien).

Frank, E. and C. Jungwirth (2003) 'Reconciling rent-seekers and donators – The governance structure of open source', *Journal of Management and Governance*, 7, 401–21.

Frei, B. (2009) Paid Crowdsourcing Current State & Progress Toward Mainstream Business Use.

Friedman, A. (1977) *Industry and Labour* (London: Macmillan).

Fuller, L. and V. Smith (1991) 'Consumers' reports: Management by customers in the service economy.' *Work, Employment and Society*, 5, 1, 1–16.

Gamble, J. (2007) 'The rhetoric of the consumer and customer control in China', *Work, Employment and Society*, 21, 1, 7–25.

Gill, R. (2010) 'Life is a pitch: Managing the self in new media work', in D. Mark (ed.), *Managing Media Work* (London: Sage).

Gold, M. and M. Mustafa (2013) '"Work always wins": Client colonisation, time management and the anxieties of connected freelancers', *New Technology, Work and Employment*, 28, 3, 197–211.

Hammon, L. and H. Hippner (2012) 'Crowdsourcing', *Wirtschaftsinformatik*, 54, 3, 165–8.

Helfen, M. (2014) 'Netzwerkförmige Tertialisierung und triangularisierte Beschäftigung: Braucht es eine interorganisationale Personalpolitik?' in J. Sydow, D. Sadowski and P. Conrad (eds), *Managementforschung*, 24, 171–206.

Holts, K. (2013) 'Towards a taxonomy of virtual work', in U. Huws 'Working online, living offline: Labour in the internet age'. *Work Organisation, Labour and Globalization*, 7, 1, 31–50.

Howe, J. (2006) 'The Rise of Crowdsourcing', *Wired Magazine*, 14, 6, 1–4.

Huws, U. (2006) 'The restructuring of global value chains and the creation of a cybertariat', in C. May (ed.), *Global Corporate Power: (Re)integrating Companies into the international political economy* (Boulder, CO: Lynne Rienner Publishers), pp. 65–82.

Huws, U. (2010) 'Expression and expropriation: The dialectics of autonomy and control in creative labour', *Ephemera*, 10, 3/4, 504–21.

Huws, U. (2013) 'Working online, living offline: Labour in the Internet age.' *Work Organisation, Labour and Globalisation*, 7, 1, 1–11.

Korczynski, M., K. Shire, S. Frenkel and M. Tam (2000) 'Service work in consumer capitalism: Customers, control and contradictions', *Work, Employment and Society*, 14, 4, 669–87.

Manske, A. and C. Schnell (2010) 'Arbeit und Beschäftigung in der Kultur- und Kreativwirtschaft', in F. Böhle, G. G. Voß and G. Wachtler (eds.), *Handbuch Arbeitssoziologie* (Wiesbaden: VS Verlag).

Marchington, M., D. Grimshaw, J. Rubery and H. Willmott (2005) *Fragmenting Work: Blurring Organizational Boundaries and Disordering Hierarchies* (Oxford: Oxford University Press).

Marks, A. and P. Thompson (2010) 'Beyond the Blank Slate: Identities and interests at work', in P. Thompson and C. Smith (eds), *Working Life – Renewing Labour Process Analysis* (Houndmills: Palgrave Macmillan), 316–38.

Marrs, K. (2010) 'Herrschaft und Kontrolle in der Arbeit', in F. Böhle, G. G. Voß and G. Wachtler (eds), *Handbuch Arbeitssoziologie* (Wiesbaden: VS Verlag).

Mayring, P. (2000) *Qualitative Inhaltsanalyse: Grundlagen und Techniken* (Weinheim: Beltz).

Ouchi, W. G. (1979) 'A Conceptual Framework for the design of organizational control mechanisms', *Management Science*, 25, 9, 833–48.

Pfeiffer, S. (2012) 'Technologische Grundlagen der Entgrenzung: Chancen und Risiken', in B. Badura, A. Ducki, H. Schröder, J. Klose and M. Meyer (eds), Fehlzeiten Report 2012 (Berlin and Heidelberg: Springer), pp. 15–21.

Rosa, H. (2005) *Beschleunigung. Die Veränderung der Zeitstrukturen in der Moderne* (Frankfurt am Main: Suhrkamp).

Roth-Ebner, C. (2016) 'Spatial Phenomena of Mediatised Work', in J. Flecker (ed.), *Space, Place and Global Digital Work* (London: Palgrave Macmillan), pp. 227–45.

Saxton, G. D., O. Oh and R. Kishore (2013) 'Rules of Crowdsourcing: Models, issues, and systems of control', *Information Systems Management*, 30, 1, 2–20.

Schörpf, P., J. Flecker, A. Schönauer and H. Eichmann (2017 forthcoming) 'Triangular love-hate. Management and control in creative crowdworking', in *New Technology, Work and Employment*.

Schiek, D. and B. Apitzsch (2013) 'Doing work. Atypische Arbeit in der Film- und der Automobilbranche im Vergleich', *Berliner Journal füer Soziologie*, 23, 181–204.

Schmiede, R. (2015) 'Arbeit im informierten Kapitalismus', *Aufsätze 1976–2015* (Berlin: edition sigma).

Shepherd, H. (2012) 'Crowdsourcing', *Contexts*, 11, 2, 10–11.

Siebert, S. and F. Wilson (2013) 'All work and no pay: Consequences of unpaid work in the creative industries', *Work, Employment and Society*, 27, 4, 711–21.

Sturdy, A., P. Fleming and R. Delbridge (2010) 'Normative control and Beyond in contemporary Capitalism', in P. Thompson and C. Smith (eds), *Working Life – Renewing Labour Process Analysis* (Basingstoke: Palgrave Macmillan), pp. 113–35.

Thompson, P. (1989) *The Nature of Work* (London: Macmillan).

Thompson, P., M. Jones and C. Warhurst (2007) 'From conception to consumption: Creativity and the missing managerial link', *Journal of Organizational Behavior*, 28, 625–40.

Townley, B., N. Beech and A. McKinley (2009) 'Managing in the creative industries: Manageing the motley crew', *Human Relations*, 62, 7, 939–62.

Vartiainen, M. (2006) 'Mobile Virtual Work – Concepts, Outcomes and Challenges', in E. Andriessen and M. Vartiainen (eds), *Mobile Virtual Work. A New Paradigm?* (Berlin and Heidelberg: Springer), pp. 13–44.

Workplace Cyberbullying: Insights into an Emergent Phenomenon

Premilla D'Cruz and Ernesto Noronha

Introduction

The growing reliance of contemporary workplaces on information and communications technologies and devices (ICTDs) (Holtgrewe, 2014), operating across varying degrees of virtualisation (Huws, 2013), has set the stage for the emergence of cyberbullying (Baruch, 2005; Piotrowski, 2012), adding to the existing varieties of workplace abuse (D'Cruz and Noronha, 2016a). Defined as *inappropriate and unwanted acts of hostility, intimidation, aggression and harassment via ICTDs, marked by boundarylessness, anonymity, invisibility, concreteness and permanence, with implications for the course of the misbehaviour in terms of pervasiveness, intensity, evidence and persistence, thereby affecting outcomes for victims and other protagonists like perpetrators, bystanders, employers and so on* (D'Cruz and Noronha, 2013a), workplace cyberbullying is little understood, warranting academic studies on its trajectory (Lutgen-Sandvik and Tracy, 2012), in order to provide a basis for intervention. Extant literature provides limited insights. Both Baruch (2005) and Privitera and Campbell (2009) found that workplace cyberbullying, demonstrated via email and phone conversations, coexists with traditional workplace bullying. With studies on cyberbullying in society in general and among children and youth underscoring the long-lasting and grievous harm that such misbehaviour unleashes, in addition to highlighting the reliance on various media beyond just emails and phone conversations (Rivers et al., 2011; Duffy and Sperry, 2012), the significance of systematically researching the phenomenon at work cannot be ignored.

We purport to extend available understanding by highlighting how the distinctive features of workplace cyberbullying affect victims' sense of power when they are subjected to virtual abuse. Our focus is rooted in the recognition that power constitutes an essential feature of bullying behaviour (Einarsen et al., 2011), which has a pivotal role to play in victims' coping (D'Cruz, 2015). Following an elucidation of bullied individuals' agency and mastery in traditional workplace abuse, we present case studies of four victims of workplace cyberbullying through the lens of critical hermeneutic phenomenology. After the ideographic description of victims' lived experiences (van Manen, 1998), ideology-critique (Scherer, 2011) engaging coping theory (Folkman and Lazarus, 1980) and undertaken nomothetically highlights victims' autonomy and control vis-à-vis the specific attributes of workplace cyberbullying. The conclusion revisits the current conceptualisation of power in workplace bullying and offers areas of action that employers can consider in addressing workplace cyberbullying.

The case studies, drawn from a larger inquiry of victims' experiences of workplace cyberbullying in India's software and services sector (D'Cruz and Noronha, 2013a), have been selected to represent various prototypes evident in the sample such that together they optimise its theoretical generalisability (Thompson, 1999). Accordingly, the case studies demonstrate workplace cyberbullying across different media, such as emails, text messages, instant messages (IM), phone conversations and social media, in addition to describing hacking and showing the importance of SIM (subscriber identity module) cards, IP (Internet protocol) addresses and CCTVs (closed circuit televisions). That virtual abuse not only occurs downwards (superior-to-subordinate) and horizontally (peer-to-peer) from known colleagues but could also involve strangers from within the organisation is highlighted. Further, vignettes of both male and female victims depict general abuse and sexual harassment through virtual means. Moreover, employers' varied responses to the availability of evidence that supports the occurrence of cyberbullying are portrayed, in addition to instances where bullied individuals choose not to seek redress for their predicament despite the accompanying proof. It may be noted that victims of cyberbullying included in the larger inquiry were employees in conventional workplaces. That is, they belonged to organisations which combined material and virtual elements such that members worked in physical offices engaging in direct face-to-face communication with colleagues while also relying on ICTDs for task completion and job-related interactions.

Victims' Agency and Mastery in Traditional Workplace Bullying

Conventionally, workplace bullying, described as unethical behaviour that violates universal norms of socially acceptability (LaVan and Martin, 2008; Ramsay et al., 2011), encompasses covert and/or obvious negative behaviours embodying aggression, hostility, intimidation and harm, generally characterised by persistence, displayed by an individual and/or group to another individual and/or group at work, privately and/or publicly (D'Cruz, 2015). Recent literature on victim experiences in workplace bullying underscores the dialectical nature of power. Bullied individuals, in spite of the strain engendered by their experiences of abuse, address their position of being cornered with attempts to fight back and reclaim agency (Lutgen-Sandvik, 2006; Noronha and D'Cruz, 2013). Thus, despite widely held views that power in workplace bullying is unidimensional and functional where sovereignty predominates and a zero-sum game ensues, victims' attempts at mastery highlight the complex nature of power in organisational life and emphasise the presence of resistance and agency (Lutgen-Sandvik, 2006). Even if their attempts at resolution produce limited and/or delayed outcomes (Lutgen-Sandvik, 2006; Noronha and D'Cruz, 2013), victims' sense of autonomy is not completely negated. In fact, quitting the organisation where the bullying is encountered and taking up fresh employment contributes to victims' internal locus of control (D'Cruz, 2015). Further, counteraggression, possibly subsuming revenge and retaliation, which turns bullied individuals into provocative victims (Olweus, 2003), helps them regain control and self-worth (Lee and Brotheridge, 2006; Hauge et al., 2009; Jenkins et al., 2012), notwithstanding its negative dimension.

Victims seek to assert agency even when bullying is downwards, in the face of the superior's authority (Branch et al., 2013). Horizontal and upwards bullying where social affiliations, expert power, victim dependence/inadequacy and work-group dynamics undergird perpetrators' actions (Branch et al., 2013), though giving rise to a different dynamic, similarly stimulate victim action. This is in keeping with the view that, on the part of the perpetrator, bullying involves the illegitimate use of personal power and the overstepping of widely accepted limits of appropriate behaviour (Liefooghe and Mackenzie-Davey, 2001; Branch et al., 2007, 2013). In attempting to address the situation, Namie and Namie (2000) point out that bullied individuals' agency is empowering and central to feelings of control and efficacy.

Alongside the desire to maintain control and pursue well-being (D'Cruz and Noronha, 2012), bullied individuals' sense of mastery is affected by bystanders, human resource (HR) professionals and supervisors/managers/leaders within the organisation and by unions and significant others from outside. Extant literature, largely focused on bystanders and HR managers, evidences that the particularities of their responses can add to or take away from victims' sense of power. That is, supportive coworkers empower victims, whereas apathetic coworkers and bullies' allies weaken victims (Paull et al., 2012; Mulder et al., 2013). Similarly, HR managers who ensure fairness and justice in situations of abuse, rather than victimising bullied individuals and siding with perpetrators, aid victims' mastery of the situation (D'Cruz and Noronha, 2010; Harrington et al., 2012). Managerial responses which are unfavourable to bullied individuals have been found to neutralise the availability of organisational policies and procedures against abuse (Ferris, 2009; D'Cruz, 2012). Union intervention is believed to serve as an important means of resolving workplace bullying (Ironside and Seifert, 2003; Beale and Hoel, 2011), while appropriate assistance from victims' social network assuages distress and indicates possible courses of action (D'Cruz and Noronha, 2012). Further, the presence of anti-bullying legislation upholds victims' rights, though the trajectory and dynamics of litigation could unfold against bullied individuals' interests (D'Cruz, 2014). Obviously, then, apart from the micro-level of the victim, the meso-level of actors in the organisation and well-wishers beyond, and the macro-level of the organisation, unions and legislations, are relevant.

Notwithstanding the burgeoning evidence that power in workplace bullying is a polymorphous and multifaceted entity in which all actors operate as knowledgeable agents to mobilise resources and carve out spaces of autonomy for themselves, albeit to lesser or greater degrees (Lutgen-Sandvik, 2006; Noronha and D'Cruz, 2013), it remains the pre-eminent characteristic of the phenomenon (Hutchinson et al., 2010), being the pivotal feature which subsumes other attributes. Indeed, the manifestations of bullying and the issue of perpetrator intent complicate victims' quest for control. Subtle and ambiguous displays made privately to an individual victim leave room for his/her claims to be contested as misinterpretations or fabrications. The absence of evidence in such instances where episodes are oral and/or nonverbal and have no witnesses add to the possibility of refutation (D'Cruz, 2015). Perception and attribution of motives are integral to bullied individuals' assessment of their experience. Victims are convinced that bullying is not accidental but instead purports to harm them (Lutgen-Sandvik, 2005). Yet, bullies can deny intent (Rayner and Cooper, 2006), couching their behaviours as purely instrumental in achieving organisational goals (Einarsen et al., 2011). Clearly, the subjectivity dynamic can render bullied individuals helpless.

Victims' Lived Experiences of Workplace Cyberbullying

Suresh[1]

Suresh worked for a technical call centre and excelled at his work. Over the 13 months he spent at the company, he received very good appraisals for his work and his behaviour, being known as an outstanding performer. Based on his rich experience and superior profile, Suresh received an attractive offer which provided him a huge career boost and a large increase in remuneration. When he shared the news of his new position with his team leader, in the run-up to submitting his resignation, the latter's jealousy manifested as virtual abuse which lasted over the duration of the notice period. According to Suresh, since his new offer outweighed the team leader's current designation and compensation, the latter was overcome with envy. Suresh describes his experience then onwards as being victimised, thereby going through a long ordeal.

Suresh found that the team leader constantly monitored all his calls. While interacting with a customer, he would receive pop-ups on his screen from the team leader asking, 'Why did you say that? Why didn't you say this?' Apparently, all his actions on the call were questioned and countered to the extent that the practices he had been praised for earlier were now being criticised, with directives that he had to follow other alternatives. Suresh noted that the team leader, instead of any face-to-face communication, resorted to pings on the communicator though he was seated two spots away: their direct communication was minimal yet neutral. Suresh had little choice but to divide his attention between the customer on the call and the team leader's comments and queries, recounting the challenge of providing optimal service to customers under such circumstances. Additionally, the team leader would prevent Suresh from completing the after-call procedures, insisting that he take the next call in the queue. Suresh would be bombarded with messages saying that another call was waiting and had to be picked up immediately. Keeping the after-call work on hold, Suresh would comply, but he noted that this sequence would repeat itself incessantly. As a result, he was left with no time to complete the after-call procedures. Suresh believed that the indirect interactions facilitated by call centre technology emboldened the team leader to bully him, noting that the latter remained dispassionate otherwise.

Since after-call work involved fulfilling requirements promised to the customer, such as looking for and passing on information or providing a referral, Suresh found postponing such tasks disconcerting, and after a point, he started reacting to the team leader's instructions to take the next call prior to completing all aspects of the current one. He stood his ground of concluding a call in its entirety, despite the perennial interference, comments and queries from the team leader on the chat system.

Suresh reported extreme distress due to the team leader's behaviour. Being an ace performer, he had never been monitored before. Moreover, the constant micromanagement over the system reflected cyberstalking. Yet, being on his way out of the organisation, Suresh decided against escalating the issue to his superiors, though the communication thread would have supported his grievance, with the call record indicating his quality of his work.

A month prior to exiting the organisation, Suresh was informed by a colleague that the team leader had emailed a complaint against him to the manager and the HR head, indicating that since his performance and attitude was now altered following putting in his resignation papers, he should be fired at once and these developments should be included in the relieving letter. Suresh was sure of the authenticity of the email as his colleague had seen it open on the team leader's laptop. Hearing of this, Suresh's distress was aggravated, and his health and sleep began to suffer. His strain was evident to his family members, who referred him to the family physician. On the latter's recommendation, Suresh consulted a psychologist, who helped him cope with the situation. Suresh was able to survive the last few weeks of his notice period in the company despite the team leader's continual cyberabuse. The company did not take up any issues with him based on the alleged email, ostensibly because he was leaving anyway. Suresh considers himself lucky to have got away from the job without much damage to his career.

Astha

Having refused the romantic advances of a male colleague, Astha, a software engineer with a domestic information technology (IT) firm, found that when she was away from the office for a few days, the latter misused her office computer system, which was open for upgrading purposes. During a night shift when only a few employees were present in the office, the colleague entered her system, acquired remote access to it, hacked her various email and Skype accounts and gathered information from the system and the accounts. Based on the information so gathered, the colleague was able to identify Astha's prospective groom whom her family had chosen for her based on a long-standing relationship between both families, whose status as a future spouse was discernible from data on her email and Skype accounts and whose contact details were available from those accounts. The colleague then proceeded to send Astha's fiancé numerous anonymous emails as well as SMSs (short message service) over several weeks containing false messages about her character being morally loose particularly in relation to men. Being informed about the receipt of the mails and SMSs by her fiancé, Astha guessed the identity of sender, linking the events to her earlier rejection of the colleague's romantic interests based on the contents of the emails and SMSs. Using technology, Astha not only confirmed her suspicions about the source of the misbehaviour but also established that while the retaliation was initiated in the office, its continuity was maintained beyond office premises, time and resources. That is, when the emails and SMSs continued, Astha and her fiancé decided to trace their origins to firmly establish the identity of the sender.

While relying on the IP addresses of the emails did not help in providing any clues and the SIM cards of the numbers from which the SMSs were sent, being traced to various Indian cities, were not useful in giving any insights, Astha took two of her seniors at work into confidence, requesting their help so that her present and future personal and professional reputation and position were not jeopardised. Supporting Astha in this experience, the seniors decided to check the CCTV footage of the office and hard disk logs of her office computer system for the period when she was away. They found evidence of the colleague sitting at and using Astha's system once via CCTV footage and of him remotely accessing her system once in the office – both on a single night when she was out of town – as well as evidence of her system being remotely accessed on several occasions from locations beyond the office. Essentially, the CCTV footage and hard disk logs of remote access particularly within the office itself established the colleague's identity. Based on the data gathered, the two seniors were helpful, detailing to Astha the various extra-organisational redress options available to her. However, they did not take up her case as an organisational matter as they opined that a personal relationship was involved and the communications sent to her fiancé could not be traced to the office. Apart from the seniors' view that this was not an organisational issue, Astha was reluctant to approach the HR department despite the organisation's sexual harassment policy, since a previous case had been ineffectively handled by them such that the problem here had not only persisted but developed into an office discussion point. Astha was left to deal with the matter on her own. Using her evidence, she confronted the colleague. Though he insisted that he was innocent, Astha stood her ground such that he finally had no choice but to stop sending anonymous emails and SMSs and remotely accessing her office computer system and to refrain from contacting her. She believed that Indian legislation on sexual harassment, which is widely publicised contemporaneously, played an indirect role in influencing the colleague to cease his misbehaviour, particularly since she had proof which would serve in her favour. Notwithstanding the successful resolution of the issue, Astha opted to quit the organisation some months later, which added to her sense of relief.

Astha described her experience as harrowing, and she extolled as well as regretted the use and impact of technology. She appreciated the assistance and advice provided by her seniors but could not suppress her disappointment at their non-committal position. Despite the cessation of the harassment, Astha remained fearful that the misbehaviour could recur in the future and wreak havoc in her life. She was all too aware that technology could be used to generate false data by way of texts and images that could be spread widely and remain in circulation. Though her fiancé never doubted her, Astha harboured apprehensions that her reputation could be easily harmed at any time, with unforeseeable repercussions for her personal and professional life.

Mira

Within a few weeks of joining an offshored back-office firm, Mira received an IM from a male project member who was not a part of her team, indicating his wish that they get to know each other. Mira was completely taken aback to realise that a stranger who was not part of her group had got her IM identity out of turn (IM identities in the company were shared on an intra-team basis). Appreciating that the sender had specifically sought out her IM identity to contact her, she believed that his message was more than an offer of a simple friendship. Mira responded with questions about why he wanted to interact with her and was informed that since they were on the same project, it was good for them to get familiar. Her suspicions about the sender's ulterior motives being accentuated, Mira ignored the rejoinder. The sender continued his pursuit by calling her up on an internal line, but she insisted that she did not recognise him and hung up. Soon after, the sender/caller was present in an office elevator that Mira was travelling in and introduced himself to her – he clarified that he had used IM rather than face-to-face interactions because he did not want other colleagues to know that he had approached her. With this physical meeting confirming her view of the sender/caller's mala fide intentions, Mira directed him not to contact or speak to her again and proceeded to block him on her IM service. Once the latter avenue was unavailable, the sender/caller repeatedly reached out to Mira in person on the office premises even though she always ignored him outright. Mira was a bit distressed by his relentlessness, but she maintained a calm and firm outward demeanour. She noted that though his reliance on conventional communication as an alternative could possibly expose her to physical vulnerability, the office had CCTVs. After numerous face-to-face attempts failed, the sender/caller stopped his pursuit. Mira opined that he did not want her rejection to become publicly visible and known at the workplace. Since the sender/caller did not further meddle with her, she did not consider an informal or formal complaint, though she was fully aware that the IM trail and CCTV footage could have supported her.

Later, Mira's employer sent her onsite to the UK for six months with a team under her. She experienced sexual harassment and emotional abuse from a male colleague from the client side for two to three months. Mira had already been interacting with him virtually when she was offshore, sharing a cordial relationship. Onsite, Mira and the colleague sat adjacent to each other, with the former seeking a lot of task-related information from the latter, which she needed to bring back with her to India. In the course of these frequent interactions, the male colleague began to suggest via email that they take a break from their tasks and go out together for coffee. Interestingly, he would always send her emails for these coffee breaks and outings, though they were seated adjacent to each other and a face-to-face conversation was possible. Considering his gestures to be overtures of friendship, Mira initially readily agreed to his invitations. However, after about four to six weeks, she observed that he began to overstep his limits both during office hours when he would suggest various activities after office hours such as dancing to songs laden with double meanings at her residence as well as when he would call her up at home after office hours, sometimes even at 9 p.m. or 10 p.m. saying that he wanted to visit her there. Mira lived in a chummery with her teammates from India and usually spent the evenings in their company. To avoid arousing her teammates' suspicions, she began to store the colleague's number under another name so that her juniors would not get the wrong impression if they chanced a glimpse at her mobile's screen. After several evenings of taking his calls, Mira began to either ignore or cut off his calls even if she was alone in her room in the chummery. Nonetheless, the male colleague persisted in his attempts at calling her. But he neither stalked her physically nor attempted to come over to the chummery without her consent. Mira believed that living in a chummery protected her because the male colleague could not walk in any time, and hence his plans to visit her could not be executed unless she agreed. Even so, she was deeply disturbed by the experience. Apart from feeling constantly hounded, Mira wondered whether such behaviour would ever end, given the progress and reach of modern technology.

When the colleague's advances continued beyond a period of two months, Mira confronted him, sternly directing him to stop pursuing her. She reminded him that she had his email invitations for coffee breaks and outings and that she could report his behaviour. Though the colleague refuted Mira's capacity to effect action, he simultaneously stopped his misbehaviour. Nonetheless, he became uncooperative and affrontive with regard to task completion. Because his behaviour began to affect work adversely, Mira handled the situation in two ways. She shared the incident with his senior from the client side, and she delegated the responsibility of interacting and working with him to her junior. The senior from the client side, who was very apologetic about the incident and very supportive of Mira when he heard what had happened, discussed the matter with the male colleague who then improved in his behaviour and became more cooperative with the junior assigned to work with him. Mira, realising her luck at having a subordinate who was very competent and whom she got along well with, told the latter that she was assigning him this responsibility because he was good at his work and could maximise his learning. It was only later that she took her junior into confidence about what had actually happened, and he responded with great understanding, sensitivity and discretion.

Tarun

From his first day as a software engineer in an Indian IT multinational corporation (MNC), Tarun was the object of severe bullying behaviour through face-to-face and virtual means by his boss. Except for one of his teammates who shared a cordial relationship with the boss, the other three were similarly victimised. Yelling, berating, insulting, finding fault, maligning, back-biting, setting unmanageable deadlines and workloads and hounding for task completion, publicly and privately, individually and group-wise, through direct and virtual means including emails, phone calls and text messages was described. Indeed, so great was the pressure that once a task was assigned, the boss would not wait for even five minutes for it to be completed but would keep following up either in person or via emails, phone calls or messages. Tarun indicated that he and his teammates were subjected to this harassment during and after office hours, with the boss getting in touch with them at home, on weekends and on holidays. Putting her negative acts down not just to a disagreeable personality but more importantly to insecurity arising from incompetence, Tarun shared that his boss had been appointed to her position to due to her social connections with the top management. While being completely dependent on the team to deliver, the boss seemed to gain more in terms of skills and knowledge from her subordinates than the mentorship she could provide them. Even so, she lost no opportunity to misbehave with the team.

Tarun and his teammates were 'haunted' by their boss. They reported that 'she fills our every thought, even during office breaks and weekend leisure activities'. Their extreme distress was captured in their daily desire to turn back and go home as soon as they reached the office premises. Facing such severe emotional strain, about six months into the job, Tarun and his teammates approached HR informally about the way forward. HR, already in the know of the bully's behaviour, advised them to speak directly but informally to the boss's superior. Once the super-boss outlined his view of the situation to them, they would know the best path to follow. Informal discussions with the super-boss underscored that while he was aware of her behaviour, he could do nothing given her links with the top management. Trying to convince Tarun and his teammates, though unsuccessfully, that things would work out fine in due course, the super-boss finally decided to arrange for each of them to have individual meetings with their boss in his presence to sort out differences. Instead of ameliorating the situation, the boss's defensiveness and aggression worsened matters. Following the individual meetings, the super-boss reassured Tarun and his teammates that he would resolve the situation. However, nothing seemed forthcoming from his side, with the super-boss choosing to avoid the topic, and hence circumstances remained the same.

Tarun and his teammates concluded that even though an anti-bullying policy was in place in the organisation, the existing redress mechanisms were ineffective because of lack of employer commitment. Their boss's connection to the top management complicated grievance procedures. Observing how informal attempts had unfolded, Tarun and his teammates decided against any formal interventions despite the availability of evidence in the form of call logs, text messages and emails. Even so, they were glad that they had virtual footprints of their boss's behaviour, opining that these could be helpful in the future.

Apart from directly confronting the boss about her behaviour at some times and minimising contact with her at other times, Tarun and his teammates coped by supporting each other while also being buffered by their relatives and friends outside the workplace. Work-related travel provided some respite. Thirteen months later, as the bullying continued unabated, Tarun and his teammates felt weary and were ready to quit the organisation without a job in hand but were prevented from doing so by the super-boss who, being pleased with their performance, personally requested them to continue. For Tarun and his teammates, the boss is the only reason they wish to quit because otherwise they are happy with their jobs, realising the long-term growth potential of their employer and the losses associated with their moving out.

Ideology-Critique (Victims' Agency and Mastery in Workplace Cyberbullying)

Bullied individuals' lived experiences highlight their sense of autonomy and control in relation to the unique attributes of virtual abuse in organisations. The concreteness and permanence of workplace cyberbullying distinguish it from traditional bullying in matters of resolution. In facilitating victims' problem-focused coping and successful management of the issue, the virtual footprints of electronic abuse serve to empower them. Clearly, while technology presented bullied individuals with means of resolution, this is contingent upon the mode involved. That is, does misbehaviour have a form that can be downloaded, saved and replayed (like mails, pictures, etc.) or can remain available for viewing and replays (like posts, blogs, etc.)? Whereas phone conversations were not relevant in this regard, phone caller identities and call records, SIM cards, IM identities, text messages, emails, IP addresses and website posts were useful due to their tangible and enduring nature, which left footprints and provided proof. Their threatened or actual use by the victim independently and/or by the employer solved the problem partially/completely, immediately/over time. By capitalising on the available proof, bullied individuals could reclaim their position/protect themselves. Even so, organisational dynamics can dull the potential of virtual footprints in tackling the problem. In spite of organisational policies against negative acts, managers can choose neutral positions or provide counterarguments that side with bullies and leave victims to their own defence, enhancing the latter's vulnerability. Legislation can work in favour of victims, adding to their armour. This holds true even where available laws linked to misbehaviour do not specifically or exclusively address cyberbullying. Yet, concreteness and permanence have implications for the conceptualisation of workplace bullying. Where the material is available only to victims, even one such experience can be repeated simply by replaying it, once again calling into question the definition of bullying in terms of persistence where frequency and duration come into play. Where the material is shared publicly, its further dissemination and replays feed into persistence, apart from creating a 'buzz' marked by distortions.

The boundarylessness, anonymity and invisibility of workplace cyberbullying disempower victims due to pervasiveness, lack of bully restraint, victim isolation and lack of information about bully identity. Technology results in victims being bullied regardless of spatial, temporal and social boundaries, precipitating feelings of being 'haunted and hemmed in' and 'trapped'. Bullied individuals feel greatly disturbed to realise that perpetrators can identify and contact them, track their movements and activities, reach them any time and anywhere, get in touch with their significant others and spread information (including false and malicious information) about them to varying degrees on a public scale, possibly even in the future, and bullies can do all of this anonymously at least for some time. Women facing sexual harassment harbour fear for their physical safety and concern about their personal and professional reputation. That women could be 'picked up randomly' and 'stalked' as well as have replays of these experiences in the future if bullies get in touch with their spouses to malign them cause deep distress.

Pervasiveness implies the blurring of work–life balance such that 'the nightmare never ends', continuing 'even at home, on weekends … always', leaving bullied individuals little respite and opportunity to recuperate. Moreover, under circumstances where organisations and their employees depend on ICTDs for work, combined with the competitiveness of today's business context, spatial and temporal boundaries lose their significance as employees are expected to be available for and can be reached about work all the time, allowing for unrestricted and illimitable exposure to cyberbullying. Bullying is then experienced constantly, urging a review of its persistence conceptualisation in terms of repetition and time span. With work situations always on their minds, bullied individuals are swamped with negative thoughts and feelings and deprived of breathers through which they could replenish their emotional strength.

ICTDs facilitate the spread of cyberbullying. Audience range implies whether those privy to the bullying situation are (a) the bully(ies) and the victim(s) alone (fully confined); (b) office personnel extending from team to project to department to organisation, either directly associated as victims and observers or indirectly associated by hearing about it, and/or victims' significant others, directly associated (partially confined); or (c) society at large indirectly associated (unconfined). That is, due to technology, cyberbullying need not be limited to the parties involved or within the organisation. Either the group central to the bullying could use technology not just to bully but to publicise the bullying, or bystanders in the know of it could add to the situation by joining in directly and/or by publicising and thereby becoming accomplices. Unlike traditional bullying where the situation is more restricted spatially and hence likely to be an intra-organisational issue, technology transcends these barriers such that a bullying situation can be played out beyond organisational boundaries. Not only can group/bulk emails and public posts wreak 'wide-ranging and long-term havoc', but under such circumstances, 'even if one changes one's job to escape the bully, the past can come back to you (at) any time there (in the new organisation)'.

The indirect and sometimes anonymous nature of communication facilitated by technology not only serves as an alternate mechanism by which bullies could reach victims but also reduces bullies' inhibitions. Consequently, vindictive behaviour often at variance with direct face-to-face interaction is observable. Obviously, technology works as a shield through which the bully's true self, restrained during face-to-face meetings, emerges. Bullies' discrepant behaviour leads to confusion and distrust, adding to victims' distress. Depending on the form and mode used and the aspects of boundarylessness involved, the exposure to bullying may be available only to the victim (as in personal texts and emails) and not others (as in group texts and emails, websites, blogs) unless the victim brings it to others' notice, and this has implications for bystander behaviour, significant others' actions and victim coping. Where bystanders and well-wishers are unaware of it, they cannot respond unless victims apprise them of the situation – and victims may be reluctant to do so for various reasons, including impression management, stigmatisation and so on. Victims are then left to cope alone. Where bystanders and significant others are aware of it either because it has reached them directly or victims have informed them, the former express a range of responses from antagonism to indifference to support while the latter demonstrates various types of assistance. Further, bully identity may not be available in the immediacy of the event or at all, raising issues about source, authenticity and motive. Knowing or not knowing bully identity could work positively or negatively. When bully identity is available, victims either know or hypothesise the underlying motives, which can be instrumental in deciding the appropriate course of action. When bully identity is unavailable, victims remain uncertain by whom and why they are being bullied, increasing their vulnerability. Linked to the issues of media richness and social context cues, both ICTDs themselves and the possibility they offer of withholding identity lower accountability and raise disinhibition because they not only separate bullies from the outcomes of their actions but also promote self-dissociation (Joinson, 1998).

Bullied individuals' narratives highlighted that the feelings of power-lessness common in instances of abuse were accentuated by the use of the cyber mode, owing to its boundaryless, invisible and anonymous character. Yet, this air of defencelessness was reversed in instances where concreteness and permanence provided bullied individuals with evidence that they could use to resolve the problem, realising the benefits of the situation. Nonetheless, tangible and enduring instances of abuse fuel-ling persistence exacerbated bullied individuals' helplessness, particularly when boundarylessness was involved. Notwithstanding their consequent reclaiming of agency, the power of technology in general left victims with a residual sense of helplessness as they realised that though they were able to manage the bullying this time, technology could rear its ugly head at any point but not always provide opportunities to be nabbed.

It may be noted that the role of unions could not be ascertained through the foregoing four case studies since the majority of the work-force in the Indian software and services sector remains unwilling to engage with collective action and hence attempts at organising employ-ees have been largely unsuccessful (D'Cruz and Noronha, 2013b). Nonetheless, D'Cruz and Noronha's (2013a) inquiry reports two partic-ipants who, in their attempt to tackle workplace cyberbullying, sought and benefited from union intervention.

Conclusion

Victims' interface with workplace cyberbullying, explored via critical hermeneutic phenomenology, reaffirms the illegitimate and dialectical nature of power in workplace bullying. Virtual abuse constitutes unethical behaviour that violates universal standards of social acceptability, demon-strating the bullies' overstepping of personal power. Victims, despite their strain, fight back, displaying agency even in the case of downwards bully-ing, being aided by the availability of virtual footprints linked to the con-creteness and permanence of cyberabuse. While organisational dynamics can colour their attempts, despite the availability of an anti-bullying pol-icy, evidence complicates this, often opening the path to alternative ave-nues linked to institutional mechanisms such as legislations (and unions). Nonetheless, while moving out of the abusive situation or quitting, whether following resolution of the issue or not, does augment bullied individuals' well-being, the possibility of the misbehaviour resurfacing in the future or the episode being shared publicly to some degree cannot be ruled out, due to the nature of the digital media.

Though not described in the four narratives above, the special charac-teristics of cyberbullying, particularly boundarylessness, anonymity and invisibility, which facilitate vindictive behaviour as evidenced by bullies, can be used by victims to cope or retaliate. Relying on ICTDs, bullied individuals can either avenge or publicise their victimisation, thereby initiating counteraggression and/or support-seeking behaviour and perhaps sowing the seeds of coworker mobilisation and collectivisation.

Obviously, the form of workplace bullying adds a pertinent dimension to the understanding of power in the substantive area, apart from the issues of legitimacy versus illegitimacy and duality versus dialectics which inform current theorisation. Boundarylessness, concreteness and permanence have implications for the pervasiveness and persistence of misbehaviour while concomitantly bringing in bystanders and significant others, impinging on coping options. Invisibility and anonymity affect the manifestations of abuse, the identification of the perpetrator and the availability of witnesses and well-wishers. The ambiguity of subjectivity, and perhaps also intent, is countered, at least partially, by the contents of virtual footprints, which can highlight the frequency, tone, spread and so on of the negative acts.

The particular features of workplace cyberbullying call for special interventions, beyond those developed for traditional workplace bullying. Yet, equally important is the commitment of top management and HR to implement these measures. Such initiatives are indispensable if the organisation's HRM (human resource management) ideology wishes means to maintain its 'H' element and retain its moral economy (Bolton and Houlihan, 2007) while ensuring virtuous leadership (Havard, 2007) and ethical organisational climates anchored in benevolence and deontology (Simha and Cullen, 2012). A zero-tolerance policy towards cyberbullying, outlining the consequences in case this is violated, is the way ahead. Whereas inculcating leadership and managerial skills that cater to the demands of digital workplaces cannot be postponed, organisational policies, guidelines and training on the appropriate use of ICTDs at work, including advice on posting sensitive information, maintaining professional boundaries, privacy settings and so on (Farley et al., 2015), are called for. Further, organisations can encourage their employees to evaluate whether digital media are appropriate for the matter they wish to discuss. If there is no alternative due to spatial distance, then employees should examine the tone of their interactions (Farley et al., 2015). With employees then behaving appropriately, workplace cyberbullying can be prevented – and intervention measures made available in case they do not.

Bystanders are increasingly seen as the focal point for workplace bullying intervention (D'Cruz and Noronha, 2011, 2014; Paull et al., 2012; Mulder et al., 2013), and organisational endeavours addressing cyberabuse would do well to embrace such initiatives. Based on a sound understanding of the trajectory of workplace cyberbullying, organisations can train employees to identify and report its occurrence. Inputs to pre-empt and intervene in such incidents can also be provided. Whereas the success of bystander intervention is contingent on the creation of a safe organisational environment (D'Cruz and Noronha, 2011), witnesses' efforts can catalyse coworker mobilisation (D'Cruz and Noronha, 2014) that further supports bullied individuals.

Unions, considered to be the most effective solution to workplace bullying (Ironside and Seifert, 2003; Beale and Hoel, 2011), cannot avoid taking up the cause of online harassment, given its prevalence in the contemporary workplace. By pressing for legislations and organisational policies and representing cases of misbehaviour as part of their agenda on workplace cyberbullying, unions certainly enhance victims' empowerment. Undoubtedly, towards this end, unions must harness their influence (Gall, 2009) to usher in a modern labour movement (Spooner, 2015).

Finally but equally important, legislative backing obviously goes a long way in strengthening victims, apart from advocating primary prevention. While laws on the use of ICTDs, available in many countries (e.g. Craig, 2012; Lloyd, 2014; Blakeley and Matsuura, 2015), can provide direction, laws on workplace bullying and related issues like sexual harassment, in place or being developed in various locations (Yamada, 2011), should incorporate the issue of virtual abuse.

In closing, it should be acknowledged that the foregoing insights into cyberbullying at work come from empirical research examining conventional workplaces. Yet, the phenomenon of virtual abuse at work is even more complicated, given that D'Cruz (2017) and D'Cruz and Noronha (2016b, 2016c) have evidenced its presence and described its features in newer forms of work and workplaces such as crowdsourcing platforms and online labour markets (OLMs).

Note

1 Names of participants have been changed to maintain confidentiality.

REFERENCES

Baruch, Y. (2005) 'Bullying on the Net: Adverse Behaviour on Email and Its Impact', *Information and Management*, 42, 361–71.

Beale, D. and H. Hoel (2011) 'Workplace Bullying and the Employment Relationship', *Work, Employment and Society*, 25, 5–18.

Blakeley, C. J. and J. H. Matsuura (2015) *Global Information Technology Law 2015–2016* (Eagan, MN: Thomson Reuters).

▶

▶

Bolton, S. and M. Houlihan (2007) *Searching for the Human in Human Resource Management: Theory, Practice and Workplace Contexts* (London: Palgrave Macmillan).

Branch, S., S. Ramsay and M. Barker (2007) 'Managers in the Firing Line: Contributing Factors to Workplace Bullying by Staff–An Interview Study', *Journal of Management and Organization*, 13, 264–81.

Branch, S., S. Ramsay and M. Barker (2013) 'Workplace Bullying, Mobbing and General Harassment: A Review', *International Journal of Management Reviews*, 15, 280–99.

Craig, B. (2012) *Cyberlaw: The Law of the Internet and Information Technology* (New York: Pearson).

D'Cruz, P. (2012) *Workplace Bullying in India* (New Delhi: Routledge).

D'Cruz, P. (2014) *Addressing Workplace Bullying Through Legislation: What India Can Learn From the Netherlands* (Sponsor report presented to ICSSR and NWO. Ahmedabad: IIM Ahmedabad).

D'Cruz, P. (2015) *Depersonalized Bullying at Work: From Evidence to Conceptualization* (New Delhi: Springer).

D'Cruz, P. (2017). Partially empowering but not decent? The contradictions of online labour markets. In E. Noronha and P. D'Cruz (Eds.), *Critical Perspectives on Work and Employment in Globalising India*. New Delhi: Springer.

D'Cruz, P. and E. Noronha (2010) 'The Exit Coping Response to Workplace Bullying: The Contribution of Inclusivist and Exclusivist HRM Strategies', *Employee Relations*, 32, 102–20.

D'Cruz, P. and E. Noronha (2011) 'The Limits to Workplace Friendship: Managerialist HRM and Bystander Behaviour in the Context of Workplace Bullying', *Employee Relations*, 33, 269–88.

D'Cruz, P. and E. Noronha (2012) 'Clarifying my World: Identity Work in the Context of Workplace Bullying', *The Qualitative Report*, 17, 1–29.

D'Cruz, P. and E. Noronha (2013a) 'Navigating the Extended Reach: Target Experiences of Cyberbullying at Work', *Information and Organization*, 23, 324–43.

D'Cruz, P. and E. Noronha (2013b) 'Hope to despair: the experience of organizing Indian call centre employees', *Indian Journal of Industrial Relations*, 48, 3, 471–86.

D'Cruz, P. and E. Noronha (2014) 'Workplace Bullying in the Context of Organizational Change: The Significance of Pluralism', *Industrial Relations Journal*, 45, 2–21.

D'Cruz, P. and E. Noronha (2016a) 'Organizational Governance: A Promising Solution to Address Varieties of Workplace Bullying', *Research on Emotions in Organizations*, 12, 409–44.

D'Cruz, P., and Noronha, E. (2016b). Positives outweighing negatives: The experiences of Indian crowdsourced workers. *Work Organisation, Labour and Globalisation*, 10(1), 44–63.

D'Cruz, P., and Noronha, E. (2016c). Cyberbullying on online labour markets: Forms and features. Unpublished project report. Ahmedabad: IIM Ahmedabad.

Duffy, M. P. and L. Sperry (2012) *Mobbing: Causes, Consequences and Solutions* (New York: Oxford University Press).

Einarsen, S., H. Hoel, D. Zapf and C. L. Cooper (2011) 'The Concept of Bullying and Harassment at Work: The European Tradition', in S. Einarsen, H. Hoel, D. Zapf and C. L. Cooper (eds), *Bullying and Harassment in the Workplace* (London: Taylor and Francis).

▶

Farley, S., I. Coyne, C. Sprigg, C. Axtell and G. Subramanian (2015) 'Exploring the Impact of Workplace Cyberbullying on Trainee Doctors', *Medical Education*, 49, 436–43.

Ferris, P. A. (2009) 'The Role of the Consulting Psychologist in the Prevention, Detection and Correction of Bullying and Mobbing in the Workplace', *Consulting Psychology Journal: Practice and Research*, 61, 169–89.

Folkman, S., & Lazarus, R. S. (1980). An analysis of coping in a middle-aged community sample. *Journal of Health and Social Behaviour*, Vol. 21, No. 3, 219–239.

Gall, G. (2009) 'Union Organizing: Past, Present and Future', in G. Gall (ed.) *The Future Of Union Organizing* (Basingstoke: Palgrave Macmillan).

Harrington, S., C. Rayner and S. Warren (2012) 'Too Hot to Handle? Trust and Human Resource Practitioners' Implementation of Anti-Bullying Policy', *Human Resource Management Journal*, 22, 392–408.

Hauge, L. J., A. Skogstad and S. Einarsen (2009) 'Individual and Situational Predictors of Workplace Bullying: Why do Perpetrators Engage in the Bullying of Others?' *Work and Stress*, 23, 349–58.

Havard, R. (2007) *Virtuous Leadership* (New York: Scepter).

Holtgrewe, U. (2014) 'New New Technologies: The Future and the Present of Work in Information and Communication Technology', *New Technology, Work and Employment*, 29, 9–24.

Hutchinson, M., M. H. Vickers, D. Jackson and L. Wilkes (2010) 'Bullying as circuits of power: An Australian nursing perspective', *Administrative Theory and Praxis*, 32, 1, 25–47.

Huws, U. (2013) 'Working Online, Living Offline: Labour in the Internet Age', *Work Organization, Labour and Globalization*, 7, 1–11.

Ironside, M. and R. Seifert (2003) 'Tackling Bullying in the Workplace: The Collective Dimension', in S. Einarsen, H. Hoel, D. Zapf and C. L. Cooper (eds), *Bullying and Emotional Abuse in the Workplace* (London: Taylor and Francis).

Jenkins, M., D. Zapf, H. Winefield and A. Sarris (2012) 'Bullying Allegations from the Accused Bully's Perspective', *British Journal of Management*, 23, 489–501.

Joinson, A. (1998) 'Causes and Effects of Disinhibition on the Internet', in J. Gackenbach (ed.) *The Psychology of the Internet: Intrapersonal, Interpersonal and Transpersonal Implications* (New York, NY: Academic Press).

LaVan, H. and W. M. Martin (2008) 'Bullying in the US Workplace: Normative and Process-Oriented Ethical Approaches', *Journal of Business Ethics*, 83, 147–65.

Lee, R. T. and C. M. Brotheridge (2006) 'When Prey Turns Predatory: Workplace Bullying as a Predictor of Counteraggression/Bullying, Coping and Well-Being', *European Journal of Work and Organizational Psychology*, 15, 352–77.

Liefooghe, A. P. D. and K. Mackenzie-Davey (2001) 'Accounts of Workplace Bullying: The Role of the Organization', *European Journal of Work and Organizational Psychology*, 10, 375–92.

Lloyd, I. (2014) *Information Technology Law* (London: Oxford University Press).

Lutgen-Sandvik, P. (2005) *Water Smoothing Stones: Subordinate Resistance to Workplace Bullying*, Unpublished PhD thesis. (Tempe, AZ: University of Arizona).

▶

Lutgen-Sandvik, P. (2006) 'Take This Job and...: Quitting and Other Forms of Resistance to Workplace Bullying', *Communication Monographs*, 73, 406–33.

Lutgen-Sandvik, P. and S. J. Tracy (2012) 'Answering Five Key Questions About Workplace Bullying How Communication Scholarship Provides Thought Leadership for Transforming Abuse at Work', *Management Communication Quarterly*, 26, 3–47.

Mulder, R., M. Pouwelse, H. Lodewijkx and C. Bolman (2013) 'Workplace Mobbing and Bystanders' Helping Behaviour Towards Victims: The Role of Gender, Perceived Responsibility and Anticipated Stigma by Association', *International Journal of Psychology*, doi:10.1002/ijop.12018

Namie, G. and R. Namie (2000) *The Bully at Work: What You Can do to Stop the Hurt and Reclaim Your Dignity on the Job* (Naperville, IL: Sourcebooks).

Noronha, E. and P. D'Cruz (2013) *Routine Resistance: Limits to Reclaiming Power in the Context of Depersonalized Bullying.* Paper presented at the Academy of Management meeting, 9–13 August, Lake Buena Vista, USA.

Olweus, D. (2003) 'Bully/Victim Problems in School', in S. Einarsen, H. Hoel, D. Zapf and C. L. Cooper (eds), *Bullying and Emotional Abuse in the Workplace* (London: Taylor and Francis).

Paull, M., M. Omari and P. Standen (2012) 'When is a Bystander not a Bystander? A Typology of the Roles of Bystanders in Workplace Bullying', *Asia Pacific Journal of Human Resources*, 50, 351–66.

Piotrowski, C. (2012) 'Cyberbullying: A Research-Based Content Analysis of the Psychological Literature', *Alabama Counseling Association Journal*, 38, 13–19.

Privitera, C. and M. A. Campbell (2009) 'Cyberbullying: The New Face of Workplace Bullying?' *Cyberpsychology and Behaviour*, 12, 395–400.

Ramsay, S., A. C. Troth and S. Branch (2011) 'Workplace Bullying Through the Lens of Social Psychology: A Group Level Analysis', *Journal of Occupational and Organizational Psychology*, 84, 799–816.

Rayner, C. and C. L. Cooper (2006) 'Workplace Bullying', in E. K. Kelloway, J. Barling and J. J. Hurrell (eds), *Handbook of Workplace Violence* (Thousand Oaks, CA: Sage).

Rivers, I., T. Chesney and I. Coyne (2011) 'Cyberbullying', in C. P. Monks and I. Coyne (eds), *Bullying in Different Context* (Cambridge, UK: Cambridge University Press), pp. 211–30.

Scherer, A. G. (2011) 'Critical Theory and its Contribution to Critical Management Studies', in M. Alvesson, T. Bridgman and H. Willmott (eds), *The Oxford Handbook of Critical Management Studies* (London: Oxford University Press).

Simha, A. and J. B. Cullen (2012) 'Ethical Climates and their Effects on Organizational Outcomes: Implications from the Past and Prophecies for the Future', *Academy of Management Perspectives*, 26, 20–34.

Spooner, D. (2015) 'The Future of Decent Work', *Global Labour Journal*, 6, 245–48.

Thompson, C. (1999) 'If you Could Just Provide me With a Sample: Examining Sampling in Qualitative and Quantitative Research Papers', *Evidence Based Nursing*, 2, 68–70.

Van Manen, M. (1998) *Researching Lived Experience* (London, ON: Althouse).

Yamada, D. (2011) 'Workplace Bullying and the Law: Emerging Global Responses', in S. Einarsen, H. Hoel, D. Zapf and C. L. Cooper (eds), *Bullying and Harassment in the Workplace* (London: Taylor and Francis).

Changing Systems, Creating Conflicts: IT-Related Changes in Swedish Banking

Fredrik Movitz and Michael Allvin

'At the heart of schemes like this there's always something unreasonable, the explanation of which is that human beings are involved' (Ford, 2012)

Introduction

What processes do strategic IT-related changes in highly digitalised work organisations set in motion, and how do skilled digital workers act in relation to them? The focus of this chapter is to describe and analyse the turbulent and uncertain conditions currently facing many skilled digital workers in finance, exemplified with ongoing changes in a major Swedish full-service bank. The chapter thus relates to the origins and core of labour process analysis (Jaros, 2010) by focusing on conflicting interests, resistance and effects following technological workplace changes. Through classic works by, for example, Braverman, Edwards, Noble and others, labour process analysis has no doubt made valuable contributions to our understanding of the contingent and contested relations between new technologies and work, making it a highly suitable perspective for understanding digital labour – that is, jobs where digital solutions are integrated, ubiquitous necessities for performing, communicating and transferring working tasks.

Arguably, labour process theorists have, however, traditionally focused on conflicts between management and labour, paying less attention

to conflicts between different groups of employees during technological changes. Second, and following Braverman, researchers have tended
to emphasise more the *outcomes* for workers of technological changes in
terms of, for example, skills rather than the change processes themselves.
Third, the focus of work has mostly been placed on the situation for manual and lower-level employees, rather than higher-level employees such
as professionals and managers. Clearly, there are notable exceptions in all
three instances (Ehrensal, 1995; Thompson and Smith, 2010; Baldry, 2012).

In order to fully understand digital labour, it is necessary to adopt a
broad understanding of what constitutes technology and to pay attention
to the different meanings attached to particular solutions (Augustsson,
2005). In highly digitalised settings, there are in some cases limited structures, procedures and rules apart from those stipulated by the techno-sys-
tem (Allvin and Movitz, 2017). While change management programmes
frequently cause tensions, we argue that IT-related changes display unique
features due to the placid yet decisive nature of IT solutions in especially
highly digitalised settings. Following this, we therefore direct attention to
conflicts between different and changing collectives of skilled high-level
employees occurring during processes of defining, conceptualising and
articulating problems and solutions connected to IT-related changes.

Further, while office politics and internal struggles for resources, positions and status have no doubt been around at least since the rise of the
modern corporation (Whyte, 1957), it can be argued that contemporary
changes in many larger companies have made internal conflicts between
groups of employees more common and severe, but also less predicta-
ble, since more is at stake in terms of, for example, job security. Such
changes include shifts towards increased focus on shareholder value and
financialisation (Thompson, 2003) with the accompanying break-ups
of clear hierarchical structures and demarcated positions, repeated reorganisations, increased employment insecurity and destabilisation and
so on. When companies, like the organisation described in this chapter,
increasingly are in the hands of institutional owners aiming to maximise returns on investments with management focusing on these owner
interests, employees become a potential liability consistently at risk of
being made redundant (Movitz and Allvin, 2014, 2015, 2016a).

As will be shown in this chapter, the conflicts at the bank being
described here become highly politicised, involving quite dirty tactics
aiming to further various groups' interests. What initially was viewed as
a simple matter of implementing IT-based systems for handling information into an already highly digitalised setting soon turns into high-
stakes games directed at resources, positions, status and even jobs. In the
process, separately planned changes unexpectedly become intertwined,

creating what one informant referred to as 'multiple-front wars' between shifting alliances of opposing departments, teams, professions and experts. The results further show that even though the proposed changes were initiated by top management and the board, the ongoing conflicts between groups of employees, who repeatedly seek to gain the support of top management, contribute to hiding underlying and more persistent conflicting interests between capital and labour, which ultimately are a root cause of the manifested conflicts.

The conflicts surfacing during the changes reveal continuous underlying struggles concerning which worker collectives will be considered as the 'real' experts within domains viewed by top management as of central strategic importance, which increase employees' chances of being relatively safe – for the time being. Conflicts between employees related to IT-based changes are thus important to study in their own right, but they are also important because they function as critical incidents revealing underlying persistent tensions and conflicting interests and logics facing different groups of skilled workers in the highly digitalised financial sector (Movitz and Allvin, 2016b). Following this, observed and manifest conflicts are not necessarily about the perceived content or outcomes of change programmes per se, but about ongoing attempts by actors to position themselves in uncertain and volatile work settings.

The chapter continues with a short description of empirical data and methods. This is followed by a presentation and analysis of empirical results relating to the bank, the perceived problems warranting change, the proposed changes, the players, the game and the outcomes of change processes so far. In the concluding discussion, the broader implications for a labour process analysis of digital labour are elaborated.

Data and Methods

The empirical results are based on an extended organisational case study (Edwards et al., 2014) complemented by a critical incident analysis in a major Swedish full-service bank conducted between 2013 and 2016. The extended analysis means that we do not limit ourselves to the bank itself, but also include important external actors, institutions, regulations and technologies within the broader social field of finance. A critical incident analysis means that important events, in this case IT-based changes, are not just studied in their own right but also used as starting points to reveal underlying and transcendental causal tendencies in the bank and ultimately the financial system as a whole (cf. Sayer, 2000), such as what relations between positions and the system as a whole must be like for changes and conflicts to emerge (Fleetwood and Ackroyd, 2004; Thompson and Vincent, 2010).

The empirical data consist of face-to face and phone interviews with employees of the bank: managers, investor relations officers, other experts and; external actors such as representatives of major institutional owners, trade organisations and the Swedish Financial Regulatory Agency. We also use internal documents and communications, as well as media articles and public documents regarding, for example, EU regulations on capital requirements.

Our main source of empirical information comes from a key informant, who is a top-tier manager at the bank's headquarters and has been directly involved in all presented change initiatives, giving us in-depth knowledge of the evolving situation. We have had repeated face-to-face and phone contacts with the informant throughout, totalling more than 60 hours of communication time. Due to the nature of the contacts, the documentation largely consists of written notes during and after interviews. This key informant has further supplied us with several extensive internal and confidential presentations of the change programmes (e.g. PowerPoint presentations and progress reports), memos and email and SMS conversations.

While the key informant has been invaluable to direct our attention to the changes and inner workings of the bank, reliance on this source presents two major methodological difficulties not uncommon to workplace studies. First, due to the vital requirement for confidentiality for the bank and the key informant (who does not have explicit permission from the bank to divulge some of the information), we must refrain from presenting some of the detailed empirical findings available to us, instead having to rely on more general descriptions and a minimum of direct quotes. Readers simply must trust that the findings presented are accurate.

Second, the high reliance on one key informant naturally means that we receive selective and potentially fallible and biased information shaped by his/her subjective understandings, interests, self-image and interpretations of others' actions and motives. As far as possible, we have aimed to corroborate the information supplied by the key informant with other sources, such as via other respondents, internal and public documents and media sources. When this has not been possible, we have chosen to leave it out of the analysis or explicitly state that it cannot be controlled.

The Bank

The bank under study here has its headquarters in Stockholm and is one of the larger full-service banks in Northern Europe, with operations mainly (but not exclusively) in the Scandinavian countries. The major owners of the bank are domestic and foreign institutional owners, such as state and private pension funds and insurance companies. Like all of the four major Swedish banks, this one dates back more than a hundred years and has during that time merged with or acquired a large number of other Swedish banks, at times in relation to financial crises (Ögren, 2010). The focus here is on the bank's headquarters and not back-office operations or local bank branches.

Following IT developments, the general digitalisation of assets and transactions, the construction of more complex financial instruments, as well as increased financial regulations and increased information demands from media, analysts and rating agencies, bank headquarters (and to some extent back-office operations) have grown in the number of employees and proportionally in relation to traditional bank branches (Movitz and Allvin, 2016b). The headquarters, which strictly speaking is not a clearly demarcated formal organisational subunit, currently has several hundred employees.

The changes described above have contributed to four relevant developments. First, the operations of the headquarters have broadened to include more areas than 'merely' handling strategic decisions and overseeing local branches and have become increasingly digitalised with nearly all tasks dependent on IT systems and digitalised information. One senior manager with an engineering background described it: 'Banking today is sixty per cent IT ... but it is actually meaningless to talk about IT [as a distinct function] because IT is in everything we do'.

Following increased external demands for information from owners, analysts, the media and regulatory agencies, banks are today further forced to spend much more time on divulging and communicating information through roadshows, one-on-one meetings, analyst and investor meetings, phone calls and so on – especially in relation to quarterly reports (Movitz and Allvin, 2016a). The levels of detail and the speed with which information is to be delivered has also increased. As one investor relations officer describes it:

> These quarterly reports ... I don't know if it is a good thing. Takes a lot of time from other things. It's not like things change that much in three months. I'm thinking sometimes maybe a bank shouldn't be on the stock market.

Third, and following the above, the educational and professional composition of the labour force within finance in Sweden has shifted over time (Movitz and Allvin, 2016b). While economists still make up the majority of employees, a growing proportion consists of professionals such as engineers, mathematicians, physicists, a range of IT specialists, journalists, lawyers and even political scientists.

Fourth, the connections between employees' education, profession/ expertise, organisational placement and working tasks have become more blurred. The operations at the headquarters resemble only to a limited extent a traditional functional/bureaucratic structure with stable departments for, for example, law comprising only lawyers, an IT department having only IT specialists and so on. Moreover, several organisational units of considerable size are temporary and changing, some more or less constituting long-lasting processes or projects with nondescript names like 'Strategic Information Implementation Unit'. The hierarchical placement – that is, which unit and manager has authority and which unit is responsible for particular issues – is therefore not always clear and repeatedly contested.

A more fruitful way of understanding the bank's central organisation than classic bureaucracy is as a continuous struggle over who *owns* and has a *stake* in certain strategic issues, who can make *demands*, the *resources* (i.e. people and budget) at their disposal and who *reports to* whom and is expected to *deliver* – all italicised words were frequently mentioned in interviews with employees at the bank.

One important aspect of the above concerns the blurred lines between the headquarters, which consists of units perceived as of central strategic importance, and the more administrative and supportive back-office operations, which are often physically separated from the headquarters. Since placement at the headquarters is internally perceived as more secure and prestigious, there are continuous power struggles over which functions should remain there and which should be transferred to more remote locations.

The temporality and blurred lines of authority structures combines and contributes to recurring movements of personnel, shifting of tasks between departments, units, projects and processes, as well as physically away from the headquarters. The employees' educational backgrounds therefore have relatively limited impact on which organisational unit they currently belong to and to some extent also what tasks they perform, seemingly resulting in quite limited and shifting collective identities based on, for example, profession or organisational placement (cf. Lysgaard, 1976). Also, several central and highly digitalised functions contain different tasks with shifting requirements for competence where it is not obvious which unit or profession (in a wide sense) should have the main responsibility.

A telling example is illustrated by the IT-based systems for handling financial information concerning, among other things, risk weights of assets, which most European banks are currently developing in order to follow updated EU regulations concerning the banks' capital requirements. Given that the system contains financial information, economists at the bank argue that they should have the main responsibility for this function with others reporting to them. The lawyers claim that these systems are implemented in response to legal requirements, making them natural owners of the system. The IT experts state that they are IT systems and that ultimately IT experts are the only ones who really understand how such systems work.

The Problem: You Would Think a Bank Knows How Much Money It Has...

Before describing the actual changes in the bank and the subsequent actions of employees, it is helpful to understand the problems facing the bank that warrant such changes. To the layperson, it would seem obvious that a bank ought to know how much money it has: its current financial situation in terms of assets and liquidity and the like. One of its main lines of business is, after all, to handle people's savings and lend money. In reality, however, it is far from that simple – which became evident after the latest financial crisis (e.g. Stiglitz, 2010).

First of all, the traditional image of the local savings and loans banks is an ill-fitting description of contemporary full-service banks. Apart from savings and loans, banks are also involved in, for example, mergers and acquisitions, underwriting shares and handling IPOs (initial public offering). They function as derivatives trading houses and trade in practically all types of assets (derivatives, shares, bonds, currencies, etc.) both for customers and with the bank's own capital. This means that the value, volume and types of assets the bank and its customers hold and the related risk exposure changes several thousand times a second around the clock. Fractional reserve banking and the fluctuating value and risk of assets, including credits, further complicate matters.

Second, many if not most banks have a vast range of different IT systems which are not always directly compatible with each other, and parts of the financial information is decentralised (to countries, branches, types of business, etc.). The bank studied here has identified more than a hundred different internal IT systems and databases deemed of strategic importance, many of which cannot directly communicate with each other. This situation is largely an effect of banks' early adoption of customised computer systems (some dating back to the 1960s) and the gradual merger and acquisition of Swedish banks that have incompatible computer systems.

For day-to-day operations, having incomplete information on the 'on-and-off' balance sheet is a limited problem, and different parts of the bank are required on a regular basis to present estimates to head-quarters on the current state of affairs. The lack of systematic knowledge does, however, increasingly pose a problem as dates for quarterly and annual reports approach when the bank needs to present a credible (but not necessarily accurate) account of the current financial situation. Furthermore, and following the Swedish bank crisis of the 1990s (Larsson and Sjögren, 1995), Sweden joining the EU and of course the most recent global financial crisis, authorities have increased demands on banks to regularly provide information on capital coverage, risk levels and weights (so-called Basel III regulations) (Wood, 2005).

In order to meet increased external demands, all the decentralised information thus needs to be gathered centrally on a regular basis and compiled to form a single balance sheet revealing profits (or losses), risk exposure and weight, and proportion of owned capital. The magnitude of this task itself makes compiling the correct information from hundreds of local branches in several different countries difficult. The information also needs to be *evaluated* in terms of, for example, the value of an asset and the level of risk involved (how much is a financial asset used as collateral for a loan worth, and what is the risk that a particular lender will not be able to repay their loans?).

Although financial reports are to be produced at regular intervals and at known dates, the process of compiling the necessary information is done under extreme time pressure. Those units required to provide financial information to the department in charge of actually producing financial reports frequently fail to deliver the necessary data until a few weeks (and at times until just days) before the report is set to be made public. In that time, the figures have to double-checked and supplied to the board, who signs off on the report or demands changes. Once agreed internally, the report is handed to external accountants who make sure the report follows established accounting procedures. For example,

> They [another unit] make a prognosis which hopefully is pretty good. The IRO [Investor Relations Officer] and the CEO look at it and talk to the market analysts and investors. That kind of sets the frame. If we are lucky, it's ... realistic. Then we have to put pressure on other units to deliver the right numbers. They are always late. And also, Finansinspektionen [National Financial Regulatory Agency] must buy it.

According to the informant quoted above, who was previously directly involved in producing financial reports, the weeks before presentation are extremely hectic with an intensified workload and massive overtime, as well as high pressure and uncertainty. Each quarter, there is an intense around-the-clock race to make the figures sing the predetermined tune; to present a report that will satisfy the market.

> With the systems we have ... you might be down three billion [roughly 300 million euros] in Sweden before lunch, and in the afternoon, you find five billion in Denmark. The last weeks before [the quarterly report] are crazy. You struggle and tweak the numbers.

While the bank has to be perceived to adhere to accounting regulations and laws, the quote shows that the completion of the financial report is far from a straightforward exercise in calculation. The report might convey a sense of extreme accuracy with extensive use of diagrams and numbers down to the third decimal. But in reality, the reports are to a great extent *constructed*, manufactured to comply with specific demands and intentions. The reports are not complete fabrications without connections to reality. But there is flexibility within the imposed constraints and an understanding and *expectation* from the board that employees responsible for producing reports should deliver 'correct' results, often using sub-optimal IT systems.

The problems and high costs associated with having a multitude of incompatible IT systems has been known for decades within the bank, with only limited efforts to change having been made. Apart from the high costs of installing a new IT system (internal estimates put the costs well above 100 million euros), decision-makers have been reluctant to alter existing practice, as it is viewed as similar to 'rebuilding an airplane during flight', given that the systems must be operational at all times.

The banks are, however, increasingly under pressure to make changes due to stricter government and EU regulations concerning capital coverage that increase demands for the ratio of a bank's own assets in relation to the capital it lends out and also require banks to have continuous detailed information on the risks associated with different assets, including debts. Failure to comply with the regulations can result in a warning, hefty fines and ultimately a loss of the banking license (all of which have occurred in Sweden). At the same time, pressures from owners for increased profits, share prices and dividends have grown, such that these stakeholders pressure banks to minimise the capital they hold. According to the investor relations officers interviewed, there is limited acceptance from owners that stricter regulations and necessary IT investments negatively impact on the balance sheet or lower returns on capital. In other words, and given the digitalisation of financial information, IT systems actually need to be changed, but owners are reluctant to accept the costs of doing so.

The Proposed Changes

There are four changes under scrutiny here: the creation of a shared database for financial information; the purchase of a new system for information on collateral; changes in the control of certain R&D budgets; and changes to the common processes for handling regulatory demands. Since the observed conflicts are not mainly about the content of the proposed changes, they are only briefly described.

As stated, the bank currently has a large number of different IT systems that in some cases cannot communicate with each other without using intermediate data transformation filters or programmes, or even manual operations. In order to solve this issue and to reduce the resources required to produce financial reports which comply with regulatory requirements, one proposed *development* change concerns the development of a shared database containing key financial information intended for the use of selected key employees involved in financial reporting.

The second change, *procurement*, concerns the installation of a new IT-based system for improving the measurement of the bank's collateral in order to better comply with regulatory requirements regarding capital coverage. In this case, the decision had already been made by top management to purchase an IT system from external suppliers. What remained to be done by 2013 was to articulate the specifications for the system, compare bids, choose a supplier and ensure the selected supplier actually delivered according to contracts.

The third change, a *structural* process, purports to create a matrix-like organisation whereby representatives of different organisational units identified as stakeholders and involved in complying with regulatory requirements become integrated in a single process to decide suitable scope and content for the necessary IT systems.

The fourth change concerns the *control* over a large proportion of the development budget for existing and new IT-based financial systems at the bank. An argument for the change is that the extensive IT change within the bank necessitates more centralised control to increase cost control, avoid double work and to make certain that the new systems are indeed compatible.

From an outside perspective and given the brief descriptions above, the four change processes might be perceived as dealing with more or less the same issue, and some of the same people at the bank are indeed involved in several of the change processes. But, according to our respondents, this was initially not the common perception within the bank, a view supported by internal documents and communications. Thus in 2013 the changes were treated as separate issues.

The Players: Professionals, Managers, Units

The players, that is the employees involved in the different change processes and conflicts, can be described along the lines of professions, including semi-professions and experts, and by structure in terms of organisational units and managerial levels, where middle and senior managers play a central role, functioning as central nodes and visible combatants that insiders focus on.

Top management, including the CEO as well as the board, play a central but quite paradoxical role in the changes and conflicts, being as one informant described it 'ever present, always absent'. On the one hand, all changes described above have been formally decided or at least authorised by the CEO and the board – in some cases following suggestions from senior managers. On the other hand, top management have only rudimentary knowledge of the changes (especially regarding IT) and are therefore reliant on the information and arguments put forth by subordinates and seem reluctant to take a clear position on the design of solutions or conflicts. Instead, they leave it up to the various players involved in the change process to sort things out.

There are three relevant points to understand the emerging conflicts. First, and given the previously described temporal nature of the bank's organisation, there are no stable dividing lines between, for example, units, professions and management, but rather there are shifting alliances of employee collectives. Repeatedly, two units that side with each other in one change process are found to be opponents in another one. Second, there are tit-for-tat reciprocal tactics at play, meaning that perceived wrongdoings and back-stabbings in relation to a particular change process spill over into other changes, contributing to the multiple-front wars mentioned in the introduction to this chapter.

Given this conflict, there are, third, limited opportunities for the formation of a broader workers' collective vis-à-vis management and owners. On the contrary, the relative absence of clear directions from top management, coupled with subordinate managers' and units' attempts to get the support of the CEO, contributes to hide conflicting interests between owners/management and labour. While most employees accept the changes as necessary, the most reasonable interpretation is that they have been proposed to meet owners' interests (which are to meet regulatory and market demands without lowering profits and potentially to reduce staff numbers) with limited concern for employee's interests such as stability and employment security.

Several respondents raise moral concerns about the profit demands from owners and even about their own salary levels and bonuses and the consequences that these demands have for them in terms of work intensity and job insecurity. Further, most display a fatalistic viewpoint along the lines that the situation is absurd but that there is nothing you can do anything about; it's the way finance works.

The Game: Valid Arguments versus Dirty Tricks

Most respondents express the view that the proposed changes were initially separate issues largely constituting the implementation of strictly technical systems which in themselves were not contested and towards which there was no apparent employee resistance. But the change initiatives quite quickly turned into a rather politicised and dirty game between employees where all four proposed changes became intertwined battle fields. The changes came to represent threats to the volatile balance between groups of employees under uncertain conditions, where top management's final decisions on design and control of the new systems potentially would have crucial consequences for future positions and jobs.

With regard to the development of a shared IT system for financial information, the conflicts have centred on which groups of employees within the bank will be in charge of developing the system and, when it is completed, 'own' it. Concerning the procurement of an IT system for collateral, conflicts revolve around the specifications of the system and which supplier to choose. The proposed 'control' changes regarding the R&D budget quite predictably concern which unit will control the budget and how the budget will be allocated to different groups in the bank. The proposed structural change, intended to produce an integrated process for handling regulatory demands, leads to conflicts over who will lead the change, thereby creating competition over which groups are legitimate stakeholders and over work organisation.

In discussions and presentations about the proposed changes, those involved consistently refer to technical specifications and problems, regulatory demands, costs and savings and deadlines. Explicit arguments are largely based on seemingly objective, rational concerns about the content of changes and who has the required expertise to manage change processes, presented as what is best for the bank, its employees and owners. Many of these arguments are ostensibly valid and raised with the best intentions. Still, given that arguments consistently favour a particular position relative to others, it seems quite evident that there is a degree of politics and tactics involved. Our key informant, who quite recently had reached a higher-level management position, claimed to have initially tried to simply focus on contributing to making the best changes from the perspective of the bank, but she quickly felt forced to engage in office politics and tactical plays to regain influence and resources.

Thus, even though discussions and presentations seemingly concern the content, design and implementation of solutions, our general impression throughout the three years following the case study has been that the subtext and causes behind tactical manoeuvers largely concern different individuals and collectives of employees aiming to improve, or at least maintain, their position at the headquarters by being perceived as of strategic importance, which in highly digitalised settings becomes tied to 'owning' the vital IT systems that the bank relies on, thereby subordinating others instead of being subordinated. The battle around change becomes more about the resulting proximity to top management and the board than the technical solutions themselves.

Starting in late spring 2013, the tactical moves and conflicts gradually escalated into a rather dirty game. Some of this resembles classic power strategies of agenda-setting and gate-keeping (compare Movitz and Levinson, 2013): issues, suggestions and problems raised by opponents are dropped from meeting agendas, left out of minutes or not communicated to top management in order to make one's own position look more attractive. On several occasions, opponents have 'mistakenly' been left out of email sending lists, not briefed on important information or not invited to or even told about important meetings. On one occasion, a respondent claimed that the head of another unit deliberately scheduled an important 'emergency' budget meeting on short notice after having made sure that the respondent was due to attend another meeting abroad, just to make sure he could not attend.

The shifting and at times unclear hierarchical structure and relations between different units at the headquarters further facilitated attempts at claiming formal mandates that did not exist, especially in relation to junior staff. In one instance, the head of one unit contacted all project managers of rivalling units, demanding information on how much money remained in their budgets, presumably to ascertain which resources could be seized, and then deployed in negotiations with senior managers about the proposed changes in control of the IT-related R&D budget.

To illustrate this point further, at one time, a manager approached junior administrative staff in another unit and demanded information on the resources that unit would request in forthcoming budget negotiations (which he did not have the mandate to do, and furthermore information that the head of the unit in question had not yet received). This manager then approached the head of the unit and a senior manager for both units, calling for an immediate decision on a very different distribution of resources without disclosing the previous communications with the junior staff.

According to our key informant, documentation and other participants, there are several other instances where employees – and especially heads of organisational units – have withheld vital information and in some cases blatantly lied to senior management and the board about crucial problems and costs – actions that would most likely constitute legitimate reasons for dismissal. For instance, there is a case where a manager continued to argue for a particular technical solution despite having received information from subordinates that costs would increase dramatically and that the solution would not solve any of the targetted problems and would quite likely not work at all.

The above represent only some of the incidents revealed by our research, and it should be noted that these types of incidents have occurred throughout our case study, and indeed are still occurring. Viewed separately, they are perhaps not significant, and readers will probably recognise similar incidents in their own working lives. Moreover, they are a far cry from threats, bullying and physical violence found in other workplaces. However, considered in combination, the incidents described above suggest the emergence of a clear pattern of power struggles using dirty tricks.

At the same time, it is important to understand that managers are not Machiavellian instigators spending all of their working days plotting schemes and that they have not lost all sight of the rationale for changes. A considerable amount of managers' time and that of other employees at the bank headquarters is spent on *real* working tasks: routine administration, reporting and problem-solving. But alongside these routine tasks, positioning around and potential engagement in discussions of change repeatedly occur, as rival and at times necessary incidents to consider in the course of work. As one respondent states,

> It's like … You really can't get involved in everything. You have to pick your battles…. But you never know, there are game changers. … [S]ometimes things look small or they change [the members] in the top management. Suddenly it's like bang!

The Situation One Year Later

In the spring of 2014, more than a year after the four changes became official, only one concrete result had been achieved: a supplier for the procurement of a standardised system for handling collateral had been chosen. The actual system was not yet implemented; it had not even been procured; and there was not yet a final written contract. But at least a choice of supplier had been made.

Interestingly, the chosen supplier was not the one favoured by the accounting unit, who early on tried to take control of the process by claiming to have authority. The unit head had attempted to exclude alternative suppliers and other internal units from the process. According to one respondent, this decision was a loss of face for the unit's manager, who had been very active in several of the change programmes and in the ensuing conflicts and who also claimed to have personal ties to several members of the top management team. This decision seems to have contributed to actually *increasing* conflicts in other change processes, as other managers sensed the opportunity to increase their influence, while the manager in question aimed to regain his reputation as a key player by devoting more energy to the proposed changes.

As discussed at greater length in the conclusion, it can be argued that the intangible nature of digital changes increases the likelihood of such developments. Even though the changes are extremely costly and require concrete work in terms of system development and programming, there is considerable room for re-specifications throughout, and extensive changes can and do occur in the final stages of change processes before they just are about to 'go live' (and sometimes even after that).

The other three change processes were hardly moving forward and were on hold for quite some time. One reason was the described repeated struggles between units with ever more meetings to discuss details and to present arguments. Another important reason for the holdups is directly related to the previously described process of providing and communicating quarterly financial reports.

On two separate occasions in 2013 and 2014, the CEO and head of the board, respectively, either ignored or misunderstood internal prognoses and publicly promised increased profits when internal estimates suggested the opposite. This meant that the bank was 'missing' several hundred million euros, warranting a 'profit-warning', as it is called, and meant that it might not meet regulatory capital coverage requirements, thereby risking hefty fines. When this became known to the affected units in the bank – mostly through the media – it caused frantic action throughout the bank to 'tweak' numbers and make use of accounting techniques to produce results that were roughly in line with the unrealistic predictions, but at the same time acceptable to supervisory agencies. Eventually, the employees in both instances managed to present sufficient results and the internal crisis was never brought to outside attention.

These are interesting examples of internally produced crises and the possibility that companies construct results in line with external expectations, which in themselves have limited connections with the proposed changes but nonetheless highlight two things. First, change processes and inherent conflicts cannot be understood in isolation; rather they need to take into account contingent and even random events connected to the 'actual' business. Second, when the change processes and conflicts temporarily came to a halt as employees endeavoured to jointly resolve senior managements' mistakes, a form of workers' collective seemed to have developed. Collective discussion emerged around conflicting interests and pressures from owners and managements to increase profits with little consideration for the employees who had to deliver results. However, this situation did not last.

A Sort of Ending: Everything Changes Again

After the crises described above had been handled, the four change processes were gradually back on track and conflicts resurfaced during the second half of 2014. Although time-consuming, these change actions and the accompanying tactics were, however, unknown to practically all but a few top-level employees largelly irrelevant. During the second half of 2014, before any of the previously described change processes had been finalised, the CEO and the top management team of the bank decided to initiate a new business group-wide organisational change programme aimed at reducing and standardising technologies, processes, products and working tasks. The board and top management had come to the conclusion that the bank's history of mergers and its international presence had contributed to a vast variety of localised solutions, including products and services, that could not be attributed to national regulatory requirements or market demands. Internally, the new lean-inspired changes were thought to contribute to cost-cutting through de-bureaucratisation and standardisation. Externally, the changes hoped to increase share valuation and customer volumes by creating a clearer market position and service portfolio to customers.[1]

This new change programme constitutes an alternative digital change programme that incorporates vital aspects of, but also goes beyond, the previous four proposed changes. The new change initiative, which was gradually specified by a small team of managers and presented to employees in 2015 therefore came to have significant impacts on the four change processes we initially studied. Only one of the changes, the procurement of a standardised IT system, progressed and was finalised. With the new changes, the proposed changes in the control over R&D budget became viewed as irrelevant by the decision-makers since the R&D-projects altered. The other two changes were reinterpreted, altered and subsumed under the new large change process (which, to complicate things, is divided into a series of interlinked sub-projects).

At the point of writing this chapter, this latest change programme is (slowly) progressing, but it is far from being completed and has begun to generate new conflicts. In the end, no clear winners of the previous conflicts could be declared, although some managers lost influence under the new initiative and new battle lines are starting to emerge where previous perceived wrongdoings during the old change processes still play a role.

With regard to the temporality of organisations, it is telling that in later discussions with respondents, they had to be reminded by us of some of the specific earlier change initiatives that they, less than three years earlier, viewed as critical for their position within the bank.

Conclusion: Staying Afloat in Uncertain Territories

This chapter is largely about conflicts over changes never made, which might seem like reviewing a book that was never written. But the aim has been to analyse the role of proposed IT-related changes in highly digitalised work settings even when such initiatives have not been finalised. Our argument is that the manifest conflicts related to the changes between shifting groups of employees at the bank's headquarters are critical incidents that in fact reflect, but also contribute to hide, more persistent underlying conflicting interests between capital and labour, which only occasionally surface in relation to, for example, crises caused by top management and owner representatives. To support this argument, we point to the role of an increased focus on shareholders following financialisation, the blurred and temporal organisation of the headquarters and the central role of IT systems in highly digitalised work settings such as banking.

To argue that the financial sector is financialised might seem a moot point or even tautological. But through our research, it has become particularly evident that the growing proportion of institutional owners of banks have increased their demands for returns and that top management increasingly adhere to these demands at the expense of legitimate employee interests such as employment security and reasonable workload (Movitz and Allvin, 2014, 2015; cf. Thompson, 2013).

Following the above, continuous efforts to find new ways to create value, made possible by technical developments and changed regulations and attempts at cost-cutting and risk relocation, the organisation of the bank headquarters have become more temporal, the boundaries between the headquarters and supportive operations blurred and the domains of professions and organisational units repeatedly contested and at the mercy of top management. The consequences of these unintended changes mean that the stable bureaucratic structure that used to characterise banks has gradually been replaced by more uncertain work and employment conditions. Employees, units and processes at the headquarters are constantly under threat to be moved to supporting locations. Among employees, it is a common (and well-founded) perception that this constitutes a slippery slope towards downsizing, outsourcing or offshoring, resulting in job losses.

Under such conditions, the employees both individually and collectively aim to gain and retain their status as being of strategic importance to the bank (i.e. the shareholders) relative to other employees and groups – a status that can be granted only by top management and the board, who lack sufficient knowledge of details to judge alternative claims and seem unwilling to take a clear stand in conflicts.

Regarding technology, it is a bit late in the game to claim that the IT changes within Swedish finance, like those presented here, constitute a process of digitalisation given that the first computer systems were installed more than 60 years ago, Internet banking has been around for roughly 20 years, and most Swedish bank branches no longer handle cash. It is rather a question of making IT-related changes in an already highly digitalised work setting where digital systems are essential for the operations of the bank. In such settings, gaining status as being of strategic importance in order to decrease insecurity becomes closely tied to the systems themselves, and any proposed changes potentially disturb the temporal and volatile balance between groups of employees, which ultimately is in the hands of the ignorant and 'ever-absent/present' top management. At the same time, different groups aim to curry favour with top management, which in turn creates conflict. To paraphrase Mantel's *Wolf Hall*, everyone aims to be close to the king, but the king is fickle (and he probably does not have your best interests at heart).

From this perspective, whether or not proposed changes have been finalised is not the point; they all exist as potential threats (more than opportunities) that employees need to monitor to judge whether they warrant action at the expense of focusing on other change processes, all in the context of attending to regular work responsibilities.

As stated, office politics are no doubt as old as the modern corporation, and similar power plays and conflicts play out in most work organisations (universities hardly being an exception). Still, IT-related changes in highly digitalised work settings offer certain distinguishing (but not necessarily unique) characteristics. Key here is the intangible and plastic yet almost determinate nature of digital solutions. There is a vast variety of ways to design a functioning digital solution aimed at a particular task or problem, and even though concrete programming, systems development and testing is necessary, the majority of work time and effort in most IT projects consists of discussing the design, content and risks of the solution, as well as who should operationalise it, the resource allocation, the order of development and deadlines (cf. Movitz and Sandberg, 2009).

Given the plastic nature of digital solutions, such discussions and conflicts are more likely to continue throughout the change project with major alterations and revisions at the very end than when, for example, building a new factory. Conflict in one change process is further more likely to spill over into others. Due to the competing technical, economic and legal logics inherent in financial digital solutions, there are no given experts but rather competing groups of employees aiming to secure a position at the bank by making alternative claims to expertise (cf. Augustsson, 2005).

Still, when the systems are in place, they place a decisive, almost determinate role for the labour process of workers in terms of decisions about what is viewed as strategically important, employees' organisational placement and who it is that gets exiled to the insecure outer boundaries of the system (or even pushed over the edge). Much like how the conveyer belt dictates work in the factory, the digital systems make some organisational rules and structures redundant in highly digital settings – and the systems are designed largely to adhere to the interests of management and owners.

Note

1 Since we as external researchers were asked to comment on this new initiative, we gained access to extensive internal documents, including memos, implementation plans and presentations. While our negative comments on their plans to rely solely on cultural change programmes made an impact, we are less convinced that they paid any attention to our worries of probable de-skilling, resistance, conflict and staff reductions.

REFERENCES

Allvin, M. and F. Movitz (2017) 'Whose Side is Technology on, Really? On the Interdependence of Work and Technology', in N. Chmiel, F. Fraccaroli and M. Sverke (eds), *An Introduction to Work and Organizational Psychology: An International Perspective. 3rd ed.* (London: Wiley-Blackwell).

Augustsson, F. (2005) *They Did IT. The Formation and Organization of Interactive Media Production in Sweden* (Stockholm: National Institute for Working Life).

Baldry, C. (2012) Computers, Jobs, and Skills: The Industrial Relations of Technological Change. *Approaches to Information Technology* (Berlin: Springer Science and Business Media).

Edwards P., J. O'Mahoney and S. Vincent (eds) (2014) *Studying Organizations Using Critial Realism. a Practical Guide* (Oxford: Oxford University Press).

Ehrensal, K. N. (1995) 'Discourses of Global Competition: Obscuring the Changing Labour Processes of Managerial Work', *Journal of Organizational Change Management*, 8, 5, 5–16.

Fleetwood, S. and S. Ackroyd (eds) (2004) *Critical Realist Applications in Organisation and Management Studies* (London: Routledge).

Ford, R. (2012) *Canada* (London: Bloomsbury).

Jaros, S. (2010) 'The Core Theory: Critiques, Defences and Advances', in P. Thompson and C. Smith (eds), *Working Life. Renewing Labour Process Analysis* (Houndsmills: Palgrave Macmillan).

Larsson, M. and H. Sjögren (1995) *Vägen till och från bankkrisen. Svenska bank-systemets förändring 1969–1994* [The Road to and From the Bank Crisis] (Stockholm: Carlsson bokförlag).

Lysgaard, S. (1976) *Arbeiderkollektivet* [The Workers' Collective] (Oslo: Universitetsforlaget).

Movitz, F. and M. Allvin (2014) 'What Does Financial Derivatives Really Have To Do with Jobs? Examining Causal Mechanisms Between Aspects of Financialization, Work Intensification and Employment Security', *International Labour Process Conference*, King's College, London.

Movitz, F. and M. Allvin (2015) '(At Least) Six Degrees of Separation: Problematizing Shareholder Value and Institutional Ownership using Swedish Pension Funds as an Example', *International Labour Process Conference*, Athens.

Movitz, F. and M. Allvin (2016a) 'Bridging Capital and Labour: Shareholder Interests and the Boundary Spanning Role of Investor Relations Officers', *International Labour Process Conference*, Berlin.

Movitz, F. and M. Allvin (2016b) 'Arbetets Finansialisering' [the Financialization of Work], in E. Andersson, O. Broberg, M. Gianneschi and B. Larsson (eds), *Vardagslivets Finansialisering* (Gothenbourg: Gothenbourg University).

Movitz, F. and K. Levinson (2013) 'Employee Board Representation in the Swedish Private Sector', in Å. Sandberg (ed.), *Nordic Ligths. Work, Management and Welfare in Scandinavia* (Stockholm: SNS).

Movitz, F. and Å. Sandberg (2009) 'The Organization of Creativity: Content, Contracts and Control in Swedish Interactive Media Production', in A. McKinlay and C. Smith (eds), *Creative Labour.Working in the Creative Industries* (Houndsmills: Palgrave Macmillan).

Sayer, A. (2000) *Realism and Social Science* (London: Sage).

Stiglitz, J. E. (2010) *Free Fall. America, Free Markets, and the Sinking of the World Economy* (New York: W. W. Norton and Company).

▶

Thompson, P. (2003) 'Disconnected Capitalism: Or Why Employers Can't Keep Their Side of the Bargain', *Work, Employment and Society*, 17, 2, 359–78.

Thompson, P. (2013) 'Financialization and the Workplace: Extending and Applying the Disconnected Capitalism Thesis', *Work, Employment and Society*, 27, 3, 472–88.

Thompson, P. and C. Smith (eds) (2010) *Working Life: Renewing Labour Process Analysis* (Basingstoke: Palgrave McMillan).

Thompson, P. and S. Vincent (2010) 'Labour Process Theory and Critical Realism', in P. Thompson and C. Smith (eds), *Working Life. Renewing Labour Process Analysis* (Houndsmills: Palgrave Macmillan).

Whyte, W.H. (1957) *Organizational Man* (New York: Double Day Books).

Wood, D. (2005) *Governing Global Banking. The Basel Committee and the Politics of Financial Globalisation* (Aldershot: Ashgate).

Ögren, A. (ed.) (2010) *The Swedish Financial Revolution* (Houndsmills: Palgrave Macmillan).

The Disruptive Power of Digital Transformation

New Forms of Industrialising Knowledge Work

Andreas Boes, Tobias Kämpf, Barbara Langes and Thomas Lühr

Scope and Momentum of the Digital Transformation

Digital transformation marks a fundamental change for our society, possibly comparable to the Industrial Revolution of the nineteenth century. It has, with great momentum, also taken hold of the economy in Germany. In virtually every economic sector and industry, companies are concerned with questions such as how is digitisation changing established models of business and manufacturing; how should innovations of products and services be put into action; and how should companies understand and reconceptualise work in this context?

Thus, the debate over how to proceed with digitisation and its challenges has reached businesses and made it to the top of decision-makers' strategic agendas. The German discussion about *Industrie 4.0* (see Hirsch-Kreinsen, 2016; Pfeiffer in this publication) marks only the beginning and remains restricted to a rather small segment of the wider debate. Strategic trends such as 'the Internet of Things', 'smart services', 'cloudworking' and 'crowdsourcing' are indicative of digitisation's enormous range. Emerging models like the 'agile organisation', new development frameworks such as 'Scrum', the increasing use of social media or the rapid spread of mobile working show that 'work' and 'organisation' are subject to fundamental changes. This applies not only – and not even predominantly – to the manufacturing sectors of *Industrie 4.0* but more specifically to businesses' indirect areas and so-called knowledge

153

work.[1] These divisions are responsible for a high percentage of the jobs currently created, such as in administration or R&D, which digitisation has considerably advanced. In the area of knowledge work, objects and means of work exist predominantly and consistently in digitised form; work without digital equipment and systems can today be imagined only with great difficulty. Therefore, in order to understand digitisation in the world of work, we need to look at the changes taking place in the field of knowledge work.

In knowledge work, a new development has been taking place for quite some time. Concepts such as process orientation, standardisation and even industrialisation are applied to knowledge work more frequently than before. Whereas the effects of these concepts are well known for low-skilled work, such as call centres (see e.g. Holtgrewe et al., 2002; Holman et al., 2007; Matuschek et al., 2007), they can be increasingly observed in high-skilled knowledge work also, such as in the finance industry (see e.g. Stobbe, 2006; Speek, 2008) and particularly in IT services. Following the breakdown of the 'new economy' and the subsequent surge of globalisation in the IT sector ('offshoring'), standardisation has received a considerable boost (see Boes and Kämpf, 2011). Even in fields such as software development, one hears often that the time of the artists is over and that what is required now is 'software factories' or even 'software from the assembly line' (cf. e.g. Janßen, 2005; Greenfield and Short, 2006). This trend reaches far beyond the IT sector into the administrative divisions of big enterprise groups, who drive forward, at rapid speed, the standardisation of many work activities; for this, they employ strategies such as 'shared services' and novel factory approaches. Even in R&D, a comprehensive economisation of innovation processes is increasingly taking place. This also includes standardisation and a considerable reduction of autonomy over work (see e.g. Streckeisen, 2008; Will-Zocholl, 2011). On the whole, core principles of lean production and integrated production systems are transferred ever more comprehensively to engineering work and development units (see Boes et al., 2014).

It is no surprise that, for some time, businesses have made efforts to further exploit the potential for productivity gains and rationalisation in knowledge work. Hence, we argue that this development, in the context of the ongoing growth in the digitisation of work, leads to a disruptive change in the world of work. We make use of a theoretical approach, the informatisation approach, in order to determine what the process of digital transformation essentially means and how it affects mental activities within the work process (section 'Understanding Change: The Information Space as a Leap in Productive Forces'). We argue that the rise of a digital information space indicates a considerable leap in the social productive forces, permitting a 'new type of industrialisation' (Boes, 2004; Boes and Kämpf, 2012) that specifically targets knowledge work (sections 'Rethinking Industrialisation' and 'New Forms of Industrialising Knowledge Work: From the 'Digital Assembly Line' to Cloudworking'). Using the example of new production models for knowledge work, we want to demonstrate that an enormous disruptive energy for the future world of work originates from this leap and discuss its consequences for the development of work (section 'Disruptive Change in Knowledge Work: The World of Work at a Crossroads'). Our line of thought is based on an extensive stock of interviews conducted with experts, managers, and employees in Germany and the United States.[2]

Understanding Change: The Information Space as a Leap in Productive Forces

In order to comprehend the scope of the changes that arise from digitisation, we have to critically examine the actual content and substance of the oft-proclaimed slogan of the 'digital revolution'. Digitisation as such – as a process of transforming information into binary data so that it can be processed by machines – is not a new development. Computers, as digitisation's technological basis, were invented more than 70 years ago. Today, the use of computers in companies has become a subject for historiography. Thus, the following questions suggest themselves: what is really new in the ongoing technical developments, and which elements of digitisation could be seen as a qualitative leap?

Avoiding Technological Reductionism: Introducing the Conceptual Perspective of Informatisation

Merely referencing the ever-growing powers and capacities of computing falls short of a sufficient answer to the questions asked above. A perspective on informatisation that consistently considers the use of information systems as a component of societal productive forces is, in our view, adequate to avoid this kind of technological reductionism. Informatisation, in this sense, generally refers to the types of increases in productive forces that specifically address the mental processes of human work, thus revolutionising the processes of production (Boes, 2005). So, our reflections are based on a theoretical approach that embeds digitisation into a historical development of work and organisation rather than taking an isolated view of the digitisation process alone.

In this perspective, informatisation is much more than merely utilising information and communication technologies, and informatisation is also much more than simply an enabler for new forms of automatisation (as it is sometimes suggested in the *Industrie 4.0* debate). Instead, we understand informatisation as a social process geared to rendering mental activities and their results accessible to others. Thus, informatisation means a process of externalising mental processes and their reification in media that can be used in a social context, beyond the individual. In other words, informatisation is 'materialising the use of information' (Boes, 2005). Individual knowledge is turned into information that is suited to collective handling and becomes accessible to a sophisticated division of labour.

We can observe the emergence of a globally accessible 'information space', based on the Internet (Baukrowitz and Boes, 1996); this emergence effectively amounts to a leap in productive forces (what Marx called 'Produktivkräfte'). The information space is far more than a vast digital library or a mere network of broadband connections using algorithms. Rather, it proves to be a new *sphere of social action*. In stark contrast to information systems of the past, from double-entry accounting to the computer systems of Fordist enterprises, a 'space for social action' (Boes, 1996) has emerged, interconnecting and bringing together people (and their social actions). Within this *open* and *living* space, people can interact in manifold ways: they can exchange ideas and views and mutually refer to their respective actions. Whereas the computer systems of the past merely allowed for human–machine interaction, the information space allows for interaction between human beings.

The history of company-based informatisation, as applied here in such a comprehensive sense, began long before the invention of computers (see Baukrowitz and Boes, 1996). At the end of the nineteenth century, a dynamic development of informatisation unfolded on the basis of double-entry accounting (Sombart, 1928). As communication converted into written form (Kocka, 1969) and information systems grew in complexity (Braverman, 1974), a veritable 'paper apparatus' (Jeidels, 1907) emerged in companies, which later was transferred to computer systems. With the rise of the PC, the computer was no longer a domain of specialists but became a common tool for everyday work (Baethge and Oberbeck, 1986). From the 1970s onwards, the first network concepts were developed and gained acceptance. From that point onwards, complex networked and computer-supported information systems emerged that, again, formed the starting point for comprehensive reorganisation processes in companies and for a new type of 'systemic rationalisation' (Altmann et al., 1986; Baethge and Oberbeck, 1986).

However, computerisation and the first network concepts were only the beginning of the far-reaching change of informatisation in companies as it has been taking place from the 1990s onwards. The rise of the Internet, in particular, has marked a new level of informatisation. The Internet became the basis for a globally available 'information space' (Baukrowitz and Boes, 1996), which in turn rang the bell for a new round: as a veritable leap in productive forces, the information space takes centre stage as the motor of the development of productive forces in society as a whole.

The Information Space as a New Sphere of Social Action

The information space, as a leap in productive forces, fundamentally differs from the information systems of the past in that a new *sphere of social action* emerged. Whereas traditional computer systems offered or demanded interaction between only humans and machines, the information space opens up a novel stage for interaction between humans. Here, not only are people able to save, handle or exchange information, but they can engage in an open and lively interaction or establish manifold relationships with each other. Thus, the information space becomes a 'space of social action' (Boes, 1996).

Looking at the reality of the Internet, it is easy to see the difference between the information space and the preprogrammed and 'grey' information systems of the past. A great variety of actors move within the information space, communicating, exchanging love messages or pursuing their economic interests. The information space offers leeway for the most diverse of activities, both of private individuals and organisations and of enterprises and civic institutions (see Dolata and Schrape, 2013). In this space, social action of manifold kinds finds its place. The key precondition for such diversity is that the information space is open and not restricted to a particular kind of use – in contrast to the Fordist information systems. Its reality is by no means predefined; instead, its structure and any opportunities for social action can be modified by its users' actual activities. Thus, it is essentially not an infrastructure for information transport but an open space that is constituted only by the users' social action itself (Baukrowitz and Boes, 1996).

With the rise of the Internet, this new sphere of action has become ubiquitous. On one hand, through the propagation of information and communication infrastructures and of mobile equipment, the information space has become permanently available and accessible from virtually anywhere, provided people know how and are able to use it. On the other hand, hardly any spheres of society remain without access to the Internet. The information space has suffused society as a whole, from the world of work to the lifeworld, including interpersonal relationships. Thus, the modes of operation and forms of exchange established by the Internet are gaining new social significance; one could call them the 'operating system' of the new sphere of social action mentioned above.

With the emergence of the information space, informatisation becomes a living social process. Here the abstract world of information meets the vitality of a new sphere of social action, a vitality that feeds on the networking and interlinking of human beings and their social togetherness. Here the 'knowledge of the world', including the everyday experiences of individuals, encyclopaedic knowledge and the most diverse kinds of data are produced in enormous amounts in the information systems, finds a common ground and becomes accessible and disposable to a new extent (Boes, 2005). What Marx once called the 'general intellect' of society in his *Grundrisse* is taking material shape with this qualitative leap in the development of productive forces.

The Information Space as a New Basis for Work and Added-Value Systems

This leap in productive forces entails fundamental consequences for work and the economy. The information space increasingly forms the basis of contemporary work and added-value systems. On one hand, it turns into a new 'shop floor': considerable aspects of work and cooperation with colleagues take place within this space, either directly or indirectly. To the extent that the objects and tools of work can be digitised, a new 'space of production' (Boes, 2004) is emerging. Precisely because it is a space of social action, it enables not only processes to be organised along the 'flow of information' but also new forms of collaboration and knowledge exchange. Work thus obtains a quality of previously unknown transparency. This quality allows for feedback loops in terms of innovation and learning and a new degree of use of mental productive forces, but it also, in turn, exposes even high-skilled labour to increasingly close-knit control.

On the other hand, new ideas and models of the organisation of added-value systems are emerging with the digital transformation. The mode of how enterprises and value chains operate as a whole is changing. Today, they seamlessly take globally distributed action on the basis of the global information space. The certainties of the Fordist industrial enterprise and its organisational principles are increasingly challenged. This is particularly evident in the field of knowledge work, where examples such as cloudworking and crowdsourcing illustrate the scope of this development. Even far-reaching questions arise: what should an enterprise comprise under such circumstances; how is social integration possible if work and cooperation are no longer restricted to fixed localities; and what will be the effects on the regulation system of work and labour as a whole?

The common backdrop for these changes in work and added-value systems is a new dominance of the informational level, which, in the course of digital transformation, has become the centre of value creation. The informational sphere turns into a sphere of direct intervention and thus becomes the strategic centre for business and production models. On this basis, a 'new type of industrialisation' (Boes, 2004; see also Boes and Kämpf, 2012) is emerging. The starting point of this type of industrialisation is no longer the traditional machine system but the informational level and the digital flow of information and data.

Rethinking Industrialisation

Reconsidering this idea of a leap in productive forces to its logical conclusion, we could say that the information space plays for work the same role in the twenty-first century as the machine systems played for 'modern industry' (Marx) in the economy of the nineteenth and twentieth centuries. In order to understand how knowledge work and its organisation change in this process, we fundamentally have to rethink industrialisation. This requires not only a well-founded and differentiated notion of industrialisation but particularly a combination of industrialisation and informatisation theory.

Industrialisation as an 'Objective Process'

Marx's reflections upon 'modern industry' still provide a key starting point for understanding industrialisation. Marx developed this concept to distinguish it from the previous mode of production, which was based on individual craft and skill, the manufacture mode. He shows, however, that manufacturing prepared the groundwork for industrialisation with its highly developed division of labour. An increasing application of novel machinery made it possible to overcome the structural limits of rationalisation that were characteristic of manufacturing, limits that were rooted in the dependency on the individual's craft skills. The integration of machinery into the work process allowed for the emergence of a historically new mode of rationalisation (the industrial rationalisation mode), which finds its leverage point in the tool rather than the worker's activity: 'In manufacture, the revolution in the mode of production begins with the labour-power; in modern industry it begins with the instruments of labour' (Marx, 1887, p. 261).

However, the essential premise for the success of 'modern industry' as a new production mode lay not in the individual machine but the machine *system*. This organisational form for the production process drew, in terms of its origins, on the job specialisation in the 'manufacture period'. However, given that this new form of organisation was implemented using novel machine systems, it marked a qualitative break with the previous period:

> Nevertheless an essential difference at once manifests itself. In manufacture it is the workmen who, with their manual implements, must, either singly or in groups, carry on each particular detail process. If, on the one hand, the workman becomes adapted to the process, on the other, the process was previously made suitable to the workman. This subjective principle of the division of labour no longer exists in production by machinery. Here, the process as a whole is examined objectively, in itself, that is to say, without regard to the question of its execution by human hands, it is analysed into its constituent phases; and the problem, how to execute each detail process, and bind them all into a whole, is solved by the aid of machines, chemistry, &c. But, of course, in this case also, theory must be perfected by accumulated experience on a large scale. (ibid., p. 265)

As Braverman (1974) observed, Marx here overestimated the real state of scientific advancement but nevertheless understood the crucial qualitative change occurring in the passage from manufacture to modern industry: the work process was transformed from a 'subjective' process, based on the individual skill of the craftsman, to an 'objective' process, which was anticipated in thought and materialised in the form of the machine system and which in turn confronted the worker as a 'condition' of the work process. Following this line of thought, the transformation from a 'subjective' to an 'objective' process marked the core of industrialisation, regardless of its actual historical manifestations. Thus, industrialisation can be defined as detaching the production process from the skills and wills of individual workers and transforming it into an objective process by means of scientific methods which shape the practical labour process (see Boes and Kämpf, 2012, pp. 317 sqq.). Just to spell it out, the practical implementation and the design of industrialisation can hardly be described as an 'objective process'; in practice, the bargaining between participating actors and the dynamics of concrete power relationships result in a non-determinate process of social change.

Industrialisation as Rationalisation of Individual Operations

Taylor's (1911) observations concerning 'scientific management', seminal for the discussion of industrialisation both in practice and science (see especially Braverman, 1974), provide another view of industrialisation. Regardless of the enormous empirical variability of Taylorist rationalisation and its concrete implementation in individual companies, three basic principles rest at the core of his concept: (1) the detachment of the immediate work process from the individual workers' skills, (2) the separation between planning and execution and (3) the comprehensive control over the execution of each individual operation. The concept is based on a detailed observation and a scientific analysis of these individual operations in order to generate 'one best way' for executing a particular activity. Crucially, Taylor still linked his understanding of rationalisation and his efforts at objectification to the individual activity and operation of work rather than to the overarching process. Such a deviation from a process-focused concept also explains the dead end that Taylorist strategies confronted once applied to mental work: key elements of intellectual problem-solving are neither entirely planned nor observable from an 'outside', so they remained a black box for Taylorist engineers.

Simply identifying Taylorisation as industrialisation, combined with a failure of Taylorism to rationalise mental work, contributed to the myth – especially in the social sciences – that mental work can principally not be industrialised. Marx's key works on the subject of modern industry, in contrast, open up a new perspective. For the context under consideration here, the growth of mental work can be understood as an element of a progressive societal process of industrialisation (see Hack and Hack, 1985). Furthermore, a concept of industrialisation as developed above that defines industrialisation as a transformation from a subjective to an objective process is not restricted to manual work and traditional manufacturing but can also be applied to mental work. So the question over the conditions and forms for integrating and organising mental activities beyond the individual in an objective process becomes relevant.

Industrialisation and Informatisation

Often overlooked is the circumstance that 'modern industry' not only engendered industrial work as the dominant form of work in society but also provided the basis for a strict separation of manual and mental work, as well as a rapid growth of various forms of mental work. After all, manual work can be transformed into an objective process only with the help of mental work. On one hand, mental work is necessary to collect information and data about the work process and to appropriate the workers' experiences in order to develop an objective process and continuously rationalise this process by using scientific methods. On the other hand, it is mental work that permits the work process to be controlled and monitored beyond the limits of immediate sensual perception at the hands of a supervisor. And information systems, ever growing in complexity, are the result of mental work (cf. Baukrowitz and Boes, 1996). Thus, the industrialisation of manual labour always had an 'underbelly', a complementary growth of the number of jobs for mental workers (cf. e.g. Bahrdt, 1958; Braverman, 1974; Kocka, 1981).

A crucial observation in this context is that the relationship between manual and mental labour is characterised by the fact that these forms of labour reference each other by means of information. Mental workers, employed in specific organisational units (e.g. industrial engineering), conduct the task of planning work processes and translating them into information, which in turn underpin the machine systems, the organisational processes and the targets which eventually confront the manual workers. In this respect, informatisation can be understood as the 'underbelly' of the development of productive forces even for the 'modern industry' of the nineteenth century. From a historical perspective, informatisation is the precondition for the existence of mental work as a distinct form of human work, largely independent of manual work, and for the possibility to organise it rationally.

However, with the rise of the information space, the metaphor of an underbelly is no longer suitable. Today, the material world of machine systems no longer occupies a dominant position; now the sphere of information holds such dominance (see Boes et al., 2014). The central principle of a new type of industrialisation is the dominant position of the information sphere. Processes of industrialisation now predominantly address the information sphere. The information sphere and the digital flow of information and data provide the possibility not only to revolutionise the industrial manufacturing processes but also to industrialise mental work and knowledge work itself, both in Marx's sense and in Taylor's sense, to an unknown extent. The following section will elaborate on the implications for knowledge work, based on empirical cases (see footnote 2).

New Forms of Industrialising Knowledge Work: From the 'Digital Assembly Line' to Cloudworking

With the leap in productive forces engendered by the information space, disruptive change in the world of work centres on so-called knowledge work. The digital information space becomes the core infrastructure for mental activities in the work process and the basis for the reorganisation of work. The changes ushered in by this development are by no means restricted to the loss of certain jobs and the replacement of certain human work activities by 'algorithms' and 'computers' (see Frey and Osborne, 2013). On the contrary, new models of work organisation in the area of knowledge work emerge as a consequence. In practice, the range of these changes extends from traditional white-collar office jobs to the high-skilled tasks of software developers and engineers. In the following section, we try to combine our conceptual reflections about a new type of industrialisation with empirical findings concerning the ongoing change of office work and high-skilled knowledge work.

Process Orientation and Transparency: On the Way to a 'Digital Assembly Line' in the Office?

In the traditional, medium-skilled areas of office work, process orientation and transparency form the basis for new production models. In many companies these departments – from human resources to finances to sales, services and logistics – are consistently digitised, which means that the information space is in fact the space of production. The concrete objects that are worked on in these departments exist in the form of digitised information (as an HR file, an order or a travel expense account), handled and processed by complex information systems (e.g. SAP). An employee, responsible for the organisation and disposition of the international spare parts sales of a mechanical engineering company, provides the graphic statement: 'We only work with figures here.'[3] The consequence is that digital work flows and processes govern the work processes; predetermine the work steps, often in a very detailed manner; and determine the division of work and cooperation with colleagues along the value chain. The digitised work object 'flows' from operation to operation and eventually to the customer, as the metaphor of the digital assembly line suggests. Modern 'ticket systems' continuously assign tasks to individual employees, thus dictating the work rhythm. Individual discretion in work activities becomes smaller and smaller since process steps are inscribed in the IT system's code, rarely permitting any deviation from the preprogramming.

This trend towards standardisation and process orientation has been advanced over recent years primarily for what are called 'Shared Services concepts' (see Boes and Kämpf, 2011). From an 'outside' perspective, internal service functions (e.g. accounting, controlling, human resource services, IT services, etc.), which previously were distributed across one company's sites and locations and which possessed diverse organisational structures according to the unit they belonged to, are now merged, homogenised and concentrated in one single location (see Bergeron, 2003). This location will now supply the whole corporation with uniform services. A closer look shows a common pattern to all these processes: first, work processes are documented in a detailed manner and evaluated; afterwards they are transferred, as processes, into uniform IT systems that face the employees in the form of a rigidly standardised work flow. The more detailed the documentation, the more complete the automation possible in the digital era.[4] Consequently, the new shared services centres are called 'factories' in internal language use – factories that are, in practice, quite often relocated in low-wage countries.

Besides the introduction of shared services, the transfer of lean production methods to indirect areas plays a central role in the attempt to increase the transparency of administrative activities and processes, to standardise and to optimise them, especially in industrial companies (see Boes et al., 2014). Besides the usual methods like 5S workshops, value stream mappings and continuous process optimisation, shop floor management in particular is used to organise the work process. Again, the basis for this lies in the high degree of informatisation of processes and the digitisation of work objects and instruments: the activities are structured and controlled in continuous processes along the flow of information. This permits a very consistent and rapid implementation of 'lean production' concepts. Usually, the employees possess hardly any opportunities to exert influence upon the concrete design of methods while their core work processes are being fundamentally altered.

Simultaneously, the increasing digitisation of processes permits a degree of transparency of work that was previously unknown. Every action within the information space leaves behind a vast amount of data. This data can be recorded, evaluated and compared to one other. In practice, such actions include the movements of a mouse cursor in call centres or the tracking of processing times of 'tickets' in IT support, and even the pulse rate of employees is sometimes recorded and evaluated. Advanced enterprises in particular not only use this data for monitoring employees' work but also attempt to use them consistently for process optimisation. In one case, activities and customer contacts of all sales representatives were recorded live and continually evaluated by big data approaches. The wider goal of these approaches is to identify the 'ideal' process with the highest probability of success.

However, in practice companies go one step further still: the new transparency also allows for new forms of performance control. In one of our cases, the enterprise used the information space, in its capacity as a space for social action, to entirely renew the well-known strategy of 'management by objectives': employees are requested to document their goal achievements daily, with the help of an app. This app, accessible to all employees, shows the performance status and degree of goal achievement of every single employee visibly and transparently for all company employees at all times. As with Twitter, you can even 'follow' selected colleagues to get automatic updates about their every status change. The new transparency no longer hides how communication takes place in the company. Businesses have already started to record what is happening in social media communities to measure and control their employees' social behaviour.

These new production models, following the principles of a digital assembly line and drawing on a new degree of transparency, make us wonder whether they should be understood as contributing to a new degree of Taylorisation (see also Brown et al., 2010, especially the chapter 'Digital Taylorism'). If Taylorisation means detailed observation and measuring of work performance, refinement and a scientific approach to optimise work processes, the digital transformation might be interpreted as paving the way for a 'Taylorism 2.0': 'Taylorism 2.0' because it is not restricted to manual work but also and primarily because it addresses mental activities and even social behaviour. This scenario might call to mind dystopian ideas: Orwell's 'Big Brother', Foucault's 'Panopticon' or the monstrous world of work created by Dave Eggers in his novel 'The Circle'.

Cloudworking and the Future of High-Skilled Knowledge Work

These changes are not restricted to medium-skilled office work. Fundamental changes of work on the basis of the digital transformation also affect high-skilled work. In these types of work, the information space forms the basis of new production models, for example industrialised development processes (see Boes et al., 2014) or new forms of cloudworking (see Boes et al., 2015). This is even more remarkable as public debate often considers precisely these types of work – generally described as 'creative' – to be protected 'islands' in an economy marked by disruptive upheavals. More often than not, there is an assumption that activities that can easily be standardised would be affected while 'creative' ones supposedly remain on the winning side. However, this assumption is worth a closer look. Our empirical findings show that the disruptive powers of the digital transformation are also present in these types of work, as we shall show in our following analysis.

Rapidly growing, software development stands as the pioneering sector for new production models. Here a new organisational paradigm has emerged, based on a combination of agile development methods such as the Daily Scrum and the principles of lean production. This paradigm has entered the software industry across the whole sector and has also transferred to traditional engineering work, where it finds increasing use (see Boes et al., 2014). Contrary to the conventional 'waterfall model', the time range has changed from several-year-long development cycles to short cycles ('sprints') of two to four weeks. Within these short cycles, the development of 'usable software' is scheduled and then repeated iteratively. Development departments as large as several thousand developers are 'clocked' according to one clock pulse, cooperating synchronously in a collective work process. In order to make this possible, the software is partitioned into single work packages and tasks that are documented in what is called a 'backlog', self-organised by development teams as a kind of working memory. This new production model is based in the digital information space, where the work packages of all teams are permanently (automatically) tested within complex development environments and continuously brought together in one system. And above that, by means of an informatised backlog, the work status of every team is made transparent for the whole organisation. As a complementary feature, regular team meetings (e.g. the Daily Scrum) provide transparency within the team and allow for collectivisation of team knowledge. In practice, many variations of this new production mode are apparent: some forms highly rely on self-organisation and team empowerment; other forms dispense with any idea of worker empowerment, with teams simply 'executing' the backlog tasks, developing software, as a developer put it, 'on the assembly line'.

The new forms of cloudworking and crowdsourcing, that are currently developing into an influential model for changes in knowledge work, in contrast, rarely permit much discretion for teams (see Boes et al., 2015). Although we are used to new commodity platforms such as eBay and others, we are now confronted with new marketplaces for workers, marketplaces that are emerging on the Internet (see Leimeister and Zogaj, 2013; Benner, 2015). It is remarkable that the information space in these marketplaces is consistently used as a new 'space of production' (Boes et al., 2015). The starting point of this concept is found in many businesses' desire (inspired by the experiences of the open source movement and the ideas of 'open innovation' (Chesbrough, 2003; Von Hippel, 2005)) to exploit Internet communities' manifold activities for their value creation processes (Boes et al., 2015). Following this line of thought to its conclusion, the new model no longer relies exclusively on employees but, flexibly, tries to make use of a worldwide workforce without work contracts or fixed offices, via the 'cloud', according to transitory requirements.

One of the companies in our study runs, with the help of 1000 employees, a crowd platform with no less than 900,000 IT developers. These developers fulfil tasks for very diverse customers, not only simple or one-time tasks but also development tasks that require a high degree of skill. They form a crowd that seems to be unorganised and arbitrary but is, in reality, shaped and kept together by means of a complex organisational model. Whereas previously the stable membership of a company and the social environment of a shared workplace marked the crucial factors by which commitment and attachment were engendered, now competition is the dominant principle. All orders are advertised in form of a competition, and only the two best-rated submissions are remunerated. This kind of 'gamification', with the look and feel of a computer game where the goal is the next level, becomes the basis of the organisation. This principle is used not only for incentivisation schemes, career options and managing individual reputation but also for training organised as 'battles'. In order to cope with complex development projects in such a division of labour, a consistent decomposition into 'atomised work packages' and an industrialisation of development work is practised. The motto is, 'If we can build a brick, we can build a house, and then we can build a city.'

This example shows that the new forms of work cannot be reduced to merely moving work into a crowd setting. Essentially, this is not simply a new method of outsourcing but the establishment of a new production model, permitting businesses to permanently shift and readjust their boundaries, as well as the scope of how they create value within the information space (Boes et al., 2015). This suggests consequences for the crowdsourcees who find themselves outside the scope of labour legislation (and, instead, within the scope of civil law). However, the employees within the company are also affected by the disruptive dynamics of such developments. This may imply entirely new forms of work organisation; a scenario within which even highly skilled workers are exchangeable in the context of transparent and industrialised work processes; and a radicalised 'system of permanent probation' (Boes and Bultemeier, 2008), in which the workers 'inside' and 'outside' of the system are pitted against each other.

Disruptive Change in Knowledge Work: The World of Work at a Crossroads

The digital transformation has led not only to a fundamental upheaval in manufacturing work but also to a new mode of industrialisation. The starting point of this new mode is no longer found in traditional machine systems. Rather, the informational sphere enters the stage. It becomes the strategic centre for a new kind of industrialisation, affecting the whole value chain, the digital flow of information, and data become the dominant reference for work and organisation. On this basis, industrial manufacturing processes can be interlinked to a new extent via the Internet of Things, and white-collar work becomes amenable to industrialisation in the ways it is intersected by information, often in combination with organisational forms in the workplace, such as lean production concepts and/or agile methods. At the same time, the digital information space emerges as a new space where knowledge work can be rethought, reconceptualised and restructured.

Taking this as a starting point, companies, in their current reorganisation, pursue the goal of systematically and rationally organising mental work so that it can be planned out and the specific subjective performances of mental workers rendered reproducible. Analogous to the industrialisation of manual work during the nineteenth century, mental activities are structured in an objective process, and the work processes in the office are organised in ways that make them independent from the individual skills of a single worker. Processes in digital information systems might assume the character of a 'modern assembly line' – however, this development is not an automatic process. The establishment and design of the new type of industrialisation in the office are not merely a 'technological' matter but one of social practice which shapes new forms of work organisation. Currently, two variations can be identified as distinct manifestations of this new type of industrialisation, apparent in different types of mental work.

1. In medium-skilled administrative jobs, a kind of 'digital Taylorisation' seems to forge ahead, following the principles of the assembly line. IT-based ticket systems, shared services centres and shop floor management ensure a consistent process orientation, at the same time

introducing increased transparency in the office. It thus becomes possible – quite in Taylor's original sense – to establish exact monitoring, measurement and a data-based evaluation for administrative white-collar work in order to refine it scientifically. This in turn allows for process optimisation and allows organisations to generalise different activities in a standardised, uniform 'single best way'.

2. In high-skilled work such as engineering or particularly in software development, entirely new production models have emerged which are based on a consistent decomposition of work packages and, again, on the principle of transparency. They draw on a combination of lean and agile methods as well as the use of new forms of cloudworking and crowdsourcing. The digital information space provides the foundation for these new production models: here, processes are kept together along the 'flow of information', and data and information about the work status of the whole organisation are provided in real time. This – sometimes combined with meetings in the workplace – leads to a new quality of transparency within the team and can collectivise team knowledge.

The digital transformation thus provides the impulse for fundamental changes and upheavals in work and production models in the realm of knowledge work. The search for a new mode of industrialisation and for the opening and exploitation of new productivity and rationalisation potential is beginning to take shape. In current practice, organisations pioneer this new mode by turning away from traditional 'expert modes' (see Boes et al., 2014, 2016a) in indirect areas: employees in the office world increasingly become part of a timed value chain where individual knowledge silos give way to a growing transparency and process orientation, not only in administrative jobs but also in software development and even in R&D. The autonomy of employees, which was a very strong feature, particularly of high-skilled, white-collar jobs, is shrinking ever further.

This disruptive change to knowledge work has far-reaching consequences for society as a whole, ranging from the experience of a world of work characterised by burn-out (Kämpf, 2015) to new insecurities and an erosion of middle-class positions within companies (see Boes et al., 2016a). The examples outlined and analysed above show that, in practice, we are reaching a crossroads. One path would be to make use of the opportunities for a new space for social action in order to support the empowerment of employees, interlinking knowledge resources and increases in mental productive forces. The other one would lead towards a negative scenario: with new production models, 'digital assembly lines', a control panopticon of data and a new extent of exchangeability even for high-skilled employees looming ahead. It is necessary to make decisions over which path to take, and a conscious and purposeful social and political shaping of the ensuing social change is vital. Naive technological reductionism will not help us, since the digital transformation is unlikely to be successful without the active participation of people. What we need here is a general guiding principle for society to assign the central role to people and their part in the digital transformation. A good starting point may be to make use of the dynamics of the leap in productive forces for a new humanisation of work (see Boes et al., 2016b).

Notes

1 'Knowledge work' is a much-used concept indicating, sensu lato, activities and areas of activity within the realm of work that are predominantly devoted to the generation of knowledge. There are several approaches to defining this term, but up to now a generally accepted definition has not been established. For instance, Drucker (1999) refers to the differentiation between 'manual-worker productivity' and 'knowledge-worker productivity', thus contributing to a first approximation. Mosco and McKercher (2007) present an overview of several approaches. These range from a narrow definition that includes exclusively 'creative labour' to wider definitions that include also the handling and distribution of information, to broad approaches which include 'all workers involved in the chain of producing and distributing knowledge products'. In our perspective, knowledge work encompasses mental work activities that require different levels of skills. Thus, under the label of knowledge work, we look at and include both routine activities and high-skilled development work, which permits us to open up productive insights into parallel developments.

2 Our empirical basis is formed by the research projects 'Wing – Designing Knowledge Work Sustainably in the Company of the Future' (www.wing-projekt.de, funded by the German Federal Ministry of Labour and Social Affairs) and 'Digit-DL – Digital Service in Modern Value-Added Systems' (www.digit-dl-projekt.de, funded by the German Federal Ministry of Education and Research). Over the past year alone, we were able to conduct around 200 expert interviews and intensive interviews with experts, managers and employees in Germany and in Silicon Valley.

3 This quotation is taken from our intensive interviews conducted in the course of the research projects named above (footnote 2). The same is true for the following quotations without in-text citations.

4 Meanwhile, this applies to large parts of human resources departments. They tend to offer more and more 'self services' to employees in the intranet, whereas personal support and advice are seldom available.

REFERENCES

Altmann, N., M. Deiß, V. Döhl and D. Sauer (1986) 'Ein "Neuer Rationalisierungstyp" – neue Anforderungen an die Industriesoziologie', *Soziale Welt*, 37, 2–3, 191–206.

Baethge, M. and H. Oberbeck (1986) *Zukunft der Angestellten. Neue Technologien und berufliche Perspektiven in Büro und Verwaltung* (Frankfurt am Main: Campus).

Bahrdt, H. (1958) *Industriebürokratie – Versuch einer Soziologie des industrialisierten Bürobetriebes und seiner Angestellten* (Stuttgart: Enke).

Baukrowitz, A. and A. Boes (1996) 'Arbeit in der "Informationsgesellschaft" – Einige grundsätzliche Überlegungen aus einer (fast schon) ungewohnten Perspektive', in R. Schmiede (ed.), *Virtuelle Arbeitswelten – Arbeit, Produktion und Subjekt in der 'Informationsgesellschaft'* (Berlin: sigma), pp. 129–58.

Benner, C. (ed.) (2015) *Crowdwork – zurück in die Zukunft? Perspektiven digitaler Arbeit* (Frankfurt am Main: Bund Verlag).

Bergeron, B. (2003) *Essentials of Shared Services* (Hoboken, New Jersey).

Boes, A. (1996) 'Formierung und Emanzipation – Zur Dialektik der Arbeit in der "Informationsgesellschaft"', in R. Schmiede (ed.), *Virtuelle Arbeitswelten – Arbeit, Produktion und Subjekt in der "Informationsgesellschaft"* (Berlin: sigma), pp. 159–78.

Boes, A. (2004) 'Offshoring in der IT-Industrie – Strategien der Internationalisierung und Auslagerung im Bereich Software und IT-Dienstleistungen', in A. Boes and M. Schwemmle (eds), *Herausforderung Offshoring – Internationalisierung und Auslagerung von IT-Dienstleistungen* (Düsseldorf: Hans-Böckler-Stiftung), pp. 9–140.

Boes, A. (2005) 'Informatisierung', in SOFI, IAB, ISF München and INIFES (eds), *Berichterstattung zur sozioökonomischen Entwicklung in Deutschland – Arbeits- und Lebensweisen. Erster Bericht* (Wiesbaden: Springer), pp. 211–44.

Boes, A. and A. Bultemeier (2008) 'Informatisierung – Unsicherheit – Kontrolle', in K. Dröge, K. Marrs and W. Menz (eds), *Die Rückkehr der Leistungsfrage. Leistung in Arbeit, Unternehmen und Gesellschaft* (Berlin: sigma), pp. 59–91.

Boes, A. and T. Kämpf (2011) *Global verteilte Kopfarbeit. Offshoring und der Wandel der Arbeitsbeziehungen* (Berlin: sigma).

Boes, A. and T. Kämpf (2012) 'Informatisierung als Produktivkraft: Der informa- tisierte Produktionsmodus als Basis einer neuen Phase des Kapitalismus', in K. Dörre, D. Sauer and V. Wittke (eds), *Kapitalismustheorie und Arbeit* (Frankfurt am Main and New York: Campus), pp. 316–35.

▶

Boes, A., T. Kämpf, T. Lühr and K. Marrs (2014) 'Kopfarbeit in der moder-nen Arbeitswelt: Auf dem Weg zu einer "Industrialisierung neuen Typs"', in J. Sydow, D. Sadowski and P. Conrad (eds), *Arbeit – eine Neubestimmung* (Wiesbaden: Springer), pp. 33–62.

Boes, A., T. Kämpf, B. Langes and T. Lühr (2015) 'Landnahme im Informationsraum. Neukonstituierung gesellschaftlicher Arbeit in der "digitalen Gesellschaft"', *WSI Mitteilungen*, 67, 2, 77–85.

Boes, A., T. Kämpf and T. Lühr (2016a) 'Neue Mittelschichten unter Druck. Die Erosion des "Expertenmodus" als Organisationsform hochqualifizierter Kopfarbeit', in T. Haipeter (ed.), *Angestellte Revisited. Arbeit, Interessen und Herausforderungen für Interessenvertretungen* (Wiesbaden: Springer), pp. 131–55.

Boes, A., A. Bultemeier, T. Kämpf and T. Lühr (2016b) 'Arbeitswelt der Zukunft – zwischen "digitalem Fließband" und neuer Humanisierung. Neue Herausforderungen für eine nachhaltige Gestaltung von Wissensarbeit', in *Jahrbuch Gute Arbeit 2016* (Berlin: Verdi/IG Metall).

Braverman, H. (1974) *Labor and Monopoly Capital: The Degradation of Work in the Twentieth Century* (New York: Monthly Review Press).

Brown, P., H. Lauder and D. Ashton (2010) *The Global Auction: The Broken Promises of Education, Jobs, and Incomes* (Oxford: Oxford University Press).

Chesbrough, H. W. (2003) *Open Innovation. The New Imperative for Creating and Profiting from Technology* (Boston, MA: Harvard Business Review Press).

Dolata, U. and J.-F. Schrape (2013) *Zwischen Individuum und Organisation. Neue kollektive Akteure und Handlungskonstellationen im Internet*, Stuttgarter Beiträge zur Organisations- und Innovationsforschung (SOI), Discussion Paper 2013–02 (Stuttgart: Universität Stuttgart).

Drucker, P. F. (1999) 'Knowledge-worker Productivity: The Biggest Challenge', *California Management Review*, 40, 2, 79–92.

Frey, C. B. and M. Osborne (2013) *The Future of Employment. How Susceptible are Jobs to Computerisation?*, http://www.oxfordmartin.ox.ac.uk/downloads/academic/ The_Future_of_Employment.pdf, date accessed 23 April 2015.

Greenfield, J. and K. Short (2006) *Software Factories. Moderne Software-Architekturen mit SOA, MDA, Patterns und agilen Methoden* (Bonn: Redline).

Hack, L. and I. Hack (1985) *Die Wirklichkeit, die Wissen schafft – Zum wechselsei-tigen Begründungsverhältnis von 'Verwissenschaftlichung der Industrie' und 'Industrialisierung der Wissenschaft'* (Frankfurt am Main: Campus).

Hirsch-Kreinsen, H. (2016) 'Zum Verhältnis von Arbeit und Technik bei Industrie 4.0', *Aus Politik und Zeitgeschichte*, 66, 18–19, 10–7.

Holman, D., R. Batt and U. Holtgrewe (2007) *The Global Call Center Report: International Perspectives on Management and Employment. A Report of the Global Call Centre Research Network*. http://www.ilr.cornell.edu/globalcallcenter/ upload/GCC-Intl-Rept-UK-Version.pdf, date accessed 13 February 2013.

Holtgrewe, U., C. Kerst and K. Shire (eds) (2002) *Re-organising Service Work in Europe: Call Centres in Germany and Britain* (Aldershot: Ashgate).

▶

Janßen, R. (2005) 'Die Psychologie des Entwicklers', *Informatik Spektrum*, 28, 4, 284–6.

Jeidels, O. (1907) *Die Methoden der Arbeiterentlohnung in der rheinisch-westfälischen Eisenindustrie* (Berlin: Simion).

Kämpf, T. (2015) 'Ausgebrannte Arbeitswelt – Wie erleben Beschäftigte neue Formen von Belastung in modernen Feldern der Wissensarbeit?', *Berliner Journal für Soziologie*, 25, 1–2, 133–59.

Kocka, J. (1969) *Unternehmensverwaltung und Angestelltenschaft am Beispiel Siemens 1874–1914. Zum Verhältnis von Kapitalismus und Bürokratie in der deutschen Industrialisierung* (Stuttgart: Klett).

Kocka, J. (1981) *Angestellte im europäischen Vergleich – Die Herausbildung angestellter Mittelschichten seit dem späten 19. Jahrhundert* (Göttingen: Beck).

Leimeister, J. M. and S. Zogaj (2013) *Neue Arbeitsorganisation durch Crowdsourcing. Eine Literaturstudie*, HBS-Arbeitspapier Nr. 287 (Düsseldorf: Hans-Böckler-Stiftung).

Marx, K. (1887) *Capital. A Critique of Political Economy. Vol. 1: The Process of Production of Capital*. Translated by Samuel Moore and Edward Aveling, edited by Frederick Engels (Moscow: Progress Publishers). https://www.marxists.org/archive/marx/works/download/pdf/Capital-Volume-I.pdf.

Matuschek, I., K. Arnold and G. Voß (2007) *Subjektivierte Taylorisierung. Organisation und Praxis medienvermittelter Dienstleistungsarbeit* (München: Hampp).

Mosco, V. and C. McKercher (2007) 'Introduction: Theorizing Knowledge Labor and the Information Society', in C. McKercher and V. Mosco (eds), *Knowledge Workers in the Information Society* (Lanham, MD: Rowman), pp. vii–xxiv.

Sombart, W. (1928) *Der moderne Kapitalismus. Historisch-systematische Darstellung des gesamteuropäischen Wirtschaftslebens von seinen Anfängen bis zur Gegenwart* (München: Duncker & Humblot).

Speek, J. (2008) 'Die Industrialisierung der Kreditbearbeitung', in C. Burger and J. U. Hagen (eds), *Strukturumbruch in der Finanzdienstleistungsindustrie. Prozessänderungen als Chance für neue Strategien und Konzepte in Banken* (Wiesbaden: Springer), pp. 45–54.

Streckeisen, P. (2008) 'Die entzauberte "Wissensarbeit", oder wie die Fabrik ins Labor eindringt', *Schweizerische Zeitschrift für Soziologie*, 34, 1, 115–29.

Stobbe, A. (2006) 'Informatisierung in der Finanzdienstleistungsbranche. Von der Hollerith-Maschine zum Straight Through Processing', in A. Baukrowitz, T. Berker, A. Boes, S. Pfeiffer, R. Schmiede and M. Will (eds), *Informatisierung der Arbeit – Gesellschaft im Umbruch* (Berlin: sigma), pp. 53–67.

Taylor, F. W. (1911) *The Principles of Scientific Management* (London: Harper & Brothers).

Von Hippel, E. (2005) *Democratizing Innovation* (Boston, MA, and London: MIT Press).

Will-Zocholl, M. (2011) *Wissensarbeit in der Automobilindustrie. Topologie der Reorganisation von Ingenieursarbeit in der globalen Produktentwicklung* (Berlin: sigma).

The Digital Workplace (Worker) – Gendered, Self-Exploitative and Vulnerable?

Women, Work and Technology: Examining the Under-Representation of Women in ICT

Gavin Maclean, Abigail Marks and Shiona Chillas

Introduction

The absence of women working in the information and communication sector is argued to be costing the European economy 9 billion euros a year in lost revenue (EC, 2013). The EC's Report on Women active in the information and communications technology (ICT) sector observed that for every 1000 women in the EU with a degree, only 29 specialise in an ICT-related subject (as compared to 95 for men) and only 0.4 per cent will work in the ICT sector. Moreover, women are more likely to leave the sector mid-career and struggle to reach senior positions. The report noted that only 19.2 per cent of ICT workers have a female superior, whereas in non-ICT work, 45.2 per cent of workers stated that there was a woman senior to them within their organisation.

Overall, just under one quarter (23 per cent) of tech industry workers in 2015 were female, compared to nearly half (47 per cent) of all workers at that time. Interestingly, female representation was slightly higher within tech manufacturing businesses (27 per cent) than in tech services firms (22 per cent), though the most even balance between male/female workers was recorded for companies providing data services, in which 51 per cent of the workforce was female (Tech Partnership, 2016).

While there are an increasing number of initiatives encouraging women to enter the workplace, we argue that the lack of representation of women in the ICT sector cannot solely be remedied by interventions at the point of entry into the labour market or during employment. Women's under-representation in ICT is emblematic of wider structural inequalities, and the place of women cannot be ignored in debates on the digitalised workplace assessed in this volume.

Even though the transformative capacity of technologies within labour process debates are viewed as materially important – and empirical studies are undeniably useful to predict the future of work – analysis of digitalisation is incomplete without paying attention to gender and the potential for technology to reinforce existing patterns of social reproduction (Bourdieu, 2001). Unlike other chapters in this collection, however, the current chapter is not going to present an empirical account of gender in the digital workplace. There are already numerous papers on women's exclusion from digital work which we will address later on in this chapter; however, we believe that in order to fully comprehend why women are no further integrated into the digital labour force than they were 20 years ago, it is necessary to consider the interaction between women and technology from school and beyond – expanding the scope of investigation. In order to do so, we will look at women's relationships with the social and technological aspects of digital work, broadly using Bourdieu's work on capitals to understand the social (e.g. Bourdieu, 1986) and developing the embryonic work on the relationship between affordances and work (e.g. MacKenzie et al., 2015). We begin the chapter by identifying where and why ICT work has become gendered, followed by an examination of remedies in the workplace and sections using affordances and capitals as fresh lenses through which to understand the problem. In the concluding section, we reflect on the implications of the study.

Gender, Work and Technology – An Overview

The intersection of gender, work and technology is at the heart of an evaluation of digital workplaces. Yet, whichever way each of these component parts is addressed, conceptually or empirically, women do not fare well (Gherardi, 2003). Work is gendered and even more so when it is technical work (Woodfield, 2000). More generally, women tend to be concentrated in lower-skilled work, and this imbalance is amplified in technical work (Grey and Healy, 2004), with extreme gender pay gaps at even the higher echelons of knowledge work (Truss et al., 2012). In the pursuit of theorising technology and work, gender has either been ignored or rendered marginal; in effect, gender has only become an issue where research subjects are female, subtly reinforcing the gendered nature of work, skills and society (Wacjman, 2000).

According to Wilson, in the domain of technology, 'continued male dominance is due in large measure to the enduring symbolic association of masculinity and technology, cultural images and representations of technology converging the prevailing images of masculinity and power' (2004, p. 128). There are parallels between the growth and development of technology and in gender relations that serve to reproduce unequal power structures to the detriment of women (Cockburn, 1999).

Computer technology, specifically, was not always gendered. In its infancy in the 1960s, large numbers of women entered the emerging profession in the United States, but since the 1980s there has been a dramatic decline in numbers working in the field and in those entering computing science degrees in the United States and in Europe (Misa, 2010). Different explanations, and perhaps justifications, emerge in analysing the relationship between computer technology and gender. In the 1980s, Beirne and Ramsay drew attention to the potential impact of the introduction of computer technology to the office, warning against a gender-blind analysis (1988, p. 199). Computing reconfigured office work quite significantly, illustrated in tracing the gender patterns of work in the computerising of data processing. Haigh (2010, p. 66) notes that computing is not a single type of work, encompassing 'hugely diverse jobs across many industries', each with its own trajectory and gender dynamics. As computing technology has advanced, however, men have selectively colonised occupations that have in turn become better paid and regarded as more highly skilled (Haigh, 2010). The history of the typewriter also illustrates the changing connotations of technological artefacts; at different points in history the typewriter has been seen as 'the instrument of the elite and the poor, a technology suitable mainly for men or mainly for women' (Sterne, 2003, p. 383)

In addition to shifting patterns of gendered work allocation and the connotations associated with technology, Ornella (2013) identifies that computing became constructed as masculine, as a result of professionalisation strategies. Professions are archetypally patriarchal, incorporating long-standing and enduring closure mechanisms that have traditionally served to exclude women from access to resources such as skills, credentials or technical competence (Witz, 1992). Professions are also said to be 'political constructs', not based on arbitrary measurements of the status of certain types of work (Ashcraft, 2009). Where women challenge the closure mechanisms of professions by, for example, achieving the required credentials for entry, closure strategies alter by, for example, operating to deny access to higher-level positions (Collins, 1979). The rising numbers of women in professions is seen by (male) members of the profession as a problem to be managed.

It is perhaps no coincidence that software engineering, for example, has held on to a connection with engineering that reaches back into a history of engineering that is connected to hard physical solutions, as Cockburn states 'making energy work for you' (1999, p. 128). Engineering has, according to Cockburn, performed 'a conceptual somersault' as it has developed. To begin with the hard, physical aspects of the work made it masculine but also posed problems in trying to relate to the 'soft' cerebral elements of the work that made the work more highly valued. An altered dichotomy was then enacted in terms of associating professional engineering with rationality – another masculine trait – as opposed to femininity that is connected to the irrational and the body (Cockburn, 1999). Cech (2014), for example, in examining perceptions of professional identity in engineering, finds that the traits of technological leadership and problem-solving, identified as masculine – and stronger in the self-perceptions of men – are positively related to intention to persist in the engineering profession. If women do enter engineering, they are swiftly excluded by colleagues, and management's poor assessment of their abilities, so they frequently leave the profession (Baldry et al., 2007). The problem of gender becomes distanced from the labour process and constructed instead around power relations and the preservation of male dominance.

Enduring structural conditions of masculine domination are thus enacted in different ways, using a variety of justifications, a point that will be returned to below in relation to Bourdieu. Problems associated with gender also persist throughout the supply and value chains in the technological sphere:

> Ascribing gender to technology thus happens in all the various stages of creating technology: from design to production processes, from marketing to the way users decide to adopt and integrate appliances into their daily lives. (Ornella, 2013, p. 201)

When seeking explanations for women's under-representation in ICT work, debates focus on choice and ability, the former arguing that women are simply not interested in computers or computer science and the latter that women do not possess the skills to work in the sector (Grey and Healy, 2004). Popular culture also appears to support the 'computer geek' image of a ponytailed male figure isolated in his bedroom playing war games, subsequently entering the world of software design. The typical Internet user is also said to be a young, white, educated male (Wacjman, 2006). The broad claim being that cultural representations of work serve to reinforce the gendered division of labour, shaping ideas of the value of work, who does that work and what they do in that work (Ashcraft, 2009). The ability argument seems to relate to a general stereotyping of men as being more likely to possess hard, technical skills and women as displaying soft skills and attributes such as empathy, communication and caring with consequent implications for the types of work suited to each gender. Indeed, the gendered division of labour is usually presented as based on natural aptitudes of men and women (Haigh, 2010). Such an essentialist and deterministic view of capabilities is heavily criticised, particularly in studies of gender and work (Adam et al., 2001).

Moreover, it has been shown that skills required in modern ICT work are highly gendered: while IT consultants may need relationship-building and technical skills, the former are seen as feminine (and therefore undervalued when displayed by women). However, when men display these same 'feminine' skills, they are rewarded (Woodfield, 2000). Joshi and Kuhn (2007) examined perceptions of skills required by IT consultants, finding that the picture was more mixed than 'masculine only' skills. While Joshi and Kuhn found that technical and leadership skills (which they identify as masculine) are necessary at all levels in IT, they do not necessarily guarantee success. Interestingly, these researchers also find that women are more likely to emphasise masculine skills – in describing a top performer – perhaps because they are under pressure to exhibit these skills (2007). Both men and women deny the complexity of skills such as building customer relationships, which requires emotion management, and these types of skills are consequently devalued, even though they are required (Kelan, 2008). This means that it is not only the type of skills that is gendered but also who displays them that matters: if a man displays excellent communication skills, he is rewarded, but that same level of skill displayed by a woman is expected and goes unrewarded.

A further explanation of the gender division in technological work has been well discussed in other work and centres on the demands of work in ICT; a long-hours culture, lack of flexible work opportunities and the constant need to upgrade skills mean that women with children cannot comply with such demands (Kelan, 2008; Guerrier et al., 2009). These are issues that will be touched upon later on in this chapter.

The Status of Digital Work

While this chapter has begun to establish the gendered nature of work, work allocation and skills, if women's under-representation in ICT were merely a result of unfair employment practices and overt discrimination, it would easily be rectified with recourse to employment legislation. However, the situation is more complex, emerging from a broader societal gender imbalance. The way in which skills are valued and women socialised is a significant barrier to entry and to success for the few who do manage to secure work in technical occupations.

For example, informal recruitment practices dominate in some sectors of the economy, which have been shown to disadvantage women (Gill, 2002). Formal practices that try to remove gender discrimination, and predominantly employed in public sector organisations which continue to have marginally higher female employment rates, are bypassed within informal recruitment practices. These practices are common in professional settings where social networks operate to the exclusion of women both at entry level and once employed (Ashcraft, 2009).

Many of the ostensibly 'flexible' work practices, designed to facilitate female participation in the workforce, actually operate against women. For example, in games manufacture, 'crunch' working practices have been observed to severely disadvantage women (Consalvo, 2008). When hard deadlines approach, workers are required to engage in long periods of unwaged overtime to ensure that products meet their launch dates. The continued reliance on women in childcare arrangements means that such work arrangements represent a further barrier to women's work in the sector. Similarly, 'bulimic' working lives (Gill and Pratt, 2008) within project-based industries such as IT and the wider 'creative industries', where periods of unemployment are filled with intense periods of project work tend to operate against people with caring responsibilities – frequently women. Such working arrangements leave women unprotected and excluded from social protections – such as maternity leave – and are often enforced by HR managers who are themselves women (Guerrier et al., 2009), and these arrangements are so entrenched that women begin to see such discriminatory practices as 'normal' in their sphere of work (Rhoton, 2011).

The explanations for the lack of representation described so far either neglect or overemphasise the structural differences in male-dominated occupations: women do not exclude themselves; instead, the closed and masculine norms and behaviours apparent in such occupations are barriers to entry (Guerrier et al., 2009). On the other hand, there are sufficient numbers of women interested in IT to counter an entirely successful closure strategy. Promoting a gender-neutral image in which skill and merit determine success is learned through professional socialisation. Moreover, gendered socialisation normalises gender bias, and women begin to see masculine practices as more professional than feminine practices (Rhoton, 2011).

The rest of this chapter will discuss two theoretical approaches to discussing the lack of women within the ICT sector. First, the chapter will consider the reasons why, before even entering the labour market, young girls and women are potentially alienated from technology. This 'affordances' approach looks at the way in which technology is designed and the manner in which people interact and engage with technology. The chapter will then consider the work of Pierre Bourdieu to explain the levels of sexism, misogyny and devaluation of women's work within the ICT sector. Because technology is a male-dominated industry, Bourdieu's work offers an approach which allows us to conceptualise women's skills in the industry as susceptible to dismissal on the basis of their perceived gender.

Technology, Education and Affordances

I was sitting in a café, which provides four iPads with preloaded games for the entertainment of child guests. However, when looking around there were six boys under the age of about seven playing with the tablets and only one girl, who was a little older, and who seemed to be responsible for her younger brother. Taking a further look around the room there were a group of girls sitting round a table making bracelets out of beads and showing no interest at all in the iPads. This is not a scientific study, but as a parent of a boy, I know that it is not a unique situation, and on many occasions the technology appeals to boys in a way that is does not seem to appeal to young girls (Abigail Marks).

Although ICT continues to be increasingly part of everyday life – and technology is included in educational activities from preschool years – as stated in previous sections, women are turning away from ICT work rather than moving towards it. What is it about technology frequently fails to appeal to women and girls? While there is a wealth of literature, described previously, examining why adult women fail to engage with ICT work, it is important to examine what is alienating younger girls from studying ICT.

Information systems researchers argue that teachers' beliefs and attitudes about appropriate behaviours and roles for boys and girls, in addition to their attitudes and beliefs about technology, can subtly influence girls not to study ICT (Barker and Aspray, 2006, p. 20). There are also some potentially dangerous arguments about the reasons that girls are alienated from studying ICT subjects. Trusty et al. (2000) argues that roles and stereotypes are learned in the home, at school and through the media, and they are a primary reason for the rejection of certain occupations.

If we look at the example of the children in the café with iPads, it would be a little simplistic to assume that the girls were necessarily discouraged from using the technology by parents and educators – whereas the boys were encouraged to feel more comfortable with the technology. For one, there were some boys as young as four in the grouping, and were thus, unlikely to have been subject to extensive education in technology. The iPads had been preloaded with a number of games, and a superficial assessment would suggest that there were many activities that should appeal to girls.

Academic arguments that go beyond simple gender stereotyping during the education process suggest that the individualistic nature of technology does not appeal to a more feminine orientation (Diekman et al., 2011). Paralleling this argument, an interview with a primary school teacher turned software development manager for Hewlett Packard, as part of a project on ICT work and skills that the authors of the chapter were involved with, stated that

> there's that classic phrase: 'when kids go to school they power down'. I think it's right. I don't think they're harnessing the technology. I don't think we're using all the exciting stuff like iPods and iPads and all the new stuff you know in an appropriate way for girls in education.

Another participant in the same project, who now works as a director for GlaxoSmithKline – who had also started her career as a primary school educator – argued that there was something about the ways that computers are designed that does not appeal to girls and therefore alienates them from an interest in technology from a very young age. This is unsurprising as the majority of digital technology is designed by men, and arguably is therefore designed for men.

The debate around 'affordances' (Hutchby, 2001; Stoffregen, 2003; Bloomfield et al., 2010; Volkoff and Strong, 2013; MacKenze et al., 2015) offers a potentially useful avenue for understanding what it is about technology that may not appeal to younger women. The affordances perspective views technological artefacts not in terms of inherent properties, or in terms of their social constructed nature, but rather in terms of the opportunities they afford social agents who interact with them (Hutchby, 2001). Hutchby (2001) uses the concept of affordances to demonstrate that technology not only enables but also constrains the ways in which individuals can use it. The classic example used to explain the affordances offered by an artefact is the fallen log that presents the affordance to sit, to those who can realise this opportunity. This affordance would be open to most people (Volkoff and Strong, 2013), but it may or may not be realised. Therefore, in addition to the capability to actualise the affordance offered by an artefact, it is argued that there also has to be an agent who has the intention or goal or actualising the affordance (Stoffregen, 2003).

If technology is designed by men for men, it is likely to present insufficient affordances to women or girls. Wajcman (2006) argues that 'technofeminism characterises the relationship between gender and technology as one of mutual shaping, in which technology is both a source and a consequence of gender relations' (p. 781). Because men design the technology – in a manner that they have an affinity with – in all likelihood they subliminally develop it to possess male-centred affordances. Hence, gender relations are materialised and embedded in digital technology, and masculine and feminine characteristics become embedded in machines. The redevelopment and reconsideration of technology is therefore essential and central to the further renegotiation of gender power relations and advancement of gender equality within society.

Computers or other forms of digital technology provide opportunities and enablements for men, yet are frequently alien to women and indeed younger girls as they are not designed with them in mind. The world of the physical relationship between technology and women has not progressed. MacKenzie et al. (2015) wrote about the relationship that telecommunication's engineers of the 1950s, 1960s, 1970s and 1980s had with the electromechanical exchange systems with which they worked. These engineers worked in a highly masculine environment, and their relationship with the technology (designed and operated by men) which was central to their work formed a key element of their occupational identity. None of this has changed.

As Wacjman (2006, p. 781) argues (like the electromechanical exchange systems), computers occupy a special place in workplace identity, 'existing as they do on the border between the inanimate and the living, an extension of the self and part of the external world'. It is the technology itself that is complicit in defining women's identities and further alienating them from the successful employment within the digital economy. Women's absence from the technology cannot be overcome solely by improved socialisation and equal opportunities policies. Women have to become central to the design process of common technologies that younger women and primary-school-aged children engage with in order to present them with technology that offers them the same interests and affordances as their male counterparts.

Looking at research on education and technology, Hanor (1998) examines girls' interactions with computers. One of the areas that she focuses on is the imaginative, creative and aesthetic opportunities that computers afford and how such opportunities impact on the learning experience. While we are not making exclusive arguments about girls, Hanor (1998) did find that for school-aged girls' use of computers, there was a priority placed on any potential for social engagement – a finding that has been also supported by Brown et al. (2015) when examining women's absence in STEM careers.

As well as the communicative process, girls also favoured programmes with the opportunity for adaption and self-initiation – Hanor (p. 67) describes this as 'choices such as color, shapes, tools, clip art, and animated sequences found within art or graphics applications and hypermedia software applications such as Hyperstudio'. Such preferences – offering creative affordances – should indicate an interest in the programming side of computing.

However, research has also found that girls' experiences of computing instruction at school has not always been positive. Heo and Myrick (2009) argued that girls, when using computers, are frequently disparaged by male classmates and have been seen to be physically blocked by the boys from using IT facilities. It was also found that girls like to spend more time on their computing activities but fail to achieve rewarded for such activities. Girls also appreciate time for free exploration with the technology, which is often not accommodated within a school environment (Hanor, 1998).

Early years education providers need to become aware of the affordances that computers can offer both girls and boys as well as how successful engagement with technology at school can contribute to future career choices.

Bourdieu, Women and Digital Work

The emphasis of the previous section has been on how young girls have perhaps been socialised away from apparently 'masculine' technologies. The aim of this section will be to show the gendered nature of technology leads to discrimination and devaluation of women's skills once they reach ICT workplaces and that this gendered nature is a reflection of wider societal inequality between genders. Utilising the theoretical framework of Pierre Bourdieu's theory of practice (Bourdieu, 1977, 1986), this section will examine work in the apparently anonymous and gender-blind online communities. In contrast to the meritocratic and libertarian ideals that many of these online communities perceive themselves to enact, this section will show how the work online reproduces 'masculine domination' (Bourdieu, 2001).

Over the past two decades, a great deal of hope has been placed on the Internet for breaking down the barriers to female participation. Yet, the hope that 'the virtuality of cyberspace is seen to spell the end of naturalized, biological embodiment as the basis for gender difference' (Wacjman, 2004, p. 7) has been superseded by increasing reports of online misogyny on various online platforms – particularly on social media. As with concerns regarding working in ICT, there are issues surrounding participation levels for women in the workplace, access to ICT work for women, employment practices that work against women and problems with how female skills are valued within the workplace.

The so-called GamerGate controversy is illustrative of the difficulties faced by women and minority groups online. The controversy – denoted through the use of the 'gate' suffix – ostensibly concerned issues of journalist ethics but has been widely reported in the media as a source of misogynistic abuse. The starting point for GamerGate surrounded a jilted ex-boyfriend of game developer Zoe Quinn. A blogpost from the ex-boyfriend argued that Quinn's game *Depression Quest* had only received favourable reviews due to alleged intimate relationships with games journalists. The resulting outcry, largely disproved, resulted in an explosion of misogynistic abuse and outcry over an apparent conspiracy led by feminists to destroy video gaming (see Chess and Shaw, 2015).

The GamerGate controversy is symbolic of the problems for women within digital work. While much of the controversy is an extreme example and does not specifically concern the workplace, the relevance to this chapter concerns the valuation of female skills once in the digital workplace. A means to theorise the problems for women in ICT work can potentially be found through the work of Pierre Bourdieu.

Bourdieu's work, primarily focused on the ways social inequalities are reproduced through culture, argued that society is stratified by the possession, or lack, of various forms of capital. The forms of capital – cultural, economic and social – are unevenly distributed throughout society. Cultural capital has perhaps represented the most enduring concept within Bourdieu's body of work, and has focused on how educational and cultural advantage are reproduced within the dominant sections of society. Cultural capital represents the knowledge and skills – effectively the labour power – of workers and can describe the 'institutionalised' educational qualifications of individuals, or their 'embodied' skills and capabilities (see Bourdieu, 1986). The value of this cultural capital is mediated within a 'field', a partially autonomous set of relationships between agents, where agents compete for the various forms of capital. There are numerous fields – a field for cultural production, a field of politics and so on – and each is guided by its own principles and accords symbolic capital – or what constitutes 'legitimacy' – within that field. Appropriate skills and dispositions are accorded 'symbolic capital' based on respect in the field.

Bourdieu's work, therefore, offers much to the study of the intersection between technology, gender and society, particularly in providing an explanation of historical patterns of male domination. He notes, 'the particular strength of the masculine sociology comes from the fact that it combines and condenses two operations: it legitimates a relationship of domination by embedding it in a biological nature that is itself a naturalized social construction' (2001, pp. 22–3). By pretending to be natural, the social division of labour between the sexes, unlike any other structure, glosses over the fact that it is social and made by humans themselves (Sterne, 2003). The social order is organised entirely in accordance with androcentric principles that are inscribed in practices such as the division of labour: collective and private rituals that serve to exclude women. Female characteristics are seen as 'different' within the androcentric view continuously legitimated by the practices that it determines. While these practices may change over time as Cockburn demonstrated in the 'conceptual somersault' performed in engineering skills, masculine domination persists as a structuring principle.

It is insufficient, Bourdieu argues, merely to describe women's exclusion from certain types of work without including the conditions of that exclusion – that is, including the reproduction of social and occupational hierarchies. The fact that women work is now 'taken for granted' as it was in pre-industrial times, yet in between there was a rupture where it was deemed unfeminine to prefer to work instead of pursuing 'domestic arts of watercolours and the piano' (2001, p. 84). These changes demonstrate different attitudes towards women and work; however, they are structured by the same guiding principle of andocentry. Access to education and economic independence and, to an extent, the transformation of family structures all represent change in the position of women in society, but that change is relative to the (dominant) position of men, and as has been shown in this chapter, surfaces continuing inequalities in society.

While Bourdieu's work engaged very little with feminist theory, and paid only limited attention to issues surrounding gender (excepting Bourdieu, 2001), his work has been adopted and advanced through the efforts of feminist researchers in recent years (e.g. McCall, 1992; Skeggs, 2004; Huppatz, 2009). For these researchers, femininity can represent a form of cultural capital in itself, and female bodies and feminine attributes represent skills and dispositions that are exchangeable within fields (Skeggs, 2004). McCall (1992), however, argues that gender can represent an asymmetric form of capital, where skills and capacities can be negatively viewed in light of a person's gender:

> An attractive woman who must interact with men at work may be perceived by heterosexual men as a distraction at best, incompetent at worst, or even a potential legal threat if she were to charge sexual harassment or sex discrimination. An attractive man however escapes connotations of incompetence and may even consider it his duty to enliven the work-place with his stimulating presence (McCall, 1992, p. 846)

Within the cultural fields, such as film and music, symbolic capital is accorded by intermediaries – including journalists, reviewers and other producers within the field (Bourdieu, 1993). Similar intermediaries operate within many digital fields, with gaming being subject to a parallel review processes. Critical acclaim from intermediaries can be then used by individuals in the field to gain access to other forms of capital, such as money through sales and royalties or through greater access to social capital. Yet, what is key from McCall's (1992) view is that technical competence is not associated with attractiveness. The legitimacy of skills and capacities within ICT fields can be seen to be contested, with various studies showing how respect is hard earned for women. Within the digital games field and in relation to the GamerGate controversy, the belief that Zoe Quinn must have had intimate relationships with journalists in order to get good reviews rather than by her own merit is a particularly striking aspect of the controversy. Yet, other forms of digital work too seem to be susceptible to similar problems. An example from Nafus (2012, p. 672) describes the difficulties women have getting mentors, especially when their gender is uncovered:

> Male mentors treated the relationship as a dating opportunity. Some told us that men would treat them as if they were their mother, asking for advice about how to dress and behave and then refusing to enter into a technical dialogue thereafter.

A study by Terrell et al. (2016) examined the role gender has in GitHub pull requests. GitHub is an online software repository which hosts and manages many open source projects. The research suggests that pull requests – proposals from users on how to improve the code of a piece of software which can be adopted or rejected – are subject to variable acceptance rates based on gender. Gender-blind requests tended to get accepted on similar – or better – rates to other users, while requests made when gender is identifiable are lower for women. Furthermore, soft skills – often portrayed as a form of 'feminine' capital – are highly valued skills within ICT professions, yet it is often men who display these dispositions who are rewarded in the industry (Chillas et al., 2015, p. 12).

Not only do many of these studies demonstrate the problems of the attainment and valuation of capital for women, but studies focusing on male-dominated professions demonstrate women's own complicity in reinforcing these gender hierarchies (e.g. Powell and Sang, 2015). This complicity and acceptance relates to what Bourdieu calls 'symbolic violence': 'the violence which is exercised upon a social agent with his or her complicity' (Bourdieu and Wacquant, 1992, p. 167). Taken-for-granted beliefs and the shared 'common sense' act to reinforce disparities and have been seen to be prevalent in male-dominated industries. The differences between the genders are 'misrecognised' as natural, based on essentialised characteristics of being male or female (Skeggs, 2004).

Within gaming communities, for instance, there is an espoused belief in libertarian politics, frequently manifested in the perception that online communities operate as a meritocracy (Reagle, 2012). While there is an anonymous and apparently gender-blind nature to online interactions, these do not, however, preclude the prevalence of sexist discourse within online communities. Criticisms over the lack of women or minorities involved in ICT work are often dismissed as a matter of rational choice, where women have made a choice not to be involved in industries (Massanari, 2015). The lack of affordances offered by technology for women, as discussed in the last section, can be seen as representing a form of symbolic violence. The belief that the ICT fields are meritocratic represents a form of 'misrecognition', where technology is seen as neutral and a leveller. The inability of many women to realise the affordances offered by technology mean that women are often unable to get started in ICT professions, and this is then later represented in an essentialised fashion: women are simply uninterested in technology. Likewise, the talk of reversing gender disparities are seen within these communities as a form of 'reverse sexism', where tackling such barriers amounts to a form of discrimination against men. The power of such discourses is to 'misrecognise' how the ICT field actually operates against female participation. As Woodfield argues, computing in general has become a site for the reproduction of masculine domination, not based on any physical differences, but due to 'the extraordinary flexibility and diversity of the ideological underpinnings of masculinity and to the extraordinary resilience of the relationship between men and technology' (2000, p. 26). While the 'hacker' trope can be seen to be tied up with notions of merit and anarchism, the character itself is an inherently male figure.

Conclusions and Recommendations

The aim of this chapter was to survey the literature on working in the ICT sector and the barriers to participation for women within the industry. The chapter also sets out to offer two theoretical frameworks to understanding the problems for women in the ICT sector – the affordances approach and Bourdieu's work on social inequality. There is also consideration of the values given to skills within the ICT sector.

It seems clear that women do not want to commit to a digital job or remain in the ICT sector, because of the structural barriers that they face. These factors include workload, long hours and ostracism by male colleagues. Moreover, there is evidence that women are often alienated from the technology itself from a very early age, as a product of hostility from boys at school and the technology itself not offering affordances that are appealing to girls.

It is therefore insufficient for policymakers to solely devise strategies to encourage women into ICT workplaces using quotas and financial incentives. The way in which technology is taught and embedded in the early years school curriculum needs to change, as well as fundamental modifications to ICT workplaces so that the structure allows women to work hours that are realistic and that support them through maternity leave, parental and other caring responsibilities. Moreover, organisational culture needs to change, too, so that women who are in the workplace remain there – managing diversity needs to be firmly established on organisational agendas. The professional bodies must develop routes that are appropriate for women's lives and that put pressure on employers to adhere to diversity policies.

It is not enough to simply propose recommendations, but strategies need to be in place to practically apply and raise awareness of these diversity policies, then monitor and measure the outcomes. Research conducted by Kodz et al. (2002) argued that there is a 'take-up' gap phenomenon with work–life balance initiatives, flexible work and part-time work being deemed as 'career suicide' by individuals, or when they were taken up being viewed by managers as a lack of commitment to a career or the organisation.

Only political action that really takes account of all the effects of domination that are exerted through [ ] the structures of the major institutions through which not only the masculine order but the whole social order is enacted and reproduced will we be able [ ] to contribute to the progressive withering away of masculine domination. (Bourdieu, 2001, p. 117)

What needs to be considered is how digital education and the ICT sector can adapt to the needs of girls and women, rather than how girls and women can adapt to ICT. Future-oriented studies of digital workplaces would do well to recognise the persistence of masculine domination.

REFERENCES

Adam, A., D. Howcroft and H. Richardson (2001) 'Absent friends? The gender dimension in information systems research', In N. Russo, B. Fitzgerald and J. DeGross (eds), *Realigning Research and Practice in Information Systems Development* (New York: Springer), pp. 333–52.

Ashcraft, K. (2009) 'Gender and diversity: other ways to "make a difference"', in M. Alvesson, T. Bridgman and H. Wilmott (eds), *The Oxford Handbook of Critical Management Studies* (Oxford: Oxford University Press), pp. 304–27.

Baldry, C., P. Bain, P. Taylor, J. Hyman, D. Scholarios, A. Marks, A. Watson, K. Gilbert, G. Gall and D. Bunzel (2007) *The Meaning of Work in the New Economy* (London: Palgrave Macmillan).

Barker, L. J. and W. Aspray (2006) *The State of Research on Girls and IT*. In J. M. Cohoon and W. Aspray (eds), *Women and information technology: Research on underrepresentation* (Cambridge, MA: MIT Press), pp. 3–54.

Beirne, M. and H. Ramsay (1988) 'Computer redesign and 'labour process' theory: towards a critical appraisal', in D. Knights and H. Willmott (eds), *New Technology and the Labour Process* (Basingstoke: Macmillan Press), pp. 197–229.

Bloomfield, B. P., Y. Latham and T. Vurdubakis (2010) 'Bodies, technologies and action possibilities: When is an affordance?', *Sociology*, 44, 3, 415–33.

Bourdieu, P. (1977), *Outline of a Theory of Practice* (Cambridge: Cambridge University Press)

Bourdieu, P. (1986) 'The forms of capital', in J. Richardson (ed.), *Handbook of Theory and Research for the Sociology of Education* (New York: Greenwood), pp. 241–58.

Bourdieu, P. (1993) *The Field of Cultural Production: Essays on Art and Literature* (Cambridge: Polity).

Bourdieu, P. (2001) *Masculine Domination* (Cambridge: Polity).

Bourdieu, P. and Wacquant, L. (1992). *An Invitation to Reflexive Sociology*. (Cambridge: Polity)

Cech, E. (2014) 'Culture of disengagement in engineering education?', *Science, Technology, & Human Values*, 39, 1, 42–72.

Chess, S. and A. Shaw (2015) 'A conspiracy of fishes, or, how we learned to stop worrying about #GamerGate and embrace hegemonic masculinity', *Journal of Broadcasting & Electronic Media*, 59, 1, 208–20.

▶

Chillas, S., A. Marks and L. Galloway (2015) 'Learning to labour: an evaluation of internships and employability in the ICT sector', *New Technology, Work and Employment*, 30, 1, 1–15.

Cockburn, C. (1999) 'Caught in the wheels: the high cost of being a female cog in the male machinery of engineering', in D. MacKenzie and J. Wacjman (eds), *The Social Shaping of Technology* (2nd edition) (Maidenhead: Open University Press), pp. 126–33.

Collins, R. (1979), *The Credential Society* (New York: Academic Press).

Diekman, A. B., E. K. Clark, A. M. Johnston, E. R. Brown and M. Steinberg (2011) 'Malleability in communal goals and beliefs influences attraction to stem careers: evidence for a goal congruity perspective', *Journal of Personality and Social Psychology*, 101, 5, 902–18.

European Commission (2013), *Women active in the ICT sector* (Madrid: European Commission).

Gherardi, S. (2003) 'Feminist theory and organization theory', in H. Tsoukas and C. Knudsen (eds), *Oxford Handbook of Organization Theory* (Oxford: Oxford University Press), pp. 210–36.

Gill, R. (2002) 'Cool, creative and egalitarian? Exploring gender in project-based new media work in Euro', *Information, Communication & Society*, 5, 1, 70–89.

Gill, R. and Pratt, A. (2008) 'In the social factory? Immaterial labour, precariousness and cultural work', *Theory, Culture & Society*, 25, 7–8, 1–30.

Grey, S. and G. Healy (2004) 'Women and IT contracting work – a testing process', *New Technology Work and Employment*, 19, 1, 30–42.

Guerrier, Y., C. Evans, J. Glover and C. Wilson (2009) '"Technical, but not very…": constructing gendered identities in IT-related employment', *Work, Employment & Society*, 23, 3, 494–511.

Haigh, T. (2010) 'Masculinity and the machine man', in T. Misa (ed.), *Gender Codes: Why Women are Leaving Computing* (Hoboken, NJ: John Wiley & Sons Inc.), pp. 51–73.

Hanor, J. H. (1998) 'Concepts and strategies learned from girls' interactions with computers', *Theory into Practice*, 37, 1, 64–71.

Heo, M. and Myrick, L. M. (2009) 'The Girls' Computing Club: Making positive changes in gender inequity in computer science with an informal, female learning community', *International Journal of Information and Communication Technology Education*, 5, 4, 44–56.

Huppatz, K. (2009) 'Reworking Bourdieu's capital: Feminine and female capitals in the field of paid caring work', *Sociology*, 43, 1, 45–66.

Hutchby, I. (2001) 'Technologies, texts and affordances,' *Sociology*, 35, 2, 441–56.

Joshi, K. and K. Kuhn (2007) 'What it takes to succeed in information technology consulting: exploring the gender typing of critical attributes', *Information Technology & People*, 20, 4, 400–24.

Kelan, E. K. (2008) 'Emotions in a rational profession: The gendering of skills in ICT work', *Gender, Work & Organization*, 15, 1, 49–71.

Kodz, J. Harper, H. and Dench, S. (2002) *Work-life balance: Beyond the rhetoric* (Brighton: Institute for Employment Studies).

▶

MacKenzie, R., A. Marks and K. Morgan (2015) 'Technology, affordances and occupational identity amongst older telecommunications engineers: from living machines to black-boxes', *Sociology*. doi:10.1177/0038038515616352.

Massanari, A. (2015) '#Gamergate and The Fappening: How Reddit's algorithm, governance, and culture support toxic technocultures', *New Media & Society*. doi:10.1177/1461444815608807.

McCall, L. (1992) 'Does gender fit? Bourdieu, feminism, and conceptions of social order', *Theory And Society*, 21, 6, 837–67

Misa, T. (2010) 'Gender codes: defining the problem', in T. Misa (ed.), *Gender Codes: Why Women are Leaving Computing* (Hoboken, NJ: John Wiley & Sons Inc.), pp. 3–25.

Nafus, D. (2012) '"Patches don't have gender": What is not open in open source software', *New Media & Society*, 14, 4, 669–83.

Ornella, A. (2013) 'It's all about sex: the peculiar case of technology and gender', *Verifiche*, 42, 183–213.

Powell, A. and K. J. Sang (2015) 'Everyday experiences of sexism in Male-dominated professions: A Bourdieusian perspective', *Sociology*, 49, 5, 919–36.

Reagle, J. (2012) '"Free as in sexist?" Free culture and the gender gap', *First Monday*, 18, 1. doi:10.5210/fm.v18i1.4291.

Rhoton, L. (2011) 'Distancing as a gendered barrier: understanding women scientists' gender practices', *Gender and Society*, 25, 6, 696–716.

Skeggs, B. (2004) *Class, Self, Culture* (London: Routledge).

Sterne, J. (2003) 'Bourdieu, technique and technology', *Cultural Studies*, 17, 3–4, 367–89.

Stoffregen, T. A. (2003) 'Affordances as properties of the animal-environment system', *Ecological Psychology*, 15, 2, 115–34.

Tech Partnership (2016) Factsheet: Tech industry workforce (February 2016), Available at: www.thetechpartnership.com.

Terrell, J., A. Kofink, J. Middleton, C. Rainear, E. Murphy-Hill and C. Parnin (2016) *Gender Bias in Open Source: Pull Request Acceptance of Women Versus Men* (No. e1733v1). PeerJ PrePrints.

Truss, C., E. Conway, A. d'Amato, G. Kelly, K. Monks, E. Hannon and P. Flood (2012) 'Knowledge work: gender-blind or gender-biased?', *Work Employment and Society*, 26, 5, 735–54.

Trusty, J., C. R. Robinson, M. Plata and K. M. Ng (2000) 'Effects of gender, socioeconomic status, and early academic performance on postsecondary educational choice', *Journal of Counseling and Development: JCD*, 78, 4, 463–72.

Volkoff, O. and D. M. Strong (2013) 'Critical realism and affordances: Theorizing IT-associated organizational change processes', *MIS Quarterly*, 37, 3, 819–34.

Wajcman, J. (2000) 'Reflections on gender and technology studies: In what state is the art?', *Social Studies of Science*, 30 3, 447–64.

Wajcman, J. (2004) *TechnoFeminism* (Cambridge: Polity Press).

Wajcman, J. (2006) 'New connections: social studies of science and technology and studies of work', *Work, Employment and Society*, 20, 4, 773–85.

Wilson, F. (2004) 'Can compute, won't compute: women's participation in the culture of computing', *New Technology, Work and Employment*, 18, 2, 127–42.

Witz, A. (1992) *Professions and Patriarchy* (London: Routledge).

Woodfield, R. (2000) *Women, Work and Computing* (Cambridge: Cambridge University Press).

Understanding Self-Exploitation in the Digital Games Sector

10

Adrian Wright

The Creative Entrepreneur

A conventional view of enterprise is that of the self-made heroic entrepreneur, centred on positive images of successful independent businesses (Casson and Casson, 2013). Such rhetoric of an 'enterprising self' has led to an ethos of enterprise that has consumed parts of entrepreneurial discourse (Du Gay, 1996). At its heart is the romanticised character of an entrepreneur displaying characteristics such as initiative, risk-taking, flexibility, independence, imagination, hard work and an internal locus of control (Gibb, 1993).

The political remodelling from the cultural to creative industries put enterprise at the heart of the creative sector (Garnham, 2005). This, alongside the drive for creative workers to develop entrepreneurial skills (Banks and Hesmondhalgh, 2009), has gone some way to altering expectations and developing a 'creative class' of entrepreneurs (Coulson, 2012). More recently, political and media discourse further reinforced the development of entrepreneurial skills celebrating and encouraging enterprise in the digital sector. Policy initiatives such as the Blueprint for Technology (Department for Business, Innovation and Skills, 2010) combined with media stories of successful tech entrepreneurs to illustrate the wealth of opportunity ostensibly available for workers willing to take up entrepreneurial activity, thus creating a 'myth of success' (Bergvall-Kåreborn and Howcroft, 2013) where individuals can become prosperous by developing products in the digital sector.

In contrast to predominantly optimistic interpretations of entrepreneurial activity a body of literature highlights the negative implications for individuals, leading us to question the true nature of entrepreneurialism in the creative industries. Emergent research points to entrepreneurial activity leading to exploitative and precarious work conditions (Haunschild and Eikhof, 2009; Coulson, 2012; Bergvall-Kåreborn and Howcroft, 2013). Recent work investigating digital games developers illustrates self-exploitation through long working hours, unpaid work and a blurring of work–life boundaries (Wright, 2015).

Self-exploitation in the creative industries has been accepted or rationalised due to self-actualisation (Ekman, 2014), workers' love of their craft (Ross, 2003) and a high level of identification with their work (DeFillippi et al., 2007). In the digital games sector a 'work as play model' (Peuter and Dyer-Witherford, 2005), high level of attachment (Thompson et al., 2015), 'passion' (Harvey and Shephard, 2016) and angst about employability appear to mitigate challenging work conditions (Peticca-Harris et al., 2015). Building on work that points to self-exploitative practices in the creative industries being rationalised due to feelings that individuals have about their work, this chapter aims to increase our understanding of how self-exploitation occurs and why individuals self-exploit, by examining the experiences of a cohort of digital games developers in a sector that is, by contemporary prescription, creatively empowered and entrepreneurial.

The Digital Games Sector

The digital games sector is valued at around £2.9 billion to the UK economy and contributes $68.3 billion to the global economy (Euromonitor, 2014). Recently, the digital games sector has adapted to major technological changes affecting product innovations, changing power relations (Parker et al., 2014) and the changing demographics of users, which has influenced consumption (Prato et al., 2010).

An accelerating trend of vertical integration in the mid 2000s, where smaller independent companies were acquired by larger publishers (Phillips et al., 2009), can be contrasted by more recent evidence suggesting that the UK sector is characterised by small development teams. The number of developers working in digital games in the UK dropped to 7000 in 2009 from an industry high of 9400 in 2004 (Skillset, 2011). The vast majority of companies (80 per cent) have fewer than four employees and a further 5 per cent have between five and nine employees. Only a small proportion of the sector (5 per cent) is made of games firms who have between 100 and 249 employees (Keynote, 2013).

A combination of advancements in technology, changing market and organisational and industry structures have been encouraging individuals to become independent developers (Martin and Deuze, 2009; Wright, 2015). The distribution of smartphones, the affordability of mobile data plans and the arrival of tablet computers have offered opportunities for developers to adapt existing and develop new types of games (Bergvall-Kåreborn and Howcroft, 2013). This has enabled third-party game developers to create and bring to market their own games and sell them in a variety of marketplaces (Parker et al., 2015), predominately on mobile platforms, for a significantly lower cost both in terms of development time and finance. In another major development, the UK government has encouraged innovation in the sector by stimulating the creation of games through tax reliefs, giving developers 25 per cent tax relief on up to 80 per cent of a game's production budget (Keynote, 2013). Perhaps changing market conditions go some way to explaining the changes to the constitution of firms in the sector and the trend towards smaller development teams. Ostensibly, these changes appear to have given developers choices in terms of work and employment: whether to work for a large game studio as an employee or to work in an independent studio as a self-employed developer.

Nascent research in the area of digital games has tended to focus on managerial tensions when reconciling creative, technical and commercial imperatives (Tschang, 2007), issues of insecurity, autonomy and identity (Thompson et al., 2015), the quality of work life and the exploitative working conditions (Robinson, 2005; Peticca-Harris et al., 2015), the employment relationships (Peuter and Dyer-Witherford, 2005), the managerial attitudes towards control (Cohendet and Simon, 2007) and the evolution of skills development (Izushi and Aoyama, 2006). However, such work has typically focused on the relationship between console game manufacturers and developers and only a limited amount of literature has recognised the new working practices in independent games production and the implications that this has had on developers (Martin and Deuze, 2009; Wright, 2015). It is in the context of limited research on entrepreneurialism in the digital games sector where this chapter aims to make a contribution.

Work Conditions

Employment within creative industries has been romanticised as flexible, liberating and 'cool' (Reeves, 2001). However, more detailed analysis into creative work suggests notions of the bohemian, autonomous creative worker enjoying a career full of excitement, flexibility and prestige appear less than convincing (Hesmondhalgh and Baker, 2009). In the creative industries, differing methods of production have influenced work arrangements, redefining the relationship that individuals have with work, resulting in employment relationships characterised by project-based work, temporary contracts and freelancing (Grabher and Ibert, 2006; Blair, 2009; Bergvall-Kåreborn and Howcroft, 2013). As a result, these changes have led to unstable labour market conditions and precarity for many creative workers (Haunschild and Eikhof, 2009) because creative work is characterised by excessive labour supply and insufficient demand (Smith and McKinlay, 2009). Insecure labour market conditions have resulted in many individuals' experiencing short term contracts, little job protection and uncertain career prospects (Hesmondhalgh and Baker, 2009). These conditions necessitate that the creative worker be 'flexible', committing themselves to the commercial imperatives of employers over and above non-work commitments (Banks, 2007). As a consequence, long hours and poor work life and the industry's 'ruthless work regiment' blur the 'cool' and 'liberating' image of working in the creative sector (Hesmondhalgh and Baker, 2009).

An emerging form of analysis in the creative industries is the use of unpaid labour in the production of creative products, or when working beyond 'normal' working hours to maintain and develop contacts or find work and develop experience. In order to 'get in', individuals are expected to work without payment (or for deferred payment) in the formative stages of their career (Hesmondhalgh and Baker, 2010; Siebert and Wilson, 2013). Percival and Hesmondhalgh (2014) note that as union power has relented, the oversupply of labour has resulted in the growth of use of unpaid labour, often in the form of 'work experience' resulting in a culture of unpaid internships and the exploitation of individuals' willingness to work cheaply in return for glamour, esteem and acclaim. Blair et al. (2003) point to the Los Angeles film industry, where working for free, deferred payment (payment depending on success of the film) or internships are common entry routes into the sector, both in terms of building networks and gaining experience. Unpaid work is also intensified by an 'economy of favours' (Ursell, 2000) that may legitimatise low pay and working for free (Umney and Kretsos, 2014). However, whether individuals deem this as exploitative is questionable: some accept unpaid work and internships as the way things are (Siebert and Wilson, 2013), and others describe such practices as 'normal' (Randle et al., 2015).

The insecurity and exploitative nature of the creative industries seems to be visible in the digital games sector. Typically, the industry is represented by project-based work, where labour is organised from one project to another (Peuter and Dyer-Witheford, 2005; Izushi and Aoyama, 2006). Employment follows a flexible employment model characterised by temporary contracts and subcontracts, no long-term employment commitment and free-agent self-guided career patterns (Cadin et al., 2006). The flexible employment model suggests labour market conditions are, at best, unstable for workers. Digital games developers have been found to engage in what is deemed to be 'extreme work' (Granter et al., 2015). Accounts of long, uncompensated working hours under 'make it or break it' conditions during periods of 'crunch' (a practice used in the sector where employees work long hours in order to finish a project) (Peuter and Dyer-Witheford, 2005) have revealed that developers can work 45–70 hours in a 'regular' week. This working intensity has been associated with accounts of unlimited and unpaid overtime, poor work–life balance and burnout (Peticca-Harris et al., 2015).

The literature discussing the work conditions of independent game developers is limited; however, recent studies suggest examples of precarious, insecure and exploitative work conditions apparent in large games studios are present in the experiences of independent developers. Increased outsourcing, growing casual employment and changing market conditions appear to have encouraged self-employment, leaving developers with little alternative other than 'involuntary entrepreneurship' (Wright, 2015). Motivations for self-employment such as a rejection of corporate control, the promise of increased autonomy (Lipkin, 2013) and a 'myth of success' (Bergvall-Kåreborn and Howcroft, 2013) can be contrasted with tensions surrounding balancing creative and commercial imperatives (Martin and Deuze, 2009) as control is eroded by market demands and power asymmetries (Bergvall-Kåreborn and Howcroft, 2013; Wright, 2015).

Examples of self-exploitation, 'whereby workers become so enamoured with their jobs that they push themselves to the limits of their physical and emotional endurance' (Hesmondhalgh and Baker, 2011, p. 6), are apparent in experiences of independent games developers, through either unpaid work or long hours. Developers have been found to work for free to gain experience or exposure in the sector, exploiting their own time, ideas and intellectual property to enhance future employability or for deferred payment in the belief a game would become commercially successful in the future (Wright, 2015). However, the unpredictability of the games market suggests that there is no guarantee that developers will receive financial payment for this work (Bergvall-Kåreborn and Howcroft, 2013). Developers also work well beyond the realms of a 'working week', either working 'day jobs' to assist in the financing of projects or by effectively being 'on call' to the demands of employers or in order to explore opportunities that may increase their potential success (Wright, 2015).

Accepting Exploitation

An emerging body of literature highlights examples of acceptance of exploitative conditions in the creative industries due to passion, attachment and self-actualising work. Ekman (2014) found that workers desire exploitation due to the opportunities it offers. Exploitation, in this sense, comes with the possibility of never-ending self-improvement, innovation and the challenge (Granter et al., 2015). Ekman describes a willing form of exploitation which broadly connects to a body of literature that highlights an acceptance of exploitative conditions due to the self-actualising nature of their work. Arvidsson's et al. (2010) study of fashion workers, Ross' (2000) investigation of dotcom working environments and Ursell's (2000) commentary on television work all highlight exploitation but propose it as a form of willing exploitation fuelled by the love of the job and involvement in their work.

Arvidsson et al. (2010) highlight that despite dire conditions, overworked and underpaid workers exhibit high levels of satisfaction. This is explained as the power of the 'ideology of creativity' linking to the popularity of the 'creative lifestyle' and the search for self-actualisation. Arvidsson et al. (2010, p. 306) also point to the absence of an alternative ideology, as the fashion workers are absorbed in their world and have little form of consciousness outside their world of fashion. Ursell (2000) explains how self-enterprising workers in television accept challenging work conditions on two levels: in one sense, workers love their jobs and rationalise these conditions by doing the job they love, enjoying the scope for creativity and relishing the challenge of working in competitive environments; alternatively, these individuals consent to their own exploitation, by recognising that their efforts may result in self-affirmation, the possibility of self-actualising work in the future or the potential rewards. What is clear from this analysis is that workers in some way contribute to their own exploitation, either due to the love and involvement in their work or because their consenting to be exploited may lead them to receive financial and psychological benefits in the future.

In a similar outcome to Ursell (2000), Ross (2000) describes workers willing to take part in exploitation of their own labour who happily discount the price of their labour for the love of their craft. Ross points to the new media industry in New York where jobs are filled by contract employees or temporary workers who work 85 hour working weeks without overtime pay. Ross' explanation of why individuals work long hours is that in the minds of these 'new slaves', it is 'cool' to be exploited.

In the digital sector, an emerging body of literature highlights how workers accepted working long hours and the central place that work takes in their lives. Barley and Kunda (2004) show that workers devoted considerable hours not only to compensated work but also to work that involved increasing their own human and social capital. In most cases workers were accepting of this because this was their choice and an investment in what would benefit them in the future. Bergvall-Kåreborn and Howcroft (2013) highlight the economic and self-actualising rationale for individuals accepting the centrality of work in their lives. Individuals would willingly self-exploit in order to deal with peaks and troughs in the market, gain success in a competitive market environment or to reap the forthcoming rewards that would come their way if they sustained this level of work. However, others felt a sense of fun due to the self-actualising nature of the work as it held a similar level of enjoyment to social activities they might have otherwise engaged in.

Literature concerning the digital games sector suggests a high level of attachment and identification to work (DeFillippi et al., 2007; Thompson et al., 2015) and a key example of passionate, effective labour (Harvey and Shephard, 2016). Digital games developers enjoy their work and to some extent see it as 'a calling' (Peuter and Dyer-Witherford, 2005; Peticca-Harris et al., 2015). A 'work as play model' appears to mitigate challenging work conditions such as unregulated long working hours (Peuter and Dyer-Witherford, 2005). This view concurs with Barrett's (2005) depiction of software work, as individuals are subjected to control strategies such as 'crunch time' to appear 'cool' and as a way of capturing creativity and collective operation.

However, an alternative view highlights the acceptance of extreme working conditions such as 'crunch' stem from angst about employability and future career prospects (Peticca-Harris et al., 2015). This analysis illustrates a complex picture of individuals consenting to or taking part in their own exploitation whether it be by the belief in future rewards, opportunities, self-improvement, love of their job or even a complex form of cultural control that makes employees feel that they must take part in exploitative work practices to further their career. This view also raises interesting questions in terms of why individuals consent. Furthermore, as much of the work in the digital games sector typically refers to those working in studios, under full-time traditional employment relationships, the research in this chapter aims to investigate how freelance or independent game developers rationalise their work conditions.

Methods

The fieldwork took place between 2012 and 2013 in various locations in North West England, including Manchester, Chester, Preston, Bolton, Wilmslow and Macclesfield. The North West has been characterised historically as a creative cluster for digital game development (Johns, 2006), which has recently gone through some notable changes regarding the structure and constitution of game development firms. A distinctive characteristic of the region was that a number of large, established development studios were acquired in the 2000s by foreign-owned publishers, whereas other regional clusters had a greater number of independent developers (Phillips et al., 2009). Therefore, the region was more exposed to changing investment strategies of large international development firms. By 2010 several large studios had downsized or closed. As a result, perhaps because the North West had a high number of highly skilled, highly paid developers (Phillips et al., 2009), there has been an increase in the formation of smaller businesses, and the sector is now characterised by a mixture of large established companies and a growing number of smaller, younger companies located predominately around Manchester and Liverpool (Nesta, 2014). The North West is thus an important context in which to examine entrepreneurial activity, as changes to the composition of firms have led to its emergence as an entrepreneurial 'cluster' for digital games development.

A qualitative approach of phased semi-structured interviews and ethnography of local networking event was undertaken. Participants were interviewed through a mixture of Skype and face-to-face discussions which lasted between 25 minutes and one hour. Respondents were contacted by 'cold call' emails and asked to participate in the study. Other respondents were gathered via a mailing list circulated after networking events, following initial face-to-face contact. While the study aimed at self-employed developers in particular, it included developers in full-time employment, graduates looking to enter the labour market, recruitment agents and game development lecturers, in order to add further context. The developers interviewed represented a varied grouping as the sample was taken from a mix of ages and roles within the sector in order to capture a wide range of experiences. There was a gender imbalance in the research given the under-representation of women, but the gender imbalance in the data collection is broadly indicative of wider trends within the software sector (Adam et al., 2006).

Initial exploratory interviews with senior management and experienced developers focused on market conditions. The interviews then focused on gaining an understanding of the working experiences and employment conditions of developers. Particular emphasis was paid to understanding reasons for working in the digital games sector, individual perceptions of the labour market, working practices, working hours and strategies for entering into and moving within the labour market.

In order to capture the wider context, the research involved an 'overt ethnography' at a number of networking events for the digital games sector. The rationale for this was the sectors reliance on social networks for attracting labour and the importance of networks for determining the industry's evolution and competitiveness (Izushi and Aoyama, 2006). At networking events, the purpose and intentions of the research were fully disclosed, allowing the researcher to provide a credible explanation for detailed probing, questioning and participation. Usually, the networking events ended with informal drinks or live music, intended to encourage attendees to interact. The events took place in various locations in North West (England), often in the function rooms of bars and hotels. The number of attendees ranged from 20 to 150 people from the software and game development sectors. Participating in these events enabled the researcher to 'forge relationships', engage in informal conversations and gather perspectives on the sector. Acting as participant, the researcher was able to go beyond interviews by meeting developers in their own domain, gathering additional insights into the culture and behaviours of the group (Creswell, 2013).

Data collection and analysis occurred simultaneously and as an ongoing reflective process and was coded by the use of a data analysis tool (NVivo). During analysis, the themes identified were then probed by the researcher to provide additional detail.

Rationalising Exploitation

This section proposes to show how the values and beliefs of developers provide a rationale to encourage developers to engage in what may be deemed by many as exploitative work conditions. It argues that exploitative conditions are tempered by a passion for the work, a commitment to a career, enterprise, the opportunity of success and a sense of belonging to a community. It suggests that the subjective beliefs developers hold about their work roles result in a lack of resistance to exploitative conditions.

A Passion for Games

The purpose of this section is to understand how a passion for games and an identification with the profession provide an explanation for why developers engage in self-exploitative activities. Respondents were overwhelmingly positive about having the opportunity to work in a sector that they considered fun, exciting and innovative. Many developers cited their childhood as the time when they realised that they wanted to work in digital games, demonstrating how they were propelled towards a career in games.

> I got a Sega Master System II. It was the end of my life that really I was just glued to the television. I just loved it. I just didn't understand how I could just be so immersed in something. And then through my life I've got consoles and just love video games. I know every game that's been made. I haven't played all of them, but I know every game. I love the idea of…It's like all mediums come together: there's music, film, books, just everything combined into one medium; that's just brilliant. I love it to bits. So that's why I wanted to be a games designer. (Owen, independent game developer, Preston)

Developers talked about their love of games and how this translated into a desire to work in games. Many pointed to the aspect of creativity when illustrating their passion for games. This enabled developers to enjoy self-expression and self-fulfilment in their occupation, which in turn has reinforced accounts of aestheticised identity in the literature (Thompson et al., 2015). These accounts also highlight how working in digital games is more than just a job: it is more a vocation or 'a calling'. Developers described their choice of a career in digital games as following their hearts and doing what they love. Working in digital games was articulated as a dream job:

> Games have got one of those sort of…dream jobs, isn't it, you know? It's like an astronaut. You know, a lot of people are very passionate about games. (Sven, game developer, Wilmslow)

This reinforces the notion that working in games fulfilled a long-term ambition and that it was much more than just a job. This developer compared working in digital games to jobs that may be beyond the reach of most individuals, categorising digital games alongside utopian presentations of creative work exempt from boredom or disaffection (Banks and Hesmondhalgh, 2009). By distinguishing work in digital games from other mundane occupations and comparing it to those of an astronaut also illustrates the personal attachment that this developer has to his work.

These feelings about work were endorsed when developers were justifying what may be deemed as exploitative working conditions. For example, when rationalising his decision to work without payment, this developer explained why he engaged in what might seem to be an exploitative practice:

> I want to make a game; this is why I'm in this. I'd love the chance to make a game, even for the sacrifice. I'm not getting paid now; I'm just purely working non-stop on it, but I love the idea of the company. (Owen, independent game developer, Preston)

This developer highlights the opportunity he was given to work on a project he was passionate about. He explains that the lack of financial remuneration and long working hours were a 'sacrifice' that he was willing to make in order to be involved in self-actualising work in an industry he loves.

Other developers compared their current role with previous experiences in alternative employment to rationalise the difficult and unstable conditions that they experienced in the digital games sector:

> I think because I worked in retail for a good few years solid that's kind of made me think, 'this is okay. I can deal with this, anything to not go back to retail.' (Gill, game developer, Bolton)

For this developer long hours and 'crunch' were contrasted with previous mundane work which lacked job satisfaction. Despite the challenging work conditions, this developer felt that working in digital games offered a creative, fun and collaborative environment that other types of work could not offer. The accounts of developers in this section not only suggest that developers are engaged in self-actualising work but also show that job satisfaction exists amid challenging working conditions. These cases suggest that attachment and self-actualising work diminishes workers' resistance (Thompson et al., 2015). Moreover, passion appears to be a form of control that enables the worker to tolerate and to some extent embrace the difficulties associated with exploitative working conditions (Ursell, 2000; McRobbie, 2002; Ross, 2003; Ardvisson et al., 2010).

To summarise, this section illustrates why developers are motivated to work in the digital games sector. It also contributes to existing literature (Ursell, 2000; McRobbie, 2002; Ross, 2003) that suggests that self-actualising work acts as a control mechanism that at least partially explains why developers self-exploit. However, the purpose of this chapter is to find additional reasons why developers appear to accept self-exploitation.

Commitment to a Career

The demands of self-employment effectively meant that developers worked well beyond the normal hours of a working week in order to establish themselves in the sector (Wright, 2015). In the following discussion, the aim is to understand how discipline and commitment allowed developers to accept exploitative practices.

Developers understood that there would be a certain level of 'sacrifice' needed in order to establish or maintain their position in the sector. Working without pay, networking practices and long working hours were seen as something that developers 'must do' in order to achieve their long-term ambitions. This was exemplified by one developer who described the reciprocal relationship between hard work and success:

> So it does sometimes get difficult, but obviously at the end of the day, the company's profit and success is basically measured on how much we want it. Obviously we're not just fooling around. (Chris, independent developer, Chester)

This view highlights that his commitment to his career is the most important indicator of future success. Corresponding in some respects to Grey (1994), this developer's pursuit of a successful career overcame his resistance towards long hours. In order to reinforce this belief, this developer has implicitly separated himself and his partner from others, suggesting others may not have engaged in the same kind of 'career project' and therefore would not have had the same commitment to work. The phrase 'we're not just fooling around' demonstrated a clear difference between this developer and others in the sector who this developer perceived as less committed and less disciplined in their work. Essentially this quote demonstrates the character of this developer, in that he suggested that hard work, discipline and commitment were prerequisites for success.

Much like working hours, both holidays and time off were balanced by self-discipline and a commitment to work:

> That's another good thing about indie: everything is very flexible; everything is very negotiable. And you're a small studio. You're all

friends, so holidays aren't a problem. It's not like we won't get holidays. … When I used to work in the bars, it was just – I'm going on holiday. The boss would say, no you're not, and then you'd just go, yes I am. Then you'd just go, and then you'd come back, and the job would be mysteriously waiting for you. But it won't be the same with our company. (Jack, independent developer, Manchester)

The telling part of this quote is last two sentences; although this developer articulates freedom and choice in holiday arrangements, it is clear that it is not solely the developer who determines his holiday time. Work time and holidays are, to some degree, normatively controlled by peers within the development team. This connects to self-policing control strategies illustrated in software work by Tapia (2004) and Kennedy (2010) that gave developers some form of responsible autonomy (Friedman, 1977) in return for commitment. However, rather than being uneasy with this form of control, this developer accepts the level of commitment desired from other members of his team.

Additional illustrations of self-discipline and commitment were demonstrated in 'crunch time'. Representative of the culture of the sector (Wright, 2015), one developer showed how this was an illustration of commitment to the occupation and a case of 'earning your stripes':

There's a bit of a macho culture. You wouldn't look at video game programmes and think there was a macho culture, but there is. There's a macho culture going, 'yeah, pulled an all-nighter.' (Alan, independent developer, Manchester)

This quotation contributes to evidence that 'crunching' was enforced not only by organisational controls. However, in contrast to accounts of the normative controls augmented by anxiety about career prospects and future employability (Peticca-Harris et al., 2015) 'crunching' is something that is admired by their peers and is a demonstration of self-discipline and the commitment required to work in the sector.

This discussion has illustrated that long hours were moderated by self-discipline and commitment. Developers are engaged in a career project to succeed in digital games. Commitment and self-discipline have displaced the desire for what might be deemed a normal working week and were seen by developers as a prerequisite for success. The individual's commitment to his or her career must be seen in combination with the normative controls to motivate developers to take part in practices that blur work–life boundaries and lead to the acceptance of exploitative working conditions.

Enterprise and the Opportunity of Success

The values of self-discipline and commitment resemble the characteristics of an enterprising person described by Du Gay (1996). The 'ethos of enterprise' and the opportunity of future success were apparent in the values and beliefs of developers. These opportunities and beliefs provided the motivation for developers to rationalise exploitative conditions.

Digital innovations and media and political discourse highlighting the opportunity for developers to become successful technology entrepreneurs have encouraged developers to start their own businesses. This resulted in a belief from developers that success was possible:

> They all live the dream of writing the next 'Temple Run', and there is something to it. (Wayne, owner of SME, Macclesfield)

Other developers highlighted the 'lottery factor' in digital games development in order to emphasise their own chances of success:

> There's enough poster boys for the indie digital revolution that everybody thinks it's feasible. ... There's a big lottery factor in the whole market. I think anything's possible now, but it's still quite stacked up against you just because there's so much competition. (Alan, independent developer, Manchester)

Although noting the strong competition, this developer cites the 'lottery factor' involved in bringing a game to market. He eschewed thinking of the 'lottery factor' as a way to demonstrate high risk but instead used it to show that success was possible, even if the odds of success are low. The rationale behind this philosophy entails that it is not the game itself that leads to success but that it is rather a case of being in the right place at the right time. The successful title Angry Birds was used as an example of a 'perfect storm' and good fortune:

> There's literally tens of thousands of games that are way better than Angry Birds that came out in the same couple of months that if they'd have got to the front they'd have been the Angry Birds. There's no reason why they couldn't have been. They were as good and as playable and as mainstream and had the characters that could've been the plushy toys and everything. But there was a perfect storm for Angry Birds. It just meant that they were the game at the time. (Alan, independent developer, Manchester)

This mentality reflects political and media rhetoric focused on the wealth of opportunity available to technology entrepreneurs. One developer when asked if he would consider full-time employment in a games studio replied,

> With our business model, if it takes off the way we are planning, I'm not sure a games company could offer a salary that would compete with the income we could potentially earn. (Bobby, independent developer, Chester)

This collection of quotations offers an insight into the enterprising mentality of developers. However, to label this solely as optimism stimulated by the media would be inaccurate. This represents the presence of entrepreneurial identities of creative workers (Hackley and Kover, 2007; Gotsi et al., 2010; Thompson et al., 2015). Some developers saw themselves as much as entrepreneurs as they were game developers: activities at networking events underlined this as enterprise became a focal point, reinforced by questions-and-answer sessions and the hero status given to developers who displayed entrepreneurial skills. This is in contrast to some areas of the creative industries where cultural and bohemian values can be seen to lie at the heart of their self-perception (Eikhof and Haunschild, 2006). The developers clearly showed that self-employment for them is not a hobby or pastime but a job and a business, and they treated it that way.

This enterprising mentality from developers contributes to explaining developers' lack of resistance to exploitative practices. Entrepreneurial characteristics in the literature such as dedication and self-reliance (Beck, 1992; Down, 2010) can be identified and enable us to understand why developers accept their working long hours networking, working additional jobs or 'crunching'. Furthermore, the entrepreneurial characteristic of risk-taking (Beck, 1992; Down, 2010) goes some way to explaining attitudes towards working for free. Working without pay demonstrates the considerable risk that developers appear to accept in the hope of future reward. The account from one developer underlines this principle when discussing his unpaid placement:

> Even before I got my degree, I found out that Craze was on an employment freeze. So I offered, just to get my foot in the door, that I'll work for free for X amount of months until there's a place open. And they went, 'oh yeah, great; jump aboard.' And that was the time of Wizard Adventure. So I worked for free for three months. I was trying to get first in line when there was an opening, and there was an

opening at the end of August. … It was very risky. I was penniless for a while. But it was worth it in the end. Now I've moved out, got a great job. It's paid off really well. (Ryan, game developer, Wilmslow)

Surprisingly this developer doesn't spend much time focusing on the lack of employment opportunities in the digital games sector but talks enthusiastically about how he was rewarded for taking a risk. In this case he secured employment despite shouldering the burden of risk (Randle and Culkin, 2009); this developer appeared to be satisfied to risk working for free in order to gain a better chance to secure a long-term position in the sector. In this case we can see how developers may desire exploitation because of the opportunities it offers to forge a successful career in the sector (Ekman, 2014).

This section has found that developers saw themselves not only as game developers but also as enterprising individuals. There was a belief from developers that they could achieve success in the right circumstances. This was strengthened by success stories of Angry Birds and Temple Run. However, the likelihood of such success was described as a 'lottery' rather than because of objective judgement of their own skills and abilities. In the previous section practices such as long working hours were seen in the context of entrepreneurial characteristics of self-discipline and commitment whereas in this section working for free was a demonstration of a positive attitude towards risk. This enterprising mentality may also partially explain a lack of resistance by developers to exploitative practices.

Belonging to the Occupational Community

An additional lens to view the acceptance of exploitative conditions is through the individual's connection to the social aspects of work. In the context of the fragmented accounts of work that point to a demise of the collective nature of employment (Beck, 1992) and a weakened connection between work and social relationships (Foster, 2012), developers believed that belonging to a community, and in turn having a social affiliation, was an important value and something they were keen to establish and maintain. As a result, developers sought out strategies to reconnect themselves with others in their occupational community.

Noting the lack of social affiliation and attachment to colleagues which results from working from home, some developers used information and communications technologies (ICTs) in order to reconnect with their colleagues as a way of recreating an office experience:

Banter, we miss playing *Call of Duty*. That's the thing we've missed the most, is all the screaming and the swearing while we were playing *Call of Duty*. The banter we kind of do on Skype now. I just finished a call with my guys, we do, when we're working we just leave it on as well, just so we can talk and go over stuff. It's about 50 per cent of the office experience. I wish I had a way of ... I think I maybe just need to set up a camera point at my desk where I can draw; the whiteboard stuff just isn't really working for us. You need to be able to go, 'no, not this, you idiot. I mean that!' So you need to be able to do stuff like that, and that kind of collaborative work's a bit harder. (Alan, independent developer, Manchester)

Alan highlights the challenge of maintaining social relations while working from home, pointing to a consequence of self-employment – the lack of attachment with colleagues (Felstead et al., 2005). Although this developer used ICTs and social media to collaborate with his peers, he felt that these methods were unable to fully recreate the office experience. This quotation demonstrates how collaboration, strong social ties and dialogue with colleagues is a key source of meaning in this developer's work.

Other developers dealt with a lack of attachment by attending networking events. This suggests normal conversations in an office environment were replicated at networking events as developers attempted to initiate, foster and/or maintain an attachment with the occupational community. Additionally, developers sought additional funding to set up their own studio (rather than work from home). This was partially motivated by a wish to reconnect with others and establish a collaborative environment with colleagues. However, the consequence of these strategies was the intensification of work for developers. This often resulted in long hours and additional 'work' tasks. It appears that developers intensified their own work to maintain social relations with their community.

An additional example of this can be seen when developers were working for free (or a share of future profits). This passage underlines the value this developer places on being part of a team and being part of a firm, this motivated him to work - without pay:

It kind of felt a bit removed, but there reached a point where they realised they couldn't pay me, you know, weekly, and they realised they were maybe tackling it the wrong way. So they kind of brought everyone together and said, look, you know, we're all sacrificing this. So now, I feel more involved, like we're part of a team. We've all got our files on the website. I've got White Paper Games on my Twitter account; I've got it on my Facebook. I feel like I'm part of this company now. (Owen, independent game developer, Preston)

For this developer being part of the project was more than a financial arrangement. The symbolism of naming him on the company website on social media connected him with others and gave meaning to his work. Payment was something he was prepared to sacrifice in order to demonstrate a social connection with others.

This section shows the importance that developers place on being part of their occupational community. The wider argument suggests that, at least for these developers, work is an important place for social relations. This view highlights work's continuing importance in individuals' lives. However, where work is fragmented, and work arrangements are changing, this has presented a challenge for developers. In order to enhance their relationship with the occupational community and recreate social relations, developers were willing to network, seek funding or work for free in order to re-establish spatial relationships to reconnect with their peers, even if this meant that they had to work harder or submit to exploitative conditions.

Conclusion

This chapter has revealed the characteristics of work that developers draw on to rationalise their own exploitative conditions. In so doing, a body of literature in the creative industries has been verified. Developers have accepted exploitative conditions because of the self-actualising nature of their work and their passion and the opportunity that exploitation offers (Ursell, 2000; McRobbie, 2002; Ross, 2003; Ekman, 2014). However, this chapter has illustrated that developers drew on other aspects of the meaning of their work to rationalise exploitative conditions.

Developers understood there was a degree of commitment needed in order to be successful. This led to the development of ideas and beliefs about how they would have to work to gain success. This mentality influenced developers to accept the need to work long hours. Developers also believed that enterprise was an important trait or characteristic that they should demonstrate, and they understood their dual role as enterprising individuals and developers. Although the presence of entrepreneurial identities in the creative sector is nothing new (Hackley and Kover, 2007; Gotsi et al., 2010; Thompson et al., 2015), by understanding themselves as enterprising individuals developers were prepared to adopt characteristics such as dedication, self-reliance and risk, which shaped their attitudes towards working practices and limited their resistance towards taking on additional jobs or working for free.

In the context of accounts of new employment relationships resulting in the demise of the collective nature of employment (Beck, 1992) and a weakened connection between work and social relationships (Foster, 2012), developers felt a loss of attachment with others, something which they felt was important because of the collaborative nature of their work. In order to establish or maintain social relationships, developers implemented various strategies to reconnect themselves with the occupational community and their peers, such as by networking, seeking out additional funding and working for free. The intensification of their work and having to work for low pay were seen as acceptable sacrifices to regain social relationships.

This analysis shows that understandings of passion, commitment to work, an entrepreneurial attitude and the need for attachment to peers were drawn on by developers to rationalise exploitative working practices. Furthermore, these characteristics appear to guide the behaviour of developers and limit their resistance to exploitative conditions.

Acknowledgment

I would like to thank Damian Hodgson and Debra Howcroft who offered guidance and support throughout the process of conducting this research. Also, I would like to thank the editors whose advice has considerably improved this chapter.

REFERENCES

Adam, A., M. Griffiths, C. Keogh, K. Moore, H. Richardson and A. Tattersall (2006) 'Being an "It" in IT: Gendered Identities in the IT', *Workplace, European Journal Of Information Systems*, 15, 4, 368–78.

Arvidsson, A. E., G. Malossi and S. Naro (2010) 'Passionate Work? Labour Conditions in the Milan Fashion Industry', *Journal for Cultural Research*, 14, 3, 295–309.

Banks, M. (2007) *The Politics Of Cultural Work* (Basingstoke: Palgrave).

Banks, M. and D. Hesmondhalgh (2009) 'Looking for Work in Creative Industries Policy'. *International Journal of Cultural Policy*, 15, 4, 415–30.

Barley, S. R. and G. Kunda (2004) *Gurus, Hired Guns, and Warm Bodies: Itinerant Experts in a Knowledge Economy* (Princeton, NJ: Princeton University Press).

Barrett, R. (2005) 'Managing the Software Development Labour Process: Direct Control, Time and Technical Autonomy', in R. Barrett (ed.), *Management, Labour Process and Software Development* (London: Routledge), pp. 76–99.

Beck, U. (1992) *Risk Society: Towards A New Modernity* (London: Sage).

Bergvall-Kåreborn, B. and D. Howcroft (2013) 'The Future's Bright, the Future's Mobile': A Study of Apple and Google Mobile Application Developers', *Work, Employment and Society*, 27, 6, 964–81.

▶

Blair, H. (2009) 'Active Networking: Action Social Structure and the Process of Networking', in C. Smith and A. Mckinlay (eds), *Creative Labour Working in the Creative Industries* (Basingstoke: Palgrave), pp. 116–35.

Blair, H., N. Culkin and K. Randle (2003) 'From London to Los Angeles: a comparison of local labour market processes in the US and UK film industries', *International Journal of Human Resource Management*, 14, 4, 619–33.

Cadin, L., F. Guerin and R. Defillippi (2006) 'HRM practices in the video game industry: industry or country contingent?', *European Management Journal*, 24, 4, 288–98.

Casson, M. and C. Casson (2013) *The Entrepreneur in History: From Medieval Merchant to Modern Business Leader* (London: Palgrave Macmillan).

Cohendet, P. and L. Simon (2007) 'Playing Across the Playground: Paradoxes of Knowledge Creation in the Videogame Firm', *Journal of Organizational Behavior*, 28, 587–605.

Coulson, S. (2012) 'Collaborating in a Competitive World: Musician's Working Lives and Understanding of Entrepreneurship', *Work, Employment and Society*, 26, 2, 246–61.

Creswell, J. (2013) *Research Design: Qualitative and Quantitative and Mixed Method Approaches* (4th edn) (Thousand Oaks: Sage).

De Peuter, G. and N. Dyer-Witheford (2005) 'A Playful Multitude? Mobilising and Counter-Mobilising Immaterial Game Labour.' *Fibreculture*, 5. http://Five. Fibreculturejournal.Org/Fcj-024, date accessed 25 July 2010.

De Prato, G., C. Feijóo, D. Nepelski, M. Bogdanowicz and J. P. Simon (2010) JRC-IPTS Report.

Defillippi, R., G. Grabher and C. Jones (2007) 'Introduction to Paradoxes of Creativity: Managerial and Organizational Challenges in the Cultural Economy', *Journal of Organizational Behaviour*, 28, 511–21.

Department for Business, Innovation and Skills (2010) Blueprint for Technology.

Deuze, M., C. B. Martin and C. Allen (2007) 'The Professional Identity of Gameworkers', *Convergence*, 13, 4, 335–53.

Down, S. (2010) *Enterprise, Entrepreneurship and Small Business* (London: Sage).

Du Gay, P. (1996) *Consumption and Identity at Work* (London: Sage).

Eikhof, D. and A. Haunschild (2006) 'Lifestyle Meets Market: Bohemian Entrepreneurs in Creative Industries', *Creativity and Innovation Management*, 15, 3, 234–41.

Ekman, S. (2014) 'Is the high-involvement worker precarious or opportunistic? Hierarchical ambiguities in late capitalism', *Organization*, 21, 2, 141–58.

Euromonitor (2014) Video Games Market Sizes. https://Www.Portal.Euromonitor. Com/Portal/Statistics/Tab, date accessed 15 November 2014.

Felstead, A., N. Jewson and S. Walters (2005) *Changing Places of Work* (Basingstoke: Palgrave Macmillan).

Foster, K. (2012) 'Work, Narrative Identity and Social Affiliation', *Work, Employment and Society*, 26, 6, 935–50.

Friedman, A. L. (1977) *Industry and Labour: Class Struggle at Work and Monopoly Capitalism* (London: Macmillan).

Garnham, N. (2005) 'From Cultural to Creative Industries', *International Journal of Cultural Policy*, 11, 1, 15–29.

Gibb, A. A. (1993) 'Enterprise Culture and Education and Its Links with Small Business, Entrepreneurship and Wider Educational Goals', *International Small Business Journal*, 11, 11–34.

Gotsi, M., C. Andriopoulos, M. W. Lewis and A. E. Ingram (2010) 'Managing Creatives: Paradoxical Approaches to Identity Regulation', *Human Relations*, 63, 6, 781–805.

Grabher, G. and O. Ibert (2006) 'Bad Company? The Ambiguity of Personal Knowledge Networks', *Journal of Economic Geography*, 6, 251–71.

Granter, E. J., L. Mccann and M. Boyle (2015) 'Extreme Work/Normal Work: Intensification, Storytelling and Hypermediation in the (re) construction of "The New Normal"', *Organization*, 22, 4, 443–56.

Grey, C. (1994). 'Career as a Project of the Self and Labour Process Discipline', *Sociology*, 28, 2, 479–97.

Hackley, C. and A. Kover (2007) 'The Trouble with Creatives: Negotiating Creative Identity in Advertising Agencies', *International Journal Of Advertising*, 26, 1, 63–78.

Harvey, A. and Shepherd, T. (2016) 'When Passion isn't Enough: Gender, Affect and Credibility in Digital Games Design.', *International Journal of Cultural Studies*, 1–17. http://journals.sagepub.com/doi/pdf/10.1177/1367877916636140, date accessed 1 June 2016.

Haunschild, A. and D. Eikhof (2009) 'Bringing Creativity to Market. Theatre Actors as Self-Employed Employees', in C. Smith and A. Mckinlay (eds), *Creative Labour. Working in the Creative Industries* (Basingstoke: Palgrave), pp. 156–73.

Hesmondhalgh, D. and S. Baker (2009) 'A very complicated version of freedom': conditions and experiences of creative labour in three cultural industries', *Poetics*, 38, 1, 4–20.

Hesmondhalgh, D. and S. Baker (2010) '"A Very Complicated Version of Freedom": Conditions and Experiences of Creative Labour in Three Cultural Industries', *Poetics*, 38, 1, 4–20.

Hesmondhalgh, D. and S. Baker (2011) *Creative Labour: Media Work in Three Cultural Industries* (London: Routledge).

Izushi, H. and Y. Aoyama (2006) 'Industry Evolution and Cross-Sectoral Skill Transfers: A Comparative Analysis of the Video Game Industry in Japan, The United States, and The United Kingdom', *Environment and Planning A*, 38, 10, 1843–61.

Johns, J. (2006) 'Video Games Production Networks: Value Capture, Power Relations and Embeddedness', *Journal of Economic Geography*, 6, 2, 151–80.

Kennedy, H. (2010) 'The Successful Self-Regulation of Web Designers', *Ephemera*, 10, 3–4, 374–89.

Keynote (2013) Market Report: Home Entertainment. Keynote.

Lipkin, N. (2013) 'Examining indie's Independence: The Meaning of "indie" Games, The Politics of Production, and Mainstream Co-optation', *Journal of the Canadian Game Studies Association*, 7, 11, 8–24.

Martin, C. and M. Deuze (2009) 'The Independent Production of Culture: A Digital Games Case Study', *Games and Culture*, 4, 3, 276–95.

Mateos–Garcia, J., H. Bakhshi and M. Lenel (2014) *A Map of the UK Games Industry* (London: NESTA).

McRobbie, A. (2002) 'From Holloway to Hollywood: Happiness at Work in the New Cultural Economy', in P. Du Gay and M. Pryke (eds), *Cultural Economy* (London: Sage), pp. 97–114.

Parker, R., S. Cox and P. Thompson (2014) 'How Technological Change Affects Power Relations in Global Markets: Remote Developers in the Console and Mobile Games Industry', *Environment and Planning A*, 46, 1, 168–85.

Percival, N. and D. Hesmondhalgh (2014) 'Unpaid Work in the UK Television and Film Industries: Resistance and Changing Attitudes', *European Journal of Communication*, 29, 2, 188–203.

Peticca-Harris, A., J. Weststar and S. Mckenna (2015) 'The Perils of Project-Based Work: Attempting Resistance to Extreme Work Practices in Video Game Development', *Organization*, 22, 4, 570–87.

Phillips, R., W. Latham, D. Hodgson, J. Corden, J. Jordan, T. Minshall and L. Wharton (2009) *In Search for Excellence: A Comparative Business Model Assessment of Value Creation Capabilities in the Computer Games Sector*. North West Development Agency.

Randle, K. and N. Culkin (2009) 'Getting in and Getting on in Hollywood: Freelance Careers in an Uncertain Industry', in Alan McKinlay and Chris Smith (eds), *The Labour Process in the Creative Industries* (London: Palgrave Macmillan).

Randle, K., C. Forson and M. Calveley (2015) 'Towards a Bourdieusian Analysis of the Social Composition of the UK Film and Television Workforce', *Work Society and Employment*, 29, 4, 590–606.

Reeves, R. (2001) *Happy Mondays - putting the pleasure back into work* (London: Momentum).

Robinson, E. (2005) Why Crunch Mode Doesn't Work: 6 Lessons, *IGDA*.

Ross, A. (2000) 'The Mental Labor Problem', *Social Text*, 63, 18, 2, 1–31.

Ross, A. (2003) *No-Collar: The Humane Workplace and Its Hidden Costs* (New York, NY: Basic Books).

Siebert, S. and F. Wilson (2013) 'All Work and No Pay: Consequences of Unpaid Work in the Creative Industries', *Work, Employment and Society*, 27, 4, 711–21.

Skillset (ed.) (2011) *Computer Games Sector: Labour Market Intelligence Digest* (London: Skillset).

Smith, C. and A. McKinlay (eds) (2009) *Creative Labour: Working in Creative Industries* (London: Palgrave Macmillan), pp. 3–28.

Tapia, A. H. (2004) 'The Power of Myth in the IT Workplace: Creating a 24 Hour Workday During the Dot-Com Bubble', *Information Technology and People*, 17, 3, 303–26.

Thompson, P., R. Parker. and S. Cox (2015) 'Interrogating Creative Theory and Creative Work: Inside the Games Studio', *Sociology*, 50, 2, 1–17.

Tschang, F. T. (2007) 'Balancing the Tensions Between Rationalization and Creativity in the Video Games Industry', *Organization Science*, 18, 6, 989–1005.

▶

Umney, C. and L. Kretsos (2014) 'Creative Labour and Collective Interaction: The Working Lives of Young Jazz Musicians in London', *Work, Employment and Society*, 28, 4, 571–88.

Ursell, G. (2000) 'Television Production: Issues of Exploitation, Commodification and Subjectivity in UK Television Labour Markets', *Media Culture and Society*, 22, 6, 805–25.

Wright, A. (2015) 'It's All About Games: Enterprise and Entrepreneurialism in Digital Games', *New Technology, Work and Employment*, 30, 32–46.

Macro-, Meso- and Micro-Level Determinants of Employment Relations in the Video Games Industry

11

Christina Teipen

Introduction

In the buzz about the 'new economy', the new media industries have been deemed pioneers of employment dynamics that will apply more generally in the future. Employees in this sector, which has been making use of hardware innovations and producing digital innovations from the start, have been at the cutting edge of technological progress. Likewise, researchers studying the creative industries have also been considered to be at the forefront of scholarship on changes in employment relations and working conditions. While there are exceptions, and no generalisations can be made for the entire economy, the significance of employees working in new media, including developers of digital entertainment software and their working conditions, is increasing due to at least three trends. First, non-material and knowledge work as a whole has risen in advanced economies (Castells, 1996). Assumptions about this type of work dialectically combine some rather optimistic features such as autonomy and self-development through work, with pessimistic features, such as insecure and short-term contracts (Pongratz and Voß, 2003). Second, the digital entertainment sector is growing in light of global technological trends like smartphone usage. An excellent illustration of this market expansion is the recent, enormous success of the movie 'Warcraft' in China, which was only made possible due to the large numbers of users of the video game of the same name. Third, due to their embeddedness in global value chains (GVCs), these developers are subject to a shifting of market risks from lead firms onto less powerful development studios – a topic that is often treated as marginal in existing research, yet eminently worthy of further scrutiny.

This chapter's research question is, what are the factors influencing working conditions in this growing labour market segment in Europe? Can we observe uniform or similar employment patterns across the industry due to global value chain characteristics and industry-specific influences? Or do different national backgrounds determine whether precarious or favourable employment characteristics are suppressed or strengthened in a given country, as the 'varieties of capitalism' (VoC) view (Hall and Soskice, 2001) would predict. I will argue that the global value chain approach (Gereffi et al., 2005) can be productively combined with elements of VoC and the labour process debate to bridge the influential macro and micro dimensions of work and employment outcomes that are so characteristic of this industry segment. Following this introduction, I will discuss these different theoretical approaches. Then, in the third section, I will introduce my own research on video game developers in Germany, Sweden and Poland. In section four, I will compare my results with other recent studies. The final section provides a theoretical conclusion.

Theoretical Discussion

In the following paragraphs, I will look at the theoretical approaches that examine how macro- and meso-level factors influence employment conditions in the video game development sector. The VoC approach (Hall and Soskice, 2001) emphasises the impact of distinct national institutional systems (i.e. macro-level factors). It argues that collective bargaining and labour law frameworks in countries such as Germany and Sweden impede the advancement of industries like the video games industry because they massively restrict corporate flexibility. The GVC approach (Gereffi et al., 2005), by contrast, stresses the impact of GVC governance on employment conditions. Regarding the video games industry, it points to the power relations between small development studios and large hardware producers and publishers (Teipen, 2008, 2016). In the following, I will briefly discuss the arguments and theses proposed by both approaches.

The core argument put forward by Hall and Soskice (2001) is that companies in liberal market economies (LMEs) favour human resource management strategies that include high external flexibility and a high level of individual employment risk (Hancké, 2009, p. 4). These employment conditions – together with complementary characteristics in other institutional systems – are said to be more favourable for radically innovative companies. Institutional conditions in coordinated market economies, in contrast, are said to support higher levels of employment protection and therefore act as barriers to the type of strategic reorientations that radically innovative companies need. The business system approach (e.g. Whitley, 2007, p. 244) also suggests that 'fluid, dynamic external labour markets' are more advantageous for companies developing risky technologies (Casper et al., 1999, p. 22).

In the debate about the creative industries and the 'new economy', several authors seem to suggest that the information and communications technology (ICT) and software development industries – to which the video games industry belongs – are radically innovative sectors that require highly flexible labour markets. Lazonick (2006) identifies a 'flexible' labour market for highly skilled employees as a necessary precondition for competitive 'new economy' work. In line with this, Florida (2002, pp. 44ff and 135f) mentions a 'new employment contract' as a characteristic element of change in the 'creative economy'. Autonomy and the liberty to pursue one's own interests are said to be more valuable in this new type of working relationship than is long-term job security.

Based on the VoC approach, we could expect the video games industry to favour LMEs. We could additionally expect video games companies to struggle with the regulatory setup in coordinated forms of capitalism like Germany and Sweden, which favour long-term employment relationships. Given that a strong video games industry has developed in both countries, even if neither country has gained a world leadership position, it is important to examine whether video games companies develop 'within' the institutional setting and adapt to the traditional employment models, which are based on stable, long-term employment, or whether they manage to establish forms of employment relations that fundamentally differ from the dominant model.

Numerous scholars have argued that the VoC approach overemphasises the role of national institutions (e.g. Allen, 2004; Hancké and Goyer, 2005, p. 56; Deeg, 2005; Schneiberg, 2007). Hollingsworth and Boyer (1997, p. 21) have argued that different 'social systems of production' often exist simultaneously within one country and that entire sectors can be organised according to principles that differ from those of the dominant social system of production.[1]

In addition to the role of institutions, we have to take into account the role of foreign companies and their influence on employment relations. This is the starting point for the second theoretical perspective that I discuss here, namely the GVC approach. It emphasises the importance of governance modes between companies and beyond national borders and explores how power is unevenly distributed across these different companies depending on their respective position in the value chain (Sturgeon, 2001, pp. 10, 11; Gereffi et al., 2005). The GVC approach focuses on vertical sequences of the value chain in industries such as hardware production, software development, publishing and distribution, in which companies are economically active (Figure 11.1.).

Gereffi et al. (2005) have identified five analytical types of value chain governance:

1. market-based governance of supplier relations, with low switching costs for focal firms to other partners;
2. modular governance, with greater importance of information transfer and supplier competences;
3. relational governance, with even more complex interactions and mutual interdependence;
4. captive governance of suppliers, with low competences depending on focal companies;
5. hierarchical governance, which is the model of vertically integrated companies.

These five firm types lie on an increasing continuum regarding power asymmetries between suppliers and focal firms: while the power imbalance is assumed to be low in the case of market-based value chain governance, it increases from one type to the next, reaching a maximum under hierarchical value chain governance.

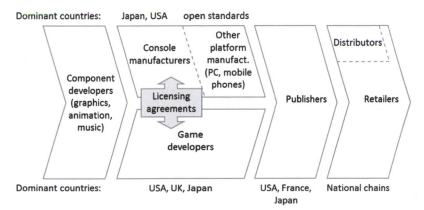

Figure 11.1 The traditional value chain structure in the video games industry

Source: Author based on Spectrum (2002).

Based on this typology by Gereffi et al. (2005), the traditional structure of the video games industry could be classified as 'market-based' or 'modular value chain governance' depending on the video game developers' competences. There is, however, one common feature of the value chain in this industry – the high dependence of the video game studios on the financing provided mainly by international publishers, who finance the often year-long process of game development. The value chain is controlled by distributors and by international publishers, which usually finance software development and hold property rights (cf. also Behrmann, 2011, p. 4). Thus, publishing companies and global hardware producers are among the key players in the video games industry: they possess power over essential resources, and they can control entry barriers to the sector, such as by financing software development staff and by owning licences for certain types of consoles (cf. Grantham and Kaplinsky, 2005; Readman and Grantham, 2006; Bouncken and Müller-Lietzkow, 2007; Teipen, 2016). The GVC approach is valuable because it highlights the development studios' lack of bargaining power in relation to publishers. It also highlights international hardware developers' capacity to establish industry standards (see Gereffi et al., 2005, p. 98).

With the exception of Lakhani et al. (2013), the GVC approach has rarely been expanded to analyse employment relations. In the past, employment relations have been discussed only on a random basis – for example, with regard to the control of process specifications by focal firms vis-à-vis suppliers, to which labour standards can also pertain (Humphrey and Schmitz, 2001, p. 22) or with reference to the control and provision of skills. There is still a question of whether power differentials have a significant impact on areas such as the staffing policies of development studios in the sector under consideration here.

Lakhani et al. (2013) have developed the first theoretical framework in this respect. In it, they aim to specify the type of employment relationships present in different value chain configurations. In the case of 'modular value chain governance', they expect a low 'influence of the lead firm on supplier employment relations', moderate skill levels at the supplier level (which is the game developers), moderate employment stability and a high influence of national institutions on the employment relations. In the case of market-based value chain governance, they expect low skill levels and low employment stability, while the other two criteria would remain the same.

Without going into more detail, we can already see that the argument from Lakhani et al. does not really capture the situation in the video games industry. Despite modular or even market-based value chain governance, the employees of development firms (which are suppliers for the publishing companies) possess high skills. Good game designers should ideally have many different competences simultaneously: technical skills such as programming, market knowledge, a capacity to empathise with gamers and creativity (Interview D5). The precarious situation of video games companies in the sectoral value chain is not the result of a low-skilled workforce and a simple product – the opposite is the case. Rather, it emerges due to the industry's high dependence on financing provided by huge international publishers, which can, however, withdraw financing at any time or refuse to award the financing necessary to develop a new project after one contract has been finished.

Lakhani et al.'s approach, although an important contribution to the analysis of employment conditions in GVCs, can be critiqued for being premised on transaction cost theory; that is, its explanations centre on supposedly efficient strategies. It avoids explanations that relate to power in labour and employment conditions. Its configurations are based on theoretical assumptions and disregard struggles and conflicts of actors that are endowed with different levels of power, which could also lead to structural changes for the employees.

An alternative approach of the kind suggested above is taken by labour process theory. The roots and origins of this theory go back a long way, although they have recently been revived with regard to value chain issues. Without retracing the whole history of this theoretical tradition, I would like to highlight a number of key points relevant to this contribution. One key point is the so-called transformation problem, which arises from the gap between the work contract and the actual job performance. This gap establishes a zone of indeterminacy regarding management's actual ability to fulfil the aims of previously agreed contracts. It is the task of management to ensure that this transformation takes place and to organise the required structures and work sequences. This marks the starting point for a discussion on the changing forms of control and corporate power. Labour process theory's contribution lies in its elucidation of the existence of consensus-based management as one of several management control strategies (Edwards, 1979). 'Market mechanisms alone are insufficient' if we are seeking 'mechanisms that transform the capacity to work into actual work' (Newsome et al., 2015, pp. 3, 4). McKinlay and Smith (2009) have applied the micro-level approach of labour process theory to the creative industries. According to them, 'employer–worker engagement' includes 'debates around how this time is used (the intensity of labour) and for how long (the extensiveness of labour)' (233). Some of these 'control strategies' appeal to the 'professional values' of employees themselves and their 'creativity' (Smith, 2015, p. 226). However, the employees' ambivalence becomes apparent when we consider this choice of a particular form of management as embedded in a fundamental power imbalance between labour and capital.

Besides this key analysis at the levels of the company and individual jobs, labour process theory also attempts to link the macro and micro dimensions of employment and work. This is true for Burawoy's (1985) distinction between politics 'in production' and 'of production' as well as for Thompson's (2013) VoC-inspired proposal to analyse different 'institutional domains'; however, Thompson places a stronger emphasis on 'financialization or new shareholder capitalism' than Hall and Soskice's earlier, and rather static, version does. The regulation of work relations has always been a 'contested terrain', with historically changing dynamics, and it has been a subject of political dispute within and beyond individual companies. A variety of different work and employment systems on the national and industry level continually compete with each other to enforce such systems. These fields of conflict between different interests and the negotiation over working conditions are emphasised by the labour process theory tradition.

Linking a comparative institutional analysis at the national level with an analysis at the meso level – that is, the level of industries, and at the transnational level – the level of value chains is still a rare theoretical and empirical endeavour,[2] to which this chapter aims to contribute. In the following section, I will first present results from my own study on the video games industry in Germany, Sweden and Poland. Based on those findings, the interrelationship between value chain configurations and working conditions seem to be characteristic for independent development studios in this industry. I will then compare this analysis to recent observations of similar value chain configurations in other countries.

Research Results from the Video Games Industry in Germany, Sweden and Poland

The following analysis is based on in-depth case studies in video games companies and interviews with representatives of industry associations in Germany, Sweden and Poland (Teipen, 2008, 2016). Twelve companies from different segments of the value chain are included: six publishers and six development studios. The case studies were conducted in 2005 as a 'snapshot' study (Thomas, 2011, p. 517). In addition,

I interviewed 23 industry experts who work outside of companies, attended industry fairs and analysed data, which allows me to describe the change dynamics until the year 2013. At the level of national institutions, I captured national characteristics as well as their change dynamics by means of a literature analysis.

Especially for smaller development companies, the conditions of product markets and traditional value chains are a cause of insecurity in the form of casualised work and insecure employment patterns. These conditions also represent barriers to employment growth and to gaining greater international market shares. One decisive factor for these outcomes is that development studios lack independent financial resources – in the form of bank loans, risk capital or other external sources. Hence they are often dependent on publishers funding their development projects. The production of entertainment software is subject to high flexibility requirements, which can be explained by high market volatility and by the high-risk position of development studios in the value chain. Large development investments have to be financed by publishers, and nobody can be certain whether a product will be successful. This results in considerable instability and pressure to work flexibly, particularly for smaller companies with limited product portfolios. Developer studios bear both the risks of unforeseeable challenges arising and the costs for any late delivery of their product. Many contracts guarantee publishers extensive co-decision power on game production, to the point of 'direct involvement' in staffing decisions, as defined for 'captive' value chain configurations by Lakhani et al. (2013, p. 450). These configurations do not, however, fit with regard to other criteria, since the supplier competences and skills of game designers are higher than Lakhani et al. (2013) theorises for 'captive' value chain configurations. Instead, the constellation would seem to combine elements of both the 'market' and the 'relational' type of 'value chain configurations'. Because of a strong power asymmetry between publishers and independent development studios, this configuration does not entirely fit into the 'market-based' category; however, since the costs of switching studios are very low for the publishers, it cannot be classified as fully 'relational' either.

All the companies included in the study showed high levels of staff turnover. These reflected the volatile economic conditions experienced by developers in the value chain and happened despite different national employment legislation in the countries under study.[3] Payroll costs accounted for 70–90 per cent of the total cost of developing game software. As one interviewee explained, 'If you have to save rapidly here, [payroll costs have] the largest potential for savings' (Interview D13).

Another interviewee described the interrelationship between insufficient financial capital and flexible forms of employment as follows:

'We have to keep a certain amount of flexibility. This is particularly important if we have to dismiss people. That has to be very fast without hesitation. … If the publisher then freezes production, at that very moment, I have to be able to react at once. Too slow a reaction would be enough to possibly signal the death of the whole firm' (Interview D11).

Due to their poor ability to attract funding through national institutions and their consistently heavy dependence on publishers, development companies were rarely able to achieve long-term growth or to implement human resource management strategies. A flop can therefore endanger a company's survival and the job security of its employees and may have immediate effects on employment.

A company case study from Germany (Interviews D13 and D14) illustrates the characteristic ways in which contexts can obstruct the most technologically able and ambitious development teams. For two to three years, this company's first successful title – its 'founding stone' – was developed with a small team: for the first four years of its existence, the company operated with no more than 20 employees. This low number of employees was the result of narrow budget constraints and the inability of the development studio to negotiate better terms with publishers. The budget limited both an expansion into international markets and prospects of contracting with other publishers. Moreover, the labour force was too small to develop the original game for other consoles with a higher market penetration.

Given this focus on external employment flexibility, to what extent can national institutions influence the employment relations in the video games sector? With reference to the VoC approach, the key issue is whether the institutional constellations that are regarded as being constitutive of a national economy play a role in the video games industry at all. Do the unfavourable regulations that exist in Germany and Sweden detrimentally affect the competitiveness of video game companies, as VoC scholars have postulated? This contribution will concentrate specifically on the flexibility of employment and the dangers of precarity. What evidence do we have about the structure of employment relationships and – in more detail – employment protection in the respective national sectors?

Let us first briefly look at the three countries under study. Sweden is characterised by a high degree of unionisation and collective bargaining, which also covers the new ICT industries and smaller firms. In Germany, however, the degree of organisation through works councils is very low in the new ICT sectors – despite the strength of works councils in core industries. In contrast, in Poland trade unions mainly exist in state-run companies. This result is confirmed by the third European company survey, in which Germany and Poland lie far behind Sweden with regard to official employee representation (Eurofound, 2013, p. 5). The share of temporary employment rose in all three countries during the 2000s. The proportion was greatest in Poland, followed by Sweden and Germany. Regarding employment protection legislation, all three countries are characterised by relatively strict rules, with Poland even topping the highest employment protection legislation index according to the OECD (2004). The monitoring and enforcement of employment protection legislation is, however, relatively weak in Poland.

In view of these different national institutions, how do companies in the video games industry deal with flexibility pressures? My analysis shows that national labour institutions influence work and employment conditions at development firms to only a small extent (see Table 11.1), which stands in stark contrast to what one might expect from a VoC perspective (Teipen, 2008, 2016). Collective forms of interest articulation are very rare in this employment segment, with the exception of the Swedish case study. The forms of employment follow industry-specific patterns but depend on resources offered by national financial systems; in addition, they are shaped by powerful players in the transnational value chain.

Table 11.1 Research outcomes regarding small, younger development studios and types of capitalism

	External labour flexibility	Corporate strategies	Regulation of external labour flexibility	Type of capitalism
Germany	High	Dualisation between core and non-core workforce	Individual	Coordinated market economy impaired by 'shareholder value'
Sweden	High	Avoiding strict labour law through dismissals in advance	Collective	Coordinated market economy/Nordic capitalism
Poland	High	Severance payments	Individual	'Dependent market economy'[4]

[4] Vliegenthart and Nölke, 2009

In Sweden – which had a very successful video games industry at the time of our study – the main development studios had active union representatives and/or collective bargaining. Most of the employment contracts were permanent. However, in the Swedish system, managers did not perceive the employment contracts or collective bargaining as obstacles to flexibility. They recalled that unions had been highly cooperative during crises: 'They understood when we had to lay somebody off' (Interview S1). During critical periods, union negotiators did not insist that the companies follow the relevant labour law – a 'last one in, first one out' policy – when selecting people to dismiss. The interviewees confirmed that strong legal protections against unfair dismissal are likewise not a problem for the video games industry in Sweden. If the future development of a company seemed uncertain, managers commonly gave advance notice to employees and withdrew such notice if the situation changed (Interview S1). Using such an approach, managers were able to work together with unions to circumvent strict national regulations that could endanger the core capabilities of a firm; they were thus able to create the appropriate space for employment flexibility in a cooperative manner.

The CEO of a Swedish development studio explained his preference for permanent employment as follows: he 'wants to keep the employees from spending time looking for other jobs. If developer S finds someone without work experience, it takes four to five months until they are at the peak of their performance. If the person comes from another game developer, it takes one to two months. In some cases, it takes years' (Interview S1).

In Germany, firms typically sought to segment their employees into core and non-core workforces. They tried to distinguish between a small permanent core, which was granted permanent contracts, and a higher number of people with temporary employment contracts. The reason for this arrangement was the firm's vulnerable position in the value chain. If a publisher dropped out at a later stage and the firm needed to find a new one, a financial bottleneck would emerge. The following case exemplifies the problems these companies face. This firm initially tried to give permanent work contracts to its staff, while additional employees were recruited from students or freelancers when required. In several cases, however, budget constraints emerged, and so the salaries of the original team of permanent staff could no longer be paid. These highly motivated employees made tremendous concessions to be able to work in their company of choice. During those periods, the company offered casual employment instead of full-time remuneration, occasionally interspersed with temporary layoffs, until the management eventually drew the logical conclusion and changed all contracts to fixed-term ones. Such precarious employment patterns are not a temporary phenomenon but instead reflect insufficient funding sources and the weak value chain positions of the companies.

The results reveal that video game developers in Germany belong to a new ICT segment, where small firms generally have the latitude to practise extremely flexible human resource management without being subject to the control of any work council. Employment relationships in this segment do not follow the dominant national model in Germany; however, they are rather similar to their Polish counterparts, where external employment flexibility is higher nationwide.

In Poland, firms resorted to dismissals when they had to adjust their employment levels. They had to pay severance payments in such cases, but Polish labour legislation limits the amount of severance payments to three months' wages at maximum. It was also not unusual to work with freelancers, but in this case, the reason was not flexibility. As one interviewee reported, about 35 per cent of the company's workforce in Poland were 'actually freelancers. To hire them on a permanent basis would be very expensive. … Developer B wants to avoid taxation. The regulation of the labour law – for example, rigid employment protection – is not the reason why permanent contracts are avoided' (Interview P2).

Thus we can conclude that in the area of employment and work, dissimilar 'varieties of capitalism' might lead to different corporate ways of dealing with flexibility pressures. Sweden's affiliation to the Nordic regime (Edlund and Grönlund, 2008; Borrás et al., 2015) could have contributed to the higher relevance of collective procedures there in comparison to Germany. Or the creative but collective avoidance strategy could also be interpreted as a better 'survival' mechanism of Sweden's 'egalitarian capitalism' compared to Germany (Thelen, 2014, p. 1). We can also observe the opposite relation: dissimilar 'varieties of capitalism', such as Germany and Poland, exhibit similar, namely individual, corporate strategies. Nonetheless, despite these differences in interest representation, in firms' responses and at the level of national work and employment institutions, companies' flexibility in terms of the people they employed was very high across all three national sectors. Therefore, this overall result does not support VoC expectations that national regulations might prevent competitiveness or that national work and employment institutions decisively influence employment patterns in this type of development studio. This statement could be interpreted in two different ways. First, the original 'varieties of capitalism' have been transformed and/or do not cover whole economies, but core segments, to which the industry studied here does not belong in any of the three countries. Or, second, there are other factors that are crucial here, which is what I will argue with respect to value chain aspects.

The low relevance of national employment institutions is also emphasised by the observation that the Swedish and German companies were typically unable to make use of 'long-term employment' traditions in national institutional systems in a way that allowed them to, among other things, achieve a leading role in the world market, as Storz (2008, p. 1488) has observed for the Japanese game software sector. Instead, due to their value chain positions and lack of financial resources, development studios in the three national sectors tried to keep highly skilled experts as core team members and to establish precarious medium-term relationships with additional developers.

Studies at the Micro Level of the Video Games and Related Industries

To what extent do our study findings represent a dominant pattern in this industry? How do they relate to studies in other countries or studies adopting different theoretical approaches? In this section, I will discuss research contributions stemming from the labour process perspective, which focuses on the work experience and subjective perceptions of employees and which places less emphasis on distinctive national institutions or corporate strategies.

Starting with examples from the United States, we can determine that the pattern of external flexibility found in the video games industry seems to follow that of older creative industries. Caves' (2000) analysis of the movie industry indicated that the long-term commitment of performers, film directors and production teams to studios had changed to 'one-shot deals' (Caves, 2000, p. 98) with a greater number of short-term and flexible contracts once the industry had successfully matured. Lampel and Shamsie (2003, p. 2206) also describe the 'hubs and networks' approaches in Hollywood's prosperous film industry. These market-based, individualised employment relationships developed to the extent that, after the model of dedicated film studios had collapsed, specific experts were mobilised for individual projects under the authority of major distributors (Randle and Culkin, 2009, p. 97). Thus, recruitment and employment are no longer organised by an independent production in the US film industry. This stands in stark contrast to development studios in Germany, Sweden and Poland, which are still seeking to prevent independent firm-based game production from being eroded and who attempt to hold development teams together (Teipen, 2016).

Regarding the internal organisation of work, management in creative industries tends to be informal and intimate rather than formal or hierarchical (McKinlay and Smith, 2009). In this type of project-based work, employees are deeply involved in the entire production process and have control over concepts. Another recurrent theme is that creative work processes are characterised by high levels of intrinsic motivation, meaning that newcomers often work for free so as to be able to access certain jobs (McKinlay and Smith, 2009).

If we want to compare research outcomes, not only do we have to consider related industries such as the movie industry; we can also look at a rich set of recent studies of the video games industry itself. A recent study on employees' values, attitudes and perceptions of their work has emphasised a negative attitude towards employment security in the German video games industry (Hoose, 2016, pp. 253–6). It is striking that Hoose's 26 interviewees put forward the view that atypical work is not just something to accept and fatalistically put up with; employees even state that it makes sense for this particular industry, while standard employment contracts often seem static and boring. In this study, a blurred line between work and leisure is often perceived as an advantage for creative activities. Employees consider it to be important to integrate inspiration and ideas into their jobs – if they arise spontaneously – at any time and anywhere.

Apitzsch (2015) provides a different account of the role of long working hours, which she found in the German film industry, with long hours also being wide-spread among digital entertainment developers. These long hours increase the employees' isolation from relationships outside their jobs and can weaken competing commitments (Apitzsch, 2015, p. 264). Long working hours, which are definitely also true for video game developers, are one of the informal forms of cooperation that exist in the absence of work councils, codified norms of professional practice or standardised professional skills. Such micro-sociological approaches offer explanations for how employers are able to ensure voluntary commitment without promising income or longer-term employment security (Apitzsch, 2015, pp. 261, 264).

The experience of working in the sector for a long time generates one of the few problematic aspects mentioned by the employees interviewed by Hoose (2016): they wonder whether the industry will ultimately be the appropriate sector for them on a permanent basis (Hoose, 2016, p. 255). And there is also another indication that suggests we should interpret the generally optimistic statements with caution: transforming a hobby into a profession – a central line of reasoning among the people interviewed by Teipen (2008, 2016) – features only for those relatively new to the industry, according to Hoose's (2016) study. The employees in his sample are conscious that their line of work is hard work and ultimately has little in common with gaming as a hobby (Hoose, 2016, p. 256). These employees' perceptions of having a high workload are even greater than those of the Hollywood script supervisor cited by Randle and Culkin (2009): 'Doing the work is fun. Finding the work is the job' (Randle and Culkin, 2009, p. 101).

Wright (2015) draws an even more sceptical picture of work and how it is subjectively experienced in the video games industry of North-West England. In contrast to Hoose (2016), he pays greater attention to how employees react to industry-specific reorganisations of the value chain such as 'outsourcing, a growing casual employment and technological changes' (Wright, 2015, p. 42) as well as the 'unpredictability of the games market' (Wright, 2015, p. 43). Against this background, he concludes that 'developers are often left with little alternative than "involuntary entrepreneurship"' and hence 'construct narratives of success and satisfaction' (Wright, 2015, p. 42). At first glance, this overall conclusion seems to be plausible, bearing in mind the complex interplay of objective circumstances and how they are subjectively evaluated. It, however, neglects the fact that there would be other opportunities for such employees, since many of them possess skills to apply to other industries with more stable labour market conditions and much higher salaries (Teipen, 2008, 2016). Still, a lot of these intrinsically motivated employees seem to accept unstable conditions in the video games industry in order to be able to carry out the work of their choice. This is the reason why they are even prepared to work 'for free' in order to ameliorate the financial crises of their companies (Teipen, 2016) or 'to establish themselves and develop their reputation in the sector' (Wright, 2015, p. 42). 'Self-commercialisation', as Wright (2015) accurately names it – based on Pongratz and Voß's (2003) work – presents only one side of the coin; extremely high professional motivation is the other. When both aspects are taken together – subjective preferences and narratives as well as adverse employment patterns in this industry – the result is the well-known phenomenon of 'self-exploitation', of which Wright is also aware.

Thompson et al. (2016) support these arguments but place different emphases in their study based on interviews with a relatively larger number of full-time and permanent employees in the Australian video games industry. On the one hand, they observe a trend towards greater standardisation and new divisions of labour in team-based development in a period of industry maturation. This restricts the degree of autonomy for individual employees. In addition, Thompson et al. quantify the share of 'freelancers' in this industry in Australia and, compared to Hoose (2016) in Germany and Wright (2015) in North-West England, find more employees seeking employment stability. On the other hand, while the industry is maturing and media giants are gaining more control across the value chain, it is still true that the creative basis, the skills and the risk of producing marketable output is delegated to small and 'more "flexible"/"expendable" firms' (Thompson et al., 2016, p. 329). All in all, they represent the view 'that games workers have a sense of themselves as creative artists, but they know they work in businesses with particular commercial logics', which results in 'a dynamic interplay of identity and interests in particular contexts' (Thompson et al., 2016). The way employees perceive these contexts is evidently less dependent on national work and employment institutions, since the micro-level findings on experiences from different countries seem to be comparable.

Conclusion

My research question was how GVCs as well as national work and employment institutions shape employment relations in independent development studios operating in the video games industry in various countries. This contribution intended to connect observations on working conditions in similar value chain configurations and to reflect systematically on the contributing factors that are specific to the national industry and micro levels as well as power constellations across value chains. According to Lakhani et al.'s (2013, p. 449) typology of value chain configurations, we should expect to find a low or moderate level of employment stability in the video games industry, but this hypothesis is based on the assumption that companies in this kind of value chain rely on a low-skilled workforce. My case studies demonstrate that even given a highly skilled workforce, companies in this kind of value chain focus their human resource management (HRM) concepts on high numerical employment flexibility. This underlines the explanatory power of the GVC approach. It is the power asymmetry between publishers and independent development studios, based on their unequal access to financial means, that submits the latter to the flexibility pressures of the former.

I also intended to address the question of to what extent institutional labour regulations influence these working conditions. Despite the fact that the countries under study here – Germany, Sweden and Poland – represent different types of capitalism according to the VoC typology, the HRM concepts in my case-study companies show very little variation. The results confirm my assumption that, despite negligible differences, the cross-national commonalities in how the sector organises work are still very visible. The impact of institutions was evident only in how the companies created high numerical flexibility in their workforce: in Sweden, this was based on bargaining procedures with the trade union; in Germany, it was based on a dualisation of the workforce between a stable core and a flexible margin of freelancers; and in Poland, it relied on a general 'hire and fire' approach.

Despite these different regulations on national levels and the different ways of creating the required flexibility, studies from the labour process perspective show that individual perceptions of employment conditions are very similar across countries. The role of enthusiasm, intrinsic motivation and identification with the product and with the creative type of work are common sources of work satisfaction. Given their risky and weak position across the value chain, this makes those digital employees susceptible to self-exploitation (see Wright in this volume), in particular when workloads are very high.

This result underlines the necessity to connect the labour process approach with a GVC analysis in order to explain the development of employment relations in high-tech and creative sectors like the video games industry. It is the particular position and vulnerability of game development studios in the sectoral value chain that explains the flexibility pressures on the companies and their search for high numerical flexibility of employment. This vulnerability shapes the employment relations under all the different national institutional settings, which explain only *how* external flexibility is achieved, but not the level of external employment flexibility. We need labour process analysis, however, to understand how video game companies still manage to retain employees and create consent and why the video game developers are willing to work under such insecure conditions and often in the face of excessive performance demands.

Notes

1 Nonetheless, based on her studies on Japanese gaming software, Storz (2009, p. 29; cf. also 2008) concludes that these firms are successful even though 'they draw upon and utilise different institutions' than the American ones.
2 The few exceptions in the field include Lane (2008) and Lane and Probert (2009), who conducted studies on leading companies active in the pharmaceutical and clothing industries in three countries.
3 This contrasts with the different value chain position of developers of business software, who are usually employed under regular contracts (Flecker and Meil, 2010, p. 687).

REFERENCES

Allen, M. (2004) 'The Varieties of Capitalism Paradigm: Not Enough Variety?', *Socio-Economic Review*, 2, 1, 87–108.

Apitzsch, B. (2015) 'Flexibilität und Inklusion: Die Integrationskraft informeller Kooperationsstrukturen', in V. von Groddeck and S. M. Wilz (eds), *Formalität und Informalität in Organisationen* (Wiesbaden: Springer-Verlag), pp. 261–76.

Behrmann, M. (2011) *Game Development and Digital Growth*. Helsinki: European Games Developer Federation (EGDF). http://www.b105.fi/egdf/wp-content/uploads/2011/06/EGDF-Policy-papers-2nd-edition-Game-Development-and-Digital-Growth-web.pdf, date accessed 24 February 2014.

Borrás, S., L. Seabrooke and V. Schmidt (2015) 'Conclusions: Sensemaking and Institutional Change in Comparative Capitalisms', in S. Borrás and L. Seabrooke (eds), *Sources of National Institutional Competitiveness. Sensemaking in Institutional Change* (Oxford: Oxford University Press), pp. 148–61.

Bouncken, R. B. and J. Müller-Lietzkow (2007) 'Machtumkehr in Projektnetzwerken der Computer- und Videospielindustrie', in G. Schreyögg and J. Sydow (eds), *Kooperation und Konkurrenz* (Wiesbaden: Gabler), pp. 75–120.

Burawoy, M. (1985) *The Politics of Production: Factory Regimes under Capitalism and Socialism* (London: Verso).

Casper, S., M. Lehrer and D. Soskice (1999) 'Can High-technology Industries Prosper in Germany? Institutional Frameworks and the Evolution of the German Software and Biotechnology Industries', *Industry and Innovation*, 6, 1, 5–24.

Castells, M. (1996) *The Network Society* (Oxford: Blackwell).

Caves, R. E. (2000) *Creative Industries: Contracts Between Art and Commerce* (Cambridge, MA: Harvard University Press).

Deeg, R. (2005) 'Path Dependency, Institutional Complementarity, and Change in National Business Systems', in G. Morgan, R. Whitley and E. Moen (eds), *Changing Capitalisms? Internationalization, Institutional Change, and Systems of Economic Organization* (Oxford: Oxford University Press), pp. 21–52.

Edlund, J. and A. Grönlund (2008) 'Protection of Mutual Interests? Employment Protection and Skill Formation in Different Labour Market Regimes', *European Journal of Industrial Relations*, 14, 3, 245–64.

Edwards, R. (1979) *Contested Terrain: The Transformation of the Workplace in the Twentieth Century* (New York: Basic).

Eurofound (2013) *Third European Company Survey. First Findings: résumé* (Luxembourg: Publications Office).

Flecker, J. and P. Meil (2010) 'Organisational Restructuring and Emerging Service Value Chains: Implications for Work and Employment', *Work, Employment & Society*, 24, 4, 680–98.

Florida, R. (2002) *The Rise of the Creative Class: And How It's Transforming Work, Leisure, Community and Everyday Life* (New York: Basic).

Gereffi, G., J. Humphrey and T. Sturgeon (2005) 'The Governance of Global Value Chains', *Review of International Political Economy*, 12, 1, 78–104.

Grantham, A. and R. Kaplinsky (2005) 'Getting the Measure of the Electronic Games Industry: Developers and the Management of Innovation', *International Journal of Innovation Management*, 9, 2, 183–213.

▶

Hall, P. and D. Soskice (2001) *Varieties of Capitalism: The Institutional Foundations of Comparative Advantage* (Oxford: Oxford University Press).

Hancké, B. (2009) *Debating Varieties of Capitalism: A Reader* (Oxford: Oxford University Press).

Hancké, B. and M. Goyer (2005) 'Degrees of Freedom: Rethinking the Institutional Analysis of Economic Change', in G. Morgan, R. Whitley and E. Moen (eds), *Changing Capitalisms? Internationalization, Institutional Change, and Systems of Economic Organization* (Oxford: Oxford University Press), pp. 53–77.

Hollingsworth, J. R. and R. Boyer (1997) 'Coordination of Economic Actors and Social Systems of Production', in J. R. Hollingsworth (ed.), *Contemporary capitalism: The Embeddedness of Institutions* (Cambridge: Cambridge University Press), pp. 1–47.

Hollingsworth, J. R. and W. Streeck (1994) 'Countries and Sectors: Concluding Remarks on Performance, Convergence, and Competitiveness', in J. R. Hollingsworth, P. C. Schmitter and W. Streeck (eds), *Governing Capitalist Economies* (New York: Oxford University Press), pp. 270–300.

Hoose, F. (2016) *Spiel als Arbeit: Arbeitsorientierungen von Beschäftigten der Gamesbranche* (Wiesbaden: Springer-Verlag).

Humphrey, J. and H. Schmitz (2001) 'Governance in Global Value Chains', *IDS Bulletin*, 32, 3, 19–29.

Lakhani, T., S. Kuruvilla and A. Avgar (2013) 'From the Firm to the Network: Global Value Chains and Employment Relations Theory', *British Journal of Industrial Relations*, 51, 3, 440–72.

Lampel, J. and J. Shamsie (2003) 'Capabilities in Motion: New Organizational Forms and the Reshaping of the Hollywood Movie Industry', *Journal of Management Studies*, 40, 8, 2189–210.

Lane, C. (2008) 'National Capitalisms and Global Production Networks: An Analysis of their Interaction in Two Global Industries', *Socio-Economic Review*, 6, 2, 227–60.

Lane, C. and J. Probert (2009) *National Capitalisms, Global Production Networks: Fashioning the Value Chain in the UK, US, and Germany* (Oxford: Oxford University Press on Demand).

Lazonick, W. (2006) 'Evolution of the New Economy Business Model', in E. Brousseau and N. Curien (eds), *Internet and Digital Economics* (Cambridge: Cambridge University Press), pp. 59–113.

McKinlay, A. and C. Smith (eds) (2009) *Creative Labour – Working in the Creative Industries* (London: Palgrave Macmillan).

Newsome, C., P. Taylor, J. Bair and A. Rainnie (eds) (2015) *Putting Labour in its Place: Labour Process Analysis and Global Value Chains* (London: Palgrave Macmillan).

Nölke, A. and A. Vliegenthart (2009) 'Enlarging the Varieties of Capitalism: The Emergence of Dependent Market Economies in East Central Europe', *World Politics*, 61, 4, 670–702.

OECD (2004) *Employment Outlook* (Paris: OECD).

Pongratz, H. J. and G. G. Voß (2003) *Arbeitskraftunternehmer. Erwerbsorientierungen in entgrenzten Arbeitsformen* (Berlin: Edition sigma).

▶

Randle, K. and N. Culkin (2009) 'Getting in and Getting on in Hollywood: Freelance Careers in an Uncertain Industry', in A. McKinlay and C. Smith (eds), *Creative Labour – Working in the Creative Industries* (London: Palgrave Macmillan), pp. 93–115.

Readman, J. and A. Grantham (2006) 'Shopping for Buyers of Product Development Expertise: How Video Games Developers Stay Ahead', *European Management Journal*, 24, 4, 256–69.

Schneiberg, M. (2007) 'What's on the Path? Path Dependence, Organizational Diversity and the Problem of Institutional Change in the US Economy, 1900–1950', *Socio-Economic Review*, 5, 1, 47–80.

Smith, C. (2015) 'Continuity and Change in Labor Process Analysis Forty Years After *Labor and Monopoly Capital*', *Labor Studies Journal*, 40, 3, 222–42.

Spectrum Strategy Consultants and DTI (Department of Trade and Industry) (2002) *From Exuberant Youth to Sustainable Maturity. Competitiveness Analysis of the UK Games Software Sector* (London: DTI). www.dti.gov.uk/cii/services/contentindustry/computer_games_leisure_software.shtml, date accessed 25 August 2008.

Storz, C. (2008) 'Dynamics in Innovation Systems: Evidence from Japan's Game Software Industry', *Research Policy*, 37, 9, 1480–91.

Storz, C. (2009) *The Emergence of New Industries between Path Dependency and Path Plasticity: The Case of Japan's Software and Biotechnology Industry* (Frankfurt/M: Interdisziplinäres Zentrum für Ostasienstudien (IZO)).

Sturgeon, T. J. (2001) 'How Do We Define Value Chains and Production Networks?', *IDS Bulletin*, 32, 3, 9–18.

Teipen, C. (2008) 'Work and Employment in Creative Industries: The Video Games Industry in Germany, Sweden and Poland', *Economic and Industrial Democracy*, 29, 3, 309–35.

Teipen, C. (2016) 'The Implications of the Value Chain and Financial Institutions for Work and Employment: Insights from the Video Game Industry in Poland, Sweden, and Germany', *British Journal of Industrial Relations*, 54, 2, 311–33.

Thelen, K. (2014) *Varieties of Liberalization and the New Politics of Social Solidarity* (Cambridge: Cambridge University Press).

Thomas, G. (2011) 'A Typology for the Case Study in Social Science Following a Review of Definition, Discourse, and Structure', *Qualitative Inquiry*, 17, 6, 511–21.

Thompson, P. (2013) 'Financialization and the Workplace: Extending and Applying the Disconnected Capitalism Thesis', *Work, Employment & Society*, 27, 3, 472–88.

Thompson P., R. Parker and S. Cox (2016) 'Interrogating Creative Theory and Creative Work: Inside the Games Studio', *Sociology*, 50, 2, 316–32.

Whitley, R. (2007) *Business Systems and Organizational Capabilities. The Institutional Structuring of Competitive Competences* (Oxford: Oxford University Press).

Wright, A. (2015) 'It's All About Games: Enterprise and Entrepreneurialism in Digital Games', *New Technology, Work and Employment*, 30, 1, 32–46.

Epilogue

Actually Existing Capitalism: Some Digital Delusions

12

Paul Thompson and Kendra Briken

Contemporary labour process analysis (LPA) emphasises the intimate connections between transformations of capitalism and trends in work and employment. Within social theory influential images of labour such as Reich's (1992 symbolic analysts or Castell's (1996) self-programmable workers, ultimately derive from conception of the broader economy, in this case informational capitalism or the knowledge economy. Their diagnosis is based on the following assumptions. First, the sources of profit, productivity and power in the new economy are said to be (variously) intangible, immaterial or weightless (e.g. knowledge, creativity, information, intellectual assets). Digital products are reproducible at low cost for high returns, enabling capitalism to overcome scarcity and 'the limits of time and space' (Castells, 2001, p. 5). Second, that knowledge-intensive, intellectual or professional work is either in the majority or becoming the majority in advanced post-industrial societies. Third, there has been a decisive shift of power from capital to labour given that knowledge 'remains with the employee and in no real sense is it ever of the firm. It is impossible to separate knowledge from the knower' (Despres and Hiltrop, 1995, p. 11). Fourth, traditional, hierarchical structures and practices of management are no longer appropriate, with the best practice being to hire talented people, then leave them alone (Florida, 2002, p. 132). Fifth, corporate forms have mutated into decentralised, flat, networked organisations. Extensive critique of these claims has been made elsewhere, and so we will not repeat them here (Thompson et al., 2001; Thompson and Harley, 2012). What we do want to do is look in more detail at a related but newer version that comes under the heading of cognitive capitalism, in part because it will facilitate a more extended engagement with issues of digital industries and labour.

Theorists of cognitive capitalism influenced by autonomist Marxism (Hardt and Negri, 1994, 2009; Böhm and Land, 2012; Moulier Boutang, 2012) build on many of these themes. Such claims significantly challenge LPA as they deny the idea of material production as a privileged site for the value extraction and antagonism between capital and labour. The policy agenda offered by more recent popularisers (Mason, 2015; Srnicek and Williams, 2015) shifts even further away from the work terrain insofar as the workplace in itself is no longer understood as a place for collective or individual resistance. This chapter counters with a detailed exposition and critique of theories of cognitive or digital capitalism. Drawing on our own and other labour process research, within that critique we offer some observations towards a more realistic picture of capitalism at work, including the importance of the financialisation of the economy.

Cognitive Capitalism

Cognitive capitalism theory (CCT) derives from a combination of Italian (post) operaismo[1] and French regulation school influences (Vercellone, 2007; Hardt and Negri, 2009; Moulier Boutang, 2012; Corsani, 2012; see Turchetto, 2008; Jeon, 2010; Boffo, 2012 for lineage and variations).

The core of the theory is that cognitive capitalism (CC) is a third type of capitalism (after mercantile, industrial) with a distinctive system of accumulation based on knowledge value: 'a mode of production in which the object of accumulation consists mainly of knowledge, which becomes the basic source of value, as well as the principal location of the process of valorisation' (Moulier Boutang, 2012, p. 57). Though CC emerges from the crisis of Fordism, theories of post-Fordism are dismissed as rooted in a neo-industrialist vision and relying on a traditional approach to the contradictions of capitalism. Instead, the new system of accumulation is characterised by a profound transformation of the antagonistic relation of capital and labour, and the conflicts that derive from it: The term 'cognitive brings to light the novel nature of labour, the sources of value and the forms of value' (Lucarelli and Vercellone, 2013, p. 7). The 'production of knowledge by knowledge' therefore puts the traditional categories of political economy – value, ownership, production and labour – in crisis (Corsani, 2012, p. 16).

Value extraction is based on knowledge that cannot be measured; thus value is produced by the 'general intellect' through socially cooperative labour or outside the workplace in the 'commons' (notably through the web and online communities) or by biopolitical labour in the production of social life itself (Hardt and Negri, 2009; Mason, 2015). Because of an abundance of use-values, increased returns and minimal cost of reproduction, scarcity disappears other than that of time and attention (Moulier Boutang, 2012, pp. 66, 72). Information 'corrodes value' in general and price mechanism for digital goods in particular (Mason, 2015, pp. 142, 143). Any account of value based on labour time in production, material production or commodity-producing labour is held to be in crisis.[2] It is here where we find the connection between CCT and 'postcapitalist' visions: 'It is impossible to properly value inputs, when they come in the form of social knowledge, knowledge-driven production tends towards the unlimited creation of wealth, independent of the labour expended' (Mason, 2016, p. 136).

As Boffo (2012, p. 265) notes, for CCT each of the above stages of the historical development of capitalism is also associated both with a specific form of a division of labour and a dominant sector of the economy. With respect to the former, CC, with its increase in abstract knowledge and intellectual powers in production, is associated with 'a radical change of the subsumption of labour to capital and indicates a third stage of the division of labour' (Vercellone, 2007, p. 15). Vercellone frames this change by using Marx's distinction between formal and real subordination of labour. Marx made this distinction to emphasise the ways in which capital's use of machinery and science in what was then the modern factory enables new and more powerful mechanisms of control and value extraction, overcoming what was previously just the general control of the employer that lacked the means to affect the actual mode of working (Marx, 1976, p. 1011). Thus three stages of the division of labour are envisaged by Vercellone: formal subsumption of labour in the early factory system; real subsumption beginning in the industrial revolution and reaching its peak in the standardised mass production and 'Smithian' division of labour of the Fordist era; and finally the general intellect under CC in which real subsumption is reversed. Whereas the concept of formal and real subsumption was developed by Marx through his analysis of the labour process in volume one of *Capital*, the general intellect is taken from the *Grundrisse* and in particular a series of unfinished notes – 'The Fragment on Machines'. Here it is envisaged that at some time in the future, knowledge developed through science and technology will become the source of real wealth rather than labour expended in production. This would mark the possibility of a transition to communism. For CCT that time has arrived. Communism, or at least its preconditions, is already in existence (see

Vercellone, 2007, p. 15), or, with Mason, postcapitalism becomes necessary and possible (2015, p. xiii).

With respect to a dominant sector, 'the new information technologies, of which the digital, the computer, and the Internet are emblematic in the same way in which the coal mine, the steam engine, the loom, and the railroad were emblematic of industrial capitalism' (Moulier Boutang 2012, p. 57). There is a particular focus on software in general and open source in particular as a model of the new capitalism and value production. Mason emphasises the growth of 'non-market production: horizontally distributed peer-production networks, that are not centrally managed, producing goods that are either completely free, or – which being Open Source – have very limited commercial value', with Wikipedia as the primary example (2016, p. 143), In addition, for some, the creative or cultural industries, particularly digital games, play a key role because of the combination of autonomous workers, collaborative work and 'free labour' in the 'outernet' to the networking of human intelligence and production of value (Terranova, 2000; de Peuter and Dyer-Witherford, 2005).

Not only is the division of labour a marker of stages of capitalism, in the operaismo tradition labour and labour process dynamics are the primary drivers of development. The crisis that ushered in CC was linked not to issues of accumulation or profits but to contradictions within capital's control of the division of labour and the need for capital to free itself of the 'mass worker' (Vercellone, 2007; see Turchetto, 2008, p. 294; Boffo, 2013, p. 264). This tradition is therefore characterised by seeking to identify an emblematic figure of labour based on a specific 'class composition'. For CC, it is immaterial labour – defined variously as that which is cerebral, affective, communicative or relational, or that which contributes to the informational or cultural content of a commodity (Lazzarato, 1996). As a result, there is a (qualitative) hegemony of intellectual labour or 'diffuse intellectuality'. Purely physical labour power is consigned to the Fordist and Taylorist era of industrial capitalism. Unlike that era, cognition and conception are no longer appropriated by capital, and living labour is no longer incorporated into science and machinery (Vercellone, 2007, p. 16). Rather, innovation is captured in interactive cognitive processes of social cooperation: 'The main source of value now lies in the creativity, versatility and ... invention of employees and not in capital assets and in the work of execution' (Vercellone, 2007, pp. 25, 26). The development of the general intellect is associated with the expansion of mass education, which develops alongside the welfare state during Fordism. It is not entirely clear what the causal links are between the two. One can only infer that diffuse intellectuality is somehow facilitated by the growth and character of educated, graduate labour. A clue can perhaps be seen in Moulier Boutang's somewhat naïve statement that 'Postgraduates cannot be commanded in the same way as high school leavers' (2012, p. 68).

To the extent that any of these theorists refer concretely to the organisation of work, the following are all said to be decreasing: specialisation, standardisation and codification. Reflecting on interactive information work, Moulier Boutang asserts that 'There is no fixed system that determines ex ante the selection of resources to be mobilised on the basis some checklist, the division of operations, or the sequence of action with agents at each stage of operations' (2012, p. 65). Assertions of autonomous immaterial labour are also linked to claims concerning measurement or more precisely its absence. Reinforcing he previous argument about labour time no longer being linked to value, autonomous labour is 'outside measurement' and beyond management: 'Immaterial labour is immeasurable because being measured means being imposed, which is in diametrical opposition to its being flexible, creative and communicative. Labour becomes life itself' (Jeon, 2009, p. 6).

Moulier Boutang links the rise of living labour to a decline of managerial interest in individual performance in the workplace (2012, p. 54). Meanwhile, Vercellone (2007, p. 33) repeats the previously noted knowledge economy argument: 'In cognitive-labour producing knowledge, the result of labour remains incorporated in the brain of the worker and is thus inseparable from the knower'. As for any engagement with ideas of managerial hierarchy or the firm, it is to repeat post-Fordist and mainstream business notions of the horizontalisation of corporate forms; an economy of variety and learning organisations; a world of small-series production (Moulier Boutang, 2012, p. 69); and networks displacing markets and hierarchies, except with an emphasis on digitalisation (see Moulier Boutang, 2012, pp. 61, 65). Mason also refers to the 'age of the network' and writes that 'Everything comes down to the struggle between network and hierarchy, between old forms of society moulded around capitalism and new forms of society that prefigure what comes next' (2016, p. xix).

Despite the Marxist language, it is irrefutable that there are many similarities to prior new economy narratives. A partial critique of the contradictions of CC emphasises the efforts by capital to offset the losses incurred in the law of value in production by enforcing it elsewhere. Capital uses its monopoly position in networks to manufacture scarcity through the extraction of rents based largely on intellectual property (see Vercellone, 2007, pp. 33, 34), or it expropriates value produced in the wider society from the 'general intellect'. The distinction between profit and rent collapses, and capital becomes purely 'parasitic' (see Boffo, 2012, p. 261). One perceived consequence is that antagonism is displaced from the labour process and employment relationship, and 'the class struggle in cognitive capitalism increasingly takes the form of a distribution struggle' (Jeon, 2010, p. 19). In slightly different terms, politics shifts from the factory to the social factory, radical demands focusing on a universal basic income and full automation replacing the 'drudgery' of wage labour (Mason, 2015; Srnicek and Williams, 2015). There are a few discussions of increased precariousness in the labour market and devaluation of labour power, but they remain relatively marginal to the main argument.

Social Theory Meets Social Facts

It would be insufficient to critique CCT empirically as 'it is not about the validity of facts and numbers, but how they are interpreted' (Jeon, 2010, p. 3). And certainly CCT is cavalier in dismissing evidence-based criticisms on the grounds that hegemony might not actually be dominant but be the start of something or the directionality of trends (Moulier Boutang, 2012, p. 54, 60). But the latter's contempt for the 'empirical approach' should not go unchallenged, for two reasons. First, specific empirical claims are made about trends that can be challenged on their own terms. Second, CCT is all too typical of the sweeping generalisations, unrepresentative exemplary industries and absence of plausible evidence that characterises much of the recent social theorising about capitalism. We will challenge the general arguments and assumptions contained in the CCT narrative by focusing on key trends in capital, employment and the division of labour.

Actually Existing Capital

Immaterial or cognitive knowledge materialises as a location of the process of valorisation. Yet we are told little or nothing about how capital is actually organised in companies or value chains, or how companies make their money through particular business models. Of equal importance, CCT overestimates the extent to which capitalism is defined and dominated by Internet-based companies. If we look at data about which industries and firms dominate the global economy, it was in 2011 that for the first time a technology firm, namely Apple, overtook

Exxon. In 2016, we find that Google's parent company Alphabet, Apple, Microsoft and Facebook are the world's most profitable companies (Myers, 2016). However, they are far from being the largest either by revenue or capitalisation, let alone by employees; and many of the other 'exemplary' Internet firms are marginal, with Uber and Airbnb not even showing up in the Fortune Global 500 list. In sum, global capitalism is dominated by energy, finance and telecoms/utilities. At the European level, financial services and supermarkets are strongly represented. In the UK, the story is similar, but with two global tobacco companies making the top 20.

Of course, such lists are limited in their explanatory value, and some of the activities producing profits for such firms will be knowledge-driven or Internet-coordinated activities. But if anyone examines how Exxon Mobil, Wal-Mart or Toyota make their money, it does offer a major corrective to the CCT narrative of immaterial production or zero-cost reproduction at the heart of economic value. The global dimension and the dynamics of value chains are also a key consideration. The example of Apple, Foxconn and the iPad is revealing. Apple's operating profit margin and stock market valuation is highly dependent on a business model based on cost control through the supply chain (Froud et al., 2014) and, specifically, very low direct labour costs in suppliers (Cleland, 2014). Foxconn is compelled to pass on the burden of cost adjustment through speed-up, contract manipulation and various forms of free labour (including unpaid overtime and the dormitory labour system). In his critique of Mason, Fuchs sums up the picture effectively: 'This analysis overestimates information economy because capitalism is not just digital and informational capitalism, but at the same time financial capitalism, hyper-industrial, fossil fuel capitalism, mobilities capitalism, etc.' (Fuchs, 2016, p. 232). He goes on to refute Mason's claim that value has collapsed in the digital sector, pointing to profits made on the basis of product innovation, exploitation of direct and indirect labour and (most significantly) targeted advertising. It is simply not true that 'capitalism can no longer adapt to technological change', as new ways to monetise and monopolise in those social media and Web 2.0 sectors show (Tyfield, 2015; Choonara, 2015).

A key trend across all sectors is the concentration of capital. In contrast to the fantasy of the global commons, concentration is particularly marked in virtual and vertical integration, Internet-based or new media (Fitzgerald, 2015). As Andrew Keen (2014) observes, the Internet, contrary to images of a sharing economy, has proven to be the perfect vehicle for free market capitalism – a 'networked kleptocracy'. Mason notes the existence of 'info-monopolies', but beyond asserting that it is a 'defence mechanism', he finds it difficult to explain if the 'spontaneous tendency' of information and the Internet is to 'dissolve markets and destroy ownership' (2015, p. xiv). It seems to us that the reverse is true. Peer production and genuine sharing economy projects exist in specialist niches, while digital platforms such as Uber and Airbnb develop hierarchical business models that invade and seek to dominate more traditional markets. It is telling that it is hard to find any substantive, collaborative peer-production example in Mason other than Wikipedia.

Employment – Job Trends and the Scope of Digital Labour

The hegemony of cognitive labour is difficult to spot among statistics on employment. Table 12.1 gives an overview from the Bureau of Labor Statistics for projected US job growth. This indicates that growth will be based largely on the expansion of personal services, retail and hospitality – sectors that are associated with significant skills under-utilisation (Wright and Sissons, 2012). CCT could argue that much of this work, while lacking 'intellectual' content, abounds with the other immaterial dimension of affectivity and allowing for the general intellect to flourish. However, the positive spin by CCT seems to ignore the weight of evidence concerning the growing regulation and standardisation of emotional and aesthetic labour power (see Warhurst et al., 2008). Indeed, it is ironic given the casting of physicality back into the Fordist era that so much interactive service work draws on embodied capacities in labour power (Wolkowitz and Warhurst, 2010).

Returning to general trends, a UK report (UKCES, 2014) estimated that the proportion of low- and middle-skilled jobs in 2022 would be 71 percent–almost no change from the 2012 figure. Of course, as Table 12.1 shows, there is also job growth among some categories of professional, managerial and technical labour that are confirming long-established observations concerning polarised labour markets (Goos et al., 2014). Scepticism concerning 'mass intellectuality' is reinforced by reports of a discrepancy between the number of graduates and 'graduate jobs' in both the US and UK (CIPD, 2015). In a commentary on the US figures, Bernick (2012) observes that 'the main point remains from these projections that most jobs in the emerging economy are not ones requiring college degrees and above'.

It may be objected that these are US and UK figures, and it's true that we need a global picture. Why not start with the fact that there are almost 100 million manufacturing jobs in China alone (Lockett, 2016)?

Table 12.1 Job growth in the US labour market 2014–24

	Total, all occupations 9,788.90	In % 6.5
Personal care aides	458.1	25.9
Registered nurses	439.3	16.0
Home health aides	348.4	38.1
Combined food preparation and serving workers, including fast food	343.5	10.9
Retail salespersons	314.2	6.8
Nursing assistants	262.0	17.6
Customer service representatives	252.9	9.8
Cooks, restaurant	158.9	14.3
General and operations managers	**151.1**	**7.1**
Construction labourers	*147.4*	*12.7*
Accountants and auditors	**142.4**	**10.7**
Medical assistants	138.9	23.5
Janitors and cleaners, except maids and housekeeping cleaners	136.3	5.8
Software developers, applications	**135.3**	**18.8**
Labourers and freight, stock, and material movers, hand	*125.1*	*5.1*
First-line supervisors of office and administrative support workers	121.2	8.3
Computer systems analysts	**118.6**	**20.9**
Licensed practical and licensed vocational nurses	117.3	16.3
Maids and housekeeping cleaners	111.7	7.7
Medical secretaries	108.2	20.5
Management analysts	**103.4**	**13.6**
Heavy and tractor-trailer truck drivers	*98.8*	*5.5*
Receptionists and information clerks	97.8	9.5
Office clerks, general	95.8	3.1
Sales representatives, wholesale and manufacturing, except technical and scientific products	93.4	6.4
Stock clerks and order fillers	*92.9*	*4.9*
Market research analysts and marketing specialists	**92.3**	**18.6**
First-line supervisors of food preparation and serving workers	88.5	9.9
Electricians	*85.9*	*13.7*
Maintenance and repair workers, general	*83.5*	*6.1*

Source: Bureau of Labor Statistics (2016), own table
Bold indicates high(er)-skilled knowledge/creative work; italics indicate manual work

As feminist critics and postcolonial critics have noted (see Federici, 2004; Huws, 2007), a dynamic analysis of the changing global divisions of labour paints a more global picture and is precisely what is missing in CCT.

What of the employment trends concerning digital-related labour itself? Given the pervasiveness of digital tools and means of communication, there is a tendency to make inflated claims of its scope and coverage (e.g. Fuchs, 2014, p. 352). We distinguish between three overlapping categories, though this list is not meant to be comprehensive. First, there is what we would describe as core digital labour defined in terms of creating and maintaining digital commodities, including software, games workers and parts of the 'creative class' (Thompson et al., 2015). While the relevant industries generate significant amounts of value, they do so largely on the basis of smaller, specialised labour forces. For example, the games industry in the UK currently generates a £1.02bn contribution to GDP, yet it employs just 9896 workers in games development and up to 18,000 indirectly. Even more starkly, WhatsApp only needs about 50 employees to reach its 900 million users worldwide (Metz, 2015).

The second category encompasses work that is allocated and/or organised through digital platforms. This is often associated with crowdsourcing, which is clearly a qualitative change with regard to employment relations, but with different business models. At one end of the spectrum, mostly non-digital labour is recruited and organised through digital platforms to provide services to individuals or organisations such as TaskRabbit (from cleaning to moving to repair services) and Uber. On the other, companies – whether digital or not – outsource work through a kind of 'internalized offshoring' (Silverman, 2014, p. 108). Much of the content – through platforms such as Amazon's Mechanical Turk – consists of microtasks, often with low skill and training requirements and minimal rewards. However, platforms can also host contests for jobs with medium-range complexity (translating articles; customer services) and even high-end jobs such as software development that are better compensated. Across the spectrum, the platforms offer the possibility of internationalising the available skill pool and evading national labour standards (Holts, 2013). This is an important new trend, but again it is worth being cautious about the scope. According to a World Bank report on online outsourcing, an estimated 48 million workers are registered on crowdsourcing platforms, but with only around approximately 10 per cent actively participating (2015, p. 9).

The third category includes the large amount of routine labour employed directly by or in digital sectors. This includes, for example, 'behind the click' workers employed by the e-tail giants in Amazon and other warehouse, distributive and logistics centres, who use digital tools to literally keep the 'value in motion' (Newsome, 2015, p. 29). Alternatively, a UK Government report (DCMS, 2014) estimates that though the proportion of jobs in the whole of the 'creative economy' is at 8.5 per cent of total employment and growing, almost one third (2.55m) were classified as 'non-creative'.

The essential point being made here is that digital-related labour is of growing significance but heterogeneous in content and context and uneven in any relationship to intellectual labour. The latter point is further illustrated in the next section.

Division of Labour – Cognition, Control and Measurement

CCT relies heavily on claims concerning the division of labour. Assertions of spontaneous social cooperation and autonomy bear little relationship to any workplace research we are aware of. European surveys report uneven trends concerning levels of employee discretion, with the majority of countries largely static (Eurofund, 2015, p. 7). The autonomy argument is intimately linked to those concerning (the absence of) time and measurement. Labour time remains a fundamental focus of managerial attention. Indeed, the use of tracking and monitoring software provides tools that F. W. Taylor could only have dreamed of. Nor is it confined to call centres and the minute measurement of call handling times. Amazon is known to use a digital platform that is multifaceted (Bergvall-Kåreborn and Howcroft, 2014), thus serving several ends simultaneously: vendors access to display and sell their wares and end customers can gain access to information on purchase and delivery status. This allows Amazon to evaluate the quantities required against in-stock availability, and managers can assess the 'hourly flow of workers required in each part of the FC, supervisory can monitor associates in real time (productivity, time targets errors, etc.)', and they are able to text messages to the handheld devices that navigate the workers through the warehouse (Briken et al., 2016, p. 10) As one worker put it, 'the targets are in your face – literally – every second, of every minute, of every day' (Maddy S. in Briken et al., 2016, p. 11). Or, more bluntly, in the words of an Amazon manager, 'You're sort of like a robot, but in human form'. 'It's human automation, if you like' (*Financial Times*, 8 February 2013).

Measurement in the service of a calculative rationality is thus wider than the question of labour time. The recent growth of 'people analytics' has been described in the *Wall Street Journal* as a trend that 'treats the humans in an organisation just like any other asset in the supply chain, as something that can be monitored, analysed and reconfigured' (Mims, 2015). This can be considered a small aspect of the wider increase in performance management in large organisations. With respect to crowd-sourcing platforms discussed earlier, Silverman notes that 'Everything they do is tracked' and that 'crowdsourced workers are expected to work seamlessly with software, following its commands' (2014, pp. 108, 109). In the private sector, it is primarily linked to cascading and often punitive targets, aided in many cases by electronic monitoring and tighter work flow (Taylor, 2013, pp. 46, 47). In the public sector, targets have accompanied the rise in 'new public management', but they are also present in the spread of audit and accountability measures. What has become fashionably known as knowledge management (KM) is also part of enhanced performance exposure. KM is particularly significant in knowledge-intensive industries, the supposed heartland of creative and cooperative labour. Of course, these characteristics *are* present, but they run alongside the use of IT systems to capture, convert and codify the tacit knowledge of expert labour in order to speed up the innovation or molecule to market process (McKinlay, 2005). This is the common language used in the KM field, and it somewhat skewers the naïve view that knowledge cannot be appropriated from the mind of the intellectual worker.

The use of IT systems to capture tacit knowledge is now part of a widespread recognition of the emergence of digital or knowledge-based Taylorism. In manufacturing this is driven by the development of engineering systems that allow global operating companies to 'calculate, to compare and to standardise processes worldwide' (Westkämper, 2007, p. 6). Brown et al. (2011) refer to digital Taylorism as the extraction, codification and digitalisation of knowledge into software prescripts and working knowledge that underpins the global auction of cheaper, high-quality, high-skilled labour. We also know that artificial intelligence and algorithms can incorporate living labour into machine systems. At the moment this is largely confined to mid-level jobs based on the collection and analysis of information, but it has the capacity, as noted in a radio interview with McAfee, to 'outsource cognitive labour' (BBC Radio 4, 2015).

Conceptual Confusions

Beyond linking these empirical limitations, a number of conceptual confusions are worth highlighting. First, despite references to systems of accumulation, the (post-)operaismo legacy defines capitalism by stages in the division of labour or the dominant 'figure of labour'. On the latter, moving from the mass worker through various intermediary categories to the contemporary 'multitude' (Hardt and Negri) or the collective worker of the general intellect' (Vercellone), the result is a politicised version of value in search of 'the transcendental political subject in struggle against capital' (Boffo, 2012, p. 279). On the wider question, defining a stage of capitalism – real subsumption – that spans more than 150 years highlights the flaws in using the division of labour as the focal point. While sociologists of work and the economy should always try to identify the ways in which capitalist political economy and the labour process are articulated, history teaches us that accumulation regimes are compatible with significant differences in the organisation of work and employment and, therefore, in the frontier of control in the workplace.

Leading contributors to CCT may try to justify their claims through Marx. 'Read(ing) the structure of capital' through the struggles of labour (Vercellone, 2007, p. 25) leads to the second issue – the disappearing capital trick. This absence is exacerbated by designating capital as purely parasitic, with accumulation taking place through rent-seeking rather than profit in production. In taking this position, CCT diminishes capital's power and evades any attempt to analyse its actual workings. It is true that in some sectors, intellectual property is a source of value capture, but rent-seeking through monopoly is not a new feature of capitalism, nor does it exhaust how firms use their power in markets and value chains. The choice to focus on value extraction through rent-seeking or outside production and in the 'totality of social life' is also at odds with contemporary employer attacks on the wages and conditions of labour (Boffo, 2012, p. 267) and, as we have already demonstrated, with the continuing centrality of extracting value from labour in supply chains.

Contemporary capitalism is read not only through labour but also through the labour theory of value, or more precisely its abolition in an era in which value and labour time cease to have relevance as knowledge is socialised and governed by the general intellect. Mason has a long defence of the labour theory of value up until the point where info goods and their associated effects throw capitalism into crisis and provide the basis for a transition to postcapitalism. Along with the autonomists, this argument is derived, as indicated earlier, from *The Fragment on Machines*. Whatever the validity of Marx's arguments about the development of science, technology and automation as a basis for a transition to a postcapitalist future, it is clear that we are far from this point. As we have shown, not only is much of value capture taking place in traditional ways and through non-digital sectors, but also capital has been extremely successful in finding new ways to valorise new ICTs and social media, both inside and outside the labour process (Pitts, 2015; Tyfield, 2015). Without this understanding, the arguments lead to determinism and/or utopianism, as mentioned by a number of his critics (Pitts, 2015; Fuchs, 2016, p. 237), attributing transformative powers to (info-)technology – in this case to dissolve markets and ownership – that it does not and cannot independently possess.

Finally, the misapprehension of the present is sustained by a misreading of the past – notably the designation of the 'industrial stage' of capitalism as based on physical labour, 'devoid of any intellectual or creative quality' (Vercellone, 2007, p. 24). As Jeon (2010, p. 15) notes, 'industrial and cognitive labour are contrasted to each other to the extent that they appear as if mutually exclusive'. As Marx (1976, p. 270) noted, labour power is always an 'aggregate of those physical and mental qualities'. Overemphasis on the role of knowledge now is matched by its underestimation in the past. Not only were there significant numbers of design, engineering or other conceptual jobs under Fordism, those involved primarily in execution still contained tacit knowledge that employers are now seeking to identify and leverage (Warhurst and Thompson, 2006).

Financialisation, Capital and the Digital

To use a term to define the character or essential logic of capitalism in general or at a particular stage is a very large claim. It is, as we have demonstrated with respect to cognitive, informational or digital, both contentious and flawed. With respect to digital, this more accurately refers to particular commodities, sectors or tools used by a wider range of companies. In contrast, we would highlight financialisation as the central dynamic in contemporary capitalist political economy (Thompson, 2013; Van der Zwan, 2014). Though it can be conceptualised in varied and broader ways, we endorse the perspective that refers to a finance-dominated regime of accumulation, with the emphasis on a shift in the interconnections and pattern of dominance in the industrial and financial circuits of capital (Stockhammer, 2008; Demirović and Sablowski, 2013). The scope of this concept includes both the role of financial assets in macroeconomic patterns of growth and household behaviour and the microeconomic consequences of partially financialised accumulation at the level of the firm and the labour process. These dynamics are, of course, always uneven and contested, especially with respect of national political economies to incentivise or constrain the opportunities of financial agents (Engelen and Konings, 2010, p. 618).

Within some of the core texts of CCT discussed in this chapter, there are occasional and brief mentions of financialisation (e.g. Vercellone, 2007, p. 23; Moulier Boutang, 2012, p. 48), but they are marginal to the central arguments and (given the GFC) inconsistent with assumptions about the relative stability of a new system of accumulation (Moulier Boutang, 212, p. 58). A partial exception among autonomist writers is Marazzi's (2010) account of the 'violence of financial capitalism'. However, while Marazzi correctly identifies the unstable nature of accumulation, he persists with the theme that sees contemporary value capture as external to production. In this instance, finance becomes a further device to capture value produced either in social life/consumption or in branding and intellectual property rights. The latter is indeed an important source of value under financialisation (Willmott, 2010), but this argument fails to understand the continuing intimate connections between financialisation, material production and the labour process. This holds true for Masons' (2015) occasional discussion of financialisation. Here it is presented largely as an *additional* income stream for firms whose sources of profits through traditional business models are squeezed, and for workers facing wage squeeze, debt and in need of credit.

CCT thus follows the dominant policy discourse and relies on the contrast between financial institutions – notably new investment funds such as private equity – and their often speculative and predatory behaviours, with the real, productive economy. This distinction is largely illusory because non-financial corporations are themselves financialised in terms of their ownership and investment patterns and because they trade in financial assets (Clark and Macey, 2015; Cushen and Thompson, 2016). Capital market actions and actors thus increasingly drive firm behaviour rather than merely act as financial intermediaries. Some accounts of the pursuit of shareholder value tend to focus on redistribution processes, including increasing investor returns via dividends, share buybacks, taking on debt and reducing internal investment and costs. Among the noted effects are perpetual restructuring, disposability of corporate assets and a bias for short-term financial engineering and value extraction as well as a bias against operational capability and innovation. Various studies have noted the increased gap between the rate of return on manufacturing investment and the rate of return on financial assets (Milburg, 2009). Whereas the loyalty of corporate executives is secured through share-option-based rewards, the influence of unit-level managerial layers and levers is weakened. Of equal importance is the weight of evidence that financialisation destroys the kinds of organisational innovation that

CCT proclaims as the source of knowledge value, even in knowledge-intensive firms (Lazonick and Mazzucato, 2013; Gleadle et al., 2014).

Of course, digital/informational tools and techniques facilitate financial flows, measurements and transactions. An example would be capital market valuation methodologies to measure performance and aid the setting of financial targets in decision-making. However, as the business analyst Simon Caulkin (2014, p. 12) notes, the effects are largely negative, 'the management innovation that is needed will not come from new communication and coordinating technologies (such as big data, the Internet of Things or social media)'. In fact, the reverse is true. In today's financialised world, these are more likely to be used to accentuate the job-stripping, winner-takes-all trend already seen with pervious techniques of outsourcing and offshoring. To return to the issue of value capture in the labour process, it is important to understand why and how these processes of financialised investment feed through to budgeting processes through which targets relating to revenue growth and cost-cutting can be disseminated and measured. As Cushen and Thompson (2016) explain, these rely strongly on cost controls, with implications for labour and the labour process. This manifests itself in two main ways. First, cost recovery takes place through removing labour, outsourcing, work intensification and a downward squeeze on wages. Second, there is a shift in control mechanisms, with an increase in the extent, intensity and punitive character of performance management. These are frequently linked to 'managed exits' of sections of the labour force and reflect the ratcheting down of financialised corporate profit targets (Clark and Macey, 2015). Among the consequences for labour and its management are increased job and role insecurity associated with perpetual restructuring and reorganisation, and falling levels of employee engagement and attachment, with corresponding increases in cynicism and dissent.

Some Concluding Comments

Significant transformation *has* taken place in the workings of capitalism, and some of those have been facilitated by digitalisation, including new sources of value and types of employment relation. However, our general examination of CCT reveals that it repeats most of the analytical mistakes of speculative grand narratives: stages as complete ruptures with the past; exemplary but atypical industries and work; technological determinism and utopianism; and evidence-light speculation. In his trenchant critique of 'post-workerism', Graeber observes that it is 'less interested in describing realities than in bringing them into being'

(2008, p. 13). The tendency to let the political goals drive or displace the empirical investigation is repeated in much of the recent post-work commentary (Mason, 2015; Srnicek and Williams, 2015). For example, after a series of definitive claims about emergent job-destroying automation, the latter admit that 'Our argument here relies largely on a normative claim rather than a descriptive one. Full automation is something that can and should be achieved, regardless of whether it is being carried out' (Srnicek and Williams, 2015, p. 117).

Hence our critique of CCT has focused on what we believe to be going on in firms and in work and labour markets. What we have given less consideration to is the more recent shift in autonomist-influenced and related claims that the rise of robot and AI-driven automation signals the end of any meaningful politics of production. It is true that some routine, mid-level and higher-value jobs are vulnerable to the impact of AI and robotics in the next few decades (Brynjolfsson and McAfee, 2014). However, that has to be set against the fact that in mid 2016, the UK employment rate (at 74.2 per cent) was the joint highest since comparable records began in 1971 (Inman, 2016). In a caustic critique of Mason, the radical economist Doug Henwood (2015) says that there is no evidence that info-tech is substantially diminishing the amount of work needed and points to the fact that employment expansion in the US is even stronger than GDP growth models would suggest. With current trends in mind, it seems a very large number of steps are ahead before we reach projections of a post-work world.[3]

The figures in Table 12.1 also underline that in many of the jobs where there is a significant upward trend, notably in human services, they will not be easy to replace by robots given their often interactive and affective character. Given that knowledge-intensive and high-discretion jobs are also unlikely to be automated, the roles with the most likely vulnerability are those (such as insurance underwriters and travel agents) where software can automate information search and manipulation. With respect to robots, manufacturing remains the main immediate market for robotics. According to the World Robotics 2015 report, the number of robot installations has increased heavily since 2010. However, this does not put into question the growth model for developing countries – low wages, cheap labour – in the near future. In developing economies, rather than replacing human labour, technology is more likely to enhance and augment human potentials (see Pfeiffer, Chapter 2 in this volume). With robots becoming more dexterous, and because they are safe enough to work alongside people, there will for sure be an increase in human–robot collaboration (Bauer et al., 2008). Also, data gloves and data glasses will be used to increase quality (and potentially workers') control.

At this stage, we don't know enough to predict with any certainty how many jobs software-driven automation and robotisation will eliminate, augment, decompose or create new demands for. What we do know is that the stock of work in any economy is not fixed (Stewart et al., 2015). It is also worth remembering that we have been here before with previous waves of technological determinist predictions from futurists and other ideational entrepreneurs of the 'end of work' (e.g. Rifkin, 1995). Such determinism lacks not only a sound empirical basis but also an appreciation of agency. To avoid the same mistakes, analysis of the future role of the digital in capitalism needs to embrace an understanding of the varied contexts, power relations, choices and decision structures and the capacity for resistance. This has always been a strong point of labour process research. In contrast, rationales for a politics of postcapitalism and post-work rest on extremely pessimistic readings of the struggles of waged workers. In recent accounts from Mason (2015) and Srnicek and Williams (2015), the *working* class (in both developed and developing economies) is presented as fragmented, divided and in thrall to consumption and debt, while the labour movement is largely defeated, demoralised and sclerotic. In doing so, they dismiss the diverse, actual struggles and concerns of labour. It is vital to understand the content of those concerns and actions. Contrary to the claim that 'For the vast majority of people, work offers no meaning, fulfilment or redemption' (Srnircek and Williams, 2015, p. 117), survey and qualitative research indicates simultaneously positive attachments to work and work identity but also critiques of and anger about insecurity, recognition, underemployment, work intensification, depressed wages and unfair rewards (Findlay and Thompson, forthcoming). It is here where the discussion about digitisation and robotisation needs to be connected to real work experiences. Workers are critical about their jobs and how work is organised, but there is evidence that they want those concrete problems addressed rather than dismissed in Fordist nostalgia.

Notes

1 Operaismo refers to an intellectual and political tradition that formed in Italy in the 1960s and 1970s and whose contemporary prominence is associated largely with the various works of Hardt and Negri. The term 'workerism' relates primarily to the orientation of linking stages of capitalism to figures of labour or class composition

of labour. Post-operaismo broadly refers to the development of this tradition in a new era after Fordism and the mass worker.

2 Though sceptical of much of the claims of new sources of value in the totality of social life and the ending of the distinction between production and reproduction, our critique here focuses on challenging the arguments that value creation and value extraction no longer take place in or are marginal to the labour process and production. This counterargument does not depend on the labour theory of value.

3 We are aware that the employment rates are contested. Looking at the data published by the World Bank, we see a global decline, with only few countries increasing their participation rates. However, the decline in some countries (China) is explained more accurately by economic crisis and not by technological transformations (World Bank, 2016).

REFERENCES

Bauer, A., D. Wollherr and M. Buss (2008) 'Human-Robot-Collaborations', *International Journal of Humanoid Robotics*, 5, 1, 47–66.

BBC 4 (2015) *When robots steal our jobs.* http://www.bbc.co.uk/programmes/b0540h85, date accessed 18 July 2016.

Boffo, M. (2012) 'Historical immaterialism: from immaterial labour to cognitive capitalism', *International Journal of Management Concepts and Philosophy*, 6, 4, 256–79.

Bergvall-Kåreborn, B. and D. Howcroft (2013) '"The future's bright, the future's mobile": a study of Apple and Google mobile application developers', *Work, Employment and Society*, 27, 6, 964–81.

Bernick, M. (2012) The Jobs with Most Openings in 2020. http://www.milkeninstitute.org/blog/view/302, date accessed 18 January 2017.

Böhm, S. and C. Land (2012) 'The new "hidden abode": reflections on value and labour in the new economy', *The Sociological Review*, 60, 2, 217–40.

Briken, K., P. Taylor and K. Newsome (2016) 'Work organisation, management control and working time in retail fulfilment centres', paper presented at the International Labour Process Conference, Berlin, Germany, 4–6 April 2016.

Brown, P., H. Lauder and D. Ashton (2011) *The Global Auction: The Broken Promise of Education, Jobs and Incomes* (Oxford: Oxford University Press).

Brynjolfsson, E. and A. McAfee (2014) *The Second Machine Age. Work, Progress, and Prosperity in a Time of Brilliant Technologies* (New York: Norton).

Bureau of Labor Statistics (2016) *Occupations with the most job growth.* http://www.bls.gov/emp/ep_table_104.htm, date accessed 18 July 2016.

Castells, M. (1996) *The Rise of the Network Society: The Information Age Economy, Society and Culture* (Vol. 1) (Oxford: Blackwell).

Castells, M. (2001) *The Internet Galaxy: Reflections on the Internet, Business, and Society* (Vol. 1) (Oxford: Oxford University Press).

▶

Caulkin, S. (2014) 'Era of management-led growth held hostage by old ideas that refuse to die', *Financial Times*, 14 September.

Choonara, J. (2015) 'Brand New, You're Retro', *International Socialism*, 48 (autumn). http://isj.org.uk/brand-new-youre-retro, date accessed 14 June 2016.

CIPD (2015) *Over-qualification and Skills Mismatch in the Graduate Labour Market* (London: Chartered Institute for Personnel and Development).

Clark, I. and R. Macey (2015) 'How is financialization contagious? What role for HR practices play in the capture of workplace outcomes in financialized firms?', paper presented to the 33rd International Labour Process Conference). Athens, 13–15 April.

Cleland, D. (2014) 'The Core of the Apple: Dark Value in Global Commodity Chains', *Journal of World Systems Research*, 20, 1, 82–111.

Corsani, A. (2012) *Wage/labour relations' in neoliberal cognitive capitalism.* http://artesliberales.spbu.ru/events/afisha/news_12_06_29txt/news12_06_29Corsani, date accessed 17 July 2016.

Cushen, J. and P. Thompson (2016) 'Financialization and value: why labour and the labour process still matter', *Work, Employment & Society*, 30, 2, 352–65.

DCMS (2014) *Creative Industries Economic Estimates 2014* (London: Department for Culture Media and Sport).

de Peuter, G. and N. Dyer-Witheford (2005) 'A playful multitude? Mobilising and counter-mobilising immaterial game labour', *Fibre Culture*, 5. http://five. fibreculturejournal.org/fcj-024-a-playful-multitude-mobilising-and-counter-m obilising-immaterial-game-labour, date accessed 18 July 2016.

Demirovic´, A. and T. Sablowski (2013) *The Finance-Dominated Regime of Accumulation and the Crisis in Europe* (Berlin: Rosa Luxemburg-Stiftung).

Despres, C. and J. M. Hiltrop (1995) 'Human resource management in the knowledge age', *Employee Relations*, 17, 1, 9–23.Eurofund (2015) First Findings. Sixth European Working Conditions Survey. EF/15/68/EN. Brussels.

Engelen, E. and M. Konings (2010) 'Financial capitalism resurgent: comparative institutionalism and the challenges of financialization', in G. Morgan, J. L. Campbell, C. Crouch and R. Pederson (eds), *The Oxford Handbook of Comparative Institutional Analysis* (Oxford: Oxford University Press), pp. 604–24.

Federici, S. (2004) *Caliban and the Witch: Women, the Body and Primitive Accumulation* (Brooklyn, NY: Autonomedia).

Findlay, T. and P. Thompson (forthcoming) 'Work and its meanings', *Journal of Industrial Relations*, 59, 2.

Fitzgerald, S. (2015) 'Structure of the Cultural Industries – Global Corporation to SMEs', in K. Oakley and J. O'Connor (eds), *The Routledge Companion to the Cultural Industries* (London: Routledge), pp. 70–85.

Florida, R. (2002) *The Rise of the Creative Class* (New York: Basic Books).

Froud, J., J. Sukhdev, A. Leaver and K. Williams (2014) 'Financialization across the pacific: Manufacturing Cost Ratios, supply chains and power', *Critical Perspectives on Accounting*, 25, 46–57.

Fuchs, C. (2014) *Digital labour and Karl Marx* (New York: Routledge).

Fuchs, C. (2016) 'Henryk Grossmann 2.0: a critique of Paul Mason's book "PostCapitalism: A Guide to Our Future"', *TripleC: Communication, Capitalism & Critique. Open Access Journal for a Global Sustainable Information Society*, 14, 1, 232–43.

Gleadle, P. (2014) 'Restructuring and innovation in pharmaceuticals and biotechs: the impact of financialisation', *Critical Perspectives on Accounting*, 25, 1, 67–77.

Goos, M., A. Manning and A. Salomons (2014) 'Explaining Job polarization: routine-biased technological change and offshoring', *American Economic Review*, 104, 8, 2509–26.

Graeber, D. (2008) The Sadness of Post-Workerism or "Art and Immaterial Labour" Conference: A Sort of Review. Tate Britain. *The Commoner*, April 2008. https://libcom.org/files/graeber_sadness.pdf, date accessed 18 July 2016.

Hardt, M. and A. Negri (1994) *Labor of Dionysus: A Critique of the State-Form* (Minneapolis, MN: University of Minnesota Press).

Hardt, M. and A. Negri (2009) *Commonwealth* (Cambridge, MA: Harvard University Press).

Henwood, D. (2015) 'Workers aren't disappearing', *The Jacobin*, 20. https://www.jacobinmag.com/2015/07/mason-guardian-capitalism-new-economy-post-work, date accessed 22 July 2016.

Holts, K. (2013) 'Towards a Taxonomy of Virtual Work', paper presented at the 31st International Labour Process Conference, 18–20 March 2013, Rutgers University.

Huws, U. (ed.) (2007) *Defragmenting: Towards a Critical Understanding of the New Global Division of Labour* (London: Merlin).

Inman, P. (2016) Unemployment at lowest level for 11 years, *The Guardian*, 16 June, p. 27.

Jeon, H. (2010) 'Cognitive capitalism or cognition in capitalism? A critique of cognitive capitalism theory', *Spectrum: Journal of Global Studies*, 3, 89–116.

Keen, A. (2015) *The Internet is Not the Answer* (London: Atlantic Books).

Lazonick, W. and M. Mazzucato (2013) 'The risk-reward nexus in the innovation-inequality relationship: who takes the risks, who gets the rewards?', in *Industrial and Corporate Change*, 27, 4, 1093–128.

Lazzarato, M. (1996) 'Immaterial labour', in P. Virno and M. Hardt (eds), *Radical Thought in Italy* (Minneapolis, MN: University of Minnesota Press), pp. 132–146.

Lockett, H. (2016) 'China's workforce faces tough year shifting gears from manufacturing to services', *China Economic review*. http://www.chinaeconomicreview.com/chinas-workforce-faces-tough-year-shifting-gears-manufacturing-services, date accessed 4 January 2017.

Lucarelli, S. and C. Vercellone (2013) 'The thesis of cognitive capitalism. New research perspectives. An introduction', *Knowledge Cultures* 1, 4, 15–27.

Marazzi, C. (2010) *The Violence of Financial Capitalism. Semiotext(e)* (Boston, MA: MIT Press).

Marx, K. (1976) *Capital* (Vol. 1) (London: Penguin Books).

Mason, P. (2015) *PostCapitalism: A Guide to our Future* (London: Allen Lane).

McKinlay, A. (2005) 'Knowledge Management', in S. Ackroyd, R. Batt, P. Thompson and P. Tolbert (eds), *The Oxford Handbook of Work and Organization* (Oxford: Oxford University Press), pp. 242–62.

Metz, C. (2015) *Why WhatsApp only needs 50 engineers for its 900M users.* 15 September. http://www.wired.com/2015/09/whatsapp-serves-900-million-users-50-engineers, date accessed 16 July 2016.

Milburg, W. (2009) 'Shifting sources and uses of profits: sustaining us financialization with global value chains', *Economy and Society*, 37, 3, 420–51.

Mims, C. (2015) 'People analytics: you're not a human, you're a data point', *Wall Street Journal*, 16 February.

Moulier Boutang, Y. (2012) *Cognitive Capitalism* (Cambridge, MA, and Malden, MA: Polity Press).

Myers, J. (2016) *What do the world's 4 biggest companies have in common?* Blog published 2 February. https://www.weforum.org/agenda/2016/02/what-do-the-world-s-4-biggest-companies-have-in-common, date accessed 16 July 2016.

Newsome, K. (2015) 'Value in motion: labour and logistics in the contemporary political economy', in K. Newsome, P. Taylor, J. Bair and A. Rainnie (eds), *Putting Labour in its Place? Labour Process Analysis and Global Value Chains* (Houndmills: Palgrave Macmillan), pp. 29–44.

O'Connor, S. (2013) 'Amazon unpacked. The online giant is creating thousands of UK jobs, so why are some employees less than happy?' *Financial Times*, 8 February 2013. https://www.ft.com/content/ed6a985c-70bd-11e2-85d0-00144feab49a, date accessed 23 January 2017.

Pitts, F. H. (2015). *Book Review: Postcapitalism: A Guide to Our Future. Author: Paul Mason. Publisher: Allen Lane* (London: Marx & Philosophy: Review of Books).

Reich, R. (1992) *The Work of Nations* (New York: Vintage Books).

Rifkin, J. (1995) *The End of Work* (New York: Putnam).Silverman, J. (2014) 'The crowdsourcing scam', *The Baffler*, 26, 106–17.

Srnicek, N. and A. Williams (2015) *Inventing the Future: Postcapitalism and a World Without Work* (London: Verso Books).

Stewart, I., D. De and A. Cole (2015) 'Technology and People: The Great Job Creating Machine', *Report* (London: Deloitte).

Stockhammer, E. (2008). 'Some stylized facts on the finance-dominated accumulation regime', *Competition & Change*, 12, 2, 184–202.

Taylor, P. (2013) *Performance Management and the New Workplace Tyranny. A Report for the Scottish Trade Union Congress* (Glasgow: University of Strathclyde).

Terranova, T. (2000) 'Free labor: producing culture for the digital economy', *Social Text*, 18, 2, 33–58.

Thompson, P. (2013) 'Financialization and the workplace: extending and applying the disconnected capitalism thesis', *Work, Employment and Society*, 27, 3, 472–88 (25th Anniversary edition).

Thompson, P. and B. Harley (2012) 'Beneath the radar: a critical realist analysis of the knowledge economy and shareholder value as competing discourses', *Organization Studies*, 33, 10, 1363–81.

Thompson, P., R. Parker and S. Cox (2015) 'Interrogating creative theory and creative work: inside the games studio', *Sociology*, 50, 2, 336–32.

Thompson, P., C. Warhurst and G. Callaghan (2001) Ignorant theory and knowledgeable workers: Interrogating the connections between knowledge, skills and services, *Journal of Management Studies*, 38, 7, 923–42.

Turchetto, M. (2008) 'From 'Mass Worker' to 'Empire': the disconcerting trajectory of Italian Operaismo', in J. Bidet and S. Kouvelakis (eds), *Critical Companion to Contemporary Marxism* (Boston, MA: Brill), pp. 285–308.

Tyfield, D. (2015) *On Paul Mason's 'Post-Capitalism' – an extended review.* http://www.lancaster.ac.uk/staff/tyfield/On_Postcapitalism_1.pdf, date accessed 14 June 2016.

UKCES (2014) Working Futures 2012–2022. Evidence Report 83. (Wath-upon-Dearne: UK Commission for Employment and Skills).

Van der Zwan, N. (2014) 'State of the art. Making sense of financialization', *Socio-Economic Review*, 12, 1, 99–129.

Vercellone, C. (2007) 'From formal subsumption to general intellect: elements for a Marxist reading of the thesis of cognitive capitalism', *Historical Materialism*, 15, 13–36.

Warhurst, C. and P. Thompson (2006) 'Mapping knowledge in work: proxies or practices?', *Work, Employment and Society*, 20, 4, 787–800.

Warhurst, C., P. Thompson and D. P. Nickson (2008). Labour process theory: putting the materialism back into the meaning of service work, in M. Korczynski and C.L. McDonald (eds), *Service work: Critical perspectives* (London: Routledge). pp. 91–112.

Westkämper, E. (2007) 'Digital manufacturing in the global era', in P. F. Cunha and P. G. Maropoulos (eds), *Digital Enterprise Technology: Perspectives and Future Challenges* (New York: Springer), pp. 3–14.

Willmott, H. (2010). 'Creating "value" beyond the point of production: branding, financialization and market capitalization', *Organization*, 17, 5, 517–42.

Wolkowitz, C. and C. Warhurst (2010) 'Embodying labour', in P. Thompson and C. Smith (eds), *Working Life: Renewing Labour Process Analysis* (Basingstoke: Palgrave Macmillan), pp. 223–43.

World Bank (2015) The Global Opportunity, Online Outsourcing. June 2015. Washington, DC: World Bank Group.

World Bank (2016) *Labor force participation rate, total (per cent of total population ages 15+) (modelled ILO estimate).* http://data.worldbank.org/indicator/SL.TLF.CACT.ZS, date accessed 18 July 2016.

Wright, J. and P. Sissons (2012) *The Skills Dilemma: Skills Under-utilisation and Low-Waged Work* (London: The Work Foundation).

Index